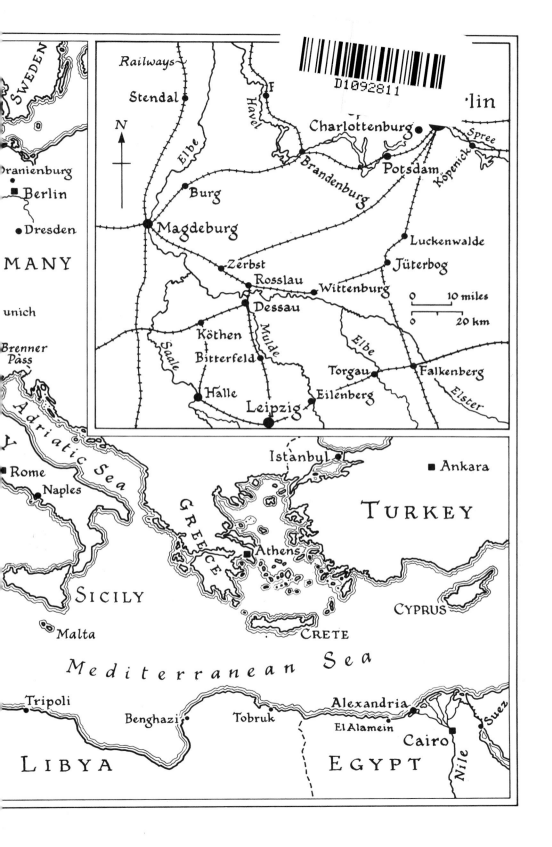

SWEDEN

Oranienburg

■ Berlin

• Dresden

MANY

unich

Brenner Pass

Adriatic Sea

■ Rome

• Naples

SICILY

• Malta

Railways

• Stendal

N

Havel

Elbe

Charlottenburg

Brandenburg

Potsdam

Spree

Köpenick

·lin

• Burg

Magdeburg

Luckenwalde

Jüterbog

• Zerbst

Rosslau

Wittenburg

Dessau

0   10 miles

0   20 km

Köthen

Mulde

Bitterfeld

Saale

Elbe

Torgau

Falkenberg

• Halle

Eilenberg

Elster

Leipzig

Istanbul

■ Ankara

GREECE

TURKEY

Athens

CYPRUS

CRETE

Mediterranean Sea

Tripoli

Benghazi

Tobruk

Alexandria

Suez

El Alamein

Cairo

Nile

LIBYA

EGYPT

NO DRUMS
- NO -
TRUMPETS

NO DRUMS
– NO –
TRUMPETS

Alec Le Vernoy

Translated from the French by
Christine Pieters Le Vernoy
and Joyce Bailey

Michael Joseph

Michael Joseph Ltd
Published by the Penguin Group
27 Wrights Lane, London W8 5TZ
Viking Penguin Inc., 40 West 23rd Street, New York, New York 10010, USA
Penguin Books Australia Ltd, Ringwood, Victoria, Australia
Penguin Books Canada Ltd, 2801 John Street, Markham, Ontario, Canada L3R 1B4
Penguin Books (NZ) Ltd, 182–190 Wairau Road, Auckland 10, New Zealand

Penguin Books Ltd, Registered Offices: Harmondsworth, Middlesex, England

First published in Great Britain in 1988

Typeset by Goodfellow & Egan Ltd, Cambridge
Made and printed in Great Britain by Butler & Tanner Ltd, Frome, Somerset

British Library Cataloguing in Publication Data
Le Vernoy, Alec
No drums, no trumpets.
1. World War. 2. Military operations by
French military forces. Personal observations
I. Title II. Sans tambours, ni trompettes.
English
940.54'81'44

ISBN 0-7181-3021-9

To my wife Christy,
the love of my life.

'. . . and they loved their lives
unto the death.'

Revelations 12.11

Contents

PROLOGUE

The Great Divide

This last day of August 1939 had been blazing and torrid. Albert, my mountain climbing companion, and I had arrived late that afternoon at the shelter, an old log cabin belonging to the Alpine Club of France situated about five miles north-east of Chamonix. It was perched on a rocky slope overlooking the Argentières Glacier, which flowed like a river surrounded by soaring mountains. We dropped our rucksacks by a low stone wall that bordered the terrace and breathed in the delight and serenity of the waning day. Albert shaded his eyes and examined the steep skyscraping ice wall, the north side of the Aguille Verte, which we planned to climb the following day. He was bursting with excitement. 'Look! Just look how beautiful she is!' The Aguille Verte was not just beautiful as she rose up massively on the opposite side of the glacier – she was overwhelming!

I knew the mountain by heart and was moved by my friend's reverence. Albert was a rare individual. He had been born in the Jura Mountains and seemed hewn out from their stone; as such, he had a bit of the peasant and a bit of the mountaineer; he had their slow patience, frugality, heartiness, and love of vast horizons. His face shone with an inner light and his intensely blue eyes sparkled with intelligence and *joie de vivre*. Although he was only twenty-seven years old, he held a Professorship in Mathematics and a Doctorate in Molecular Physics.

I looked very different – as long as a day without bread! Long-legged, long-armed, long-necked, and lanky as a foal, my long face was topped by a mop of curly brown hair. I had strong features which gave me a rather impassive look but my dark brown eyes had a dreamy, sometimes passionate, look. I had just turned twenty and felt brand new.

For four years now, Albert and I had come every summer and

set up base camp on a small ledge which overlooked the icy crevasses of the Mer de Glace. There we had been initiated into the mysteries and special techniques of Alpine climbing and had become inseparable friends, brothers, real 'rope' companions.

At the end of the afternoon the cabin keeper came up from the valley, his mule loaded down with supplies for the shelter. He had also brought the daily newspaper. The paper, usually filled with news about the villages, the local festivities, sporting results and the weather forecast, was today full of incredible news which was hard to grasp in the grandiose setting of the mountains. Its pages resounded with stamping boots and clanking weapons; there were reports of nations invaded, treaties torn to shreds, freedoms curtailed and abolished; there were detailed statistics about tanks, aeroplanes, warships, cannon and troops sprinkled with German, Czech and Polish names which evoked images of a world alien to them. The group of climbers gathered at the shelter swarmed around the one reading the paper aloud. They were outraged and disconcerted at the news and many packed up to return to the valley.

Albert and I looked at each other.

'Now what? Do we give up on it?'

'Yes, I'm afraid so. I'm certain it means war for sure!'

'Do we go back down now?'

Instinctively we raised our eyes to the Aguille Verte, glowing resplendently in the last rays of the dying sun. We had been dreaming of this expedition for a long time and had studied the Alpine climbers' little green bible, the *Guide Vallot*. We had learned the alternative routes with their recommendations and charts by heart.

'The world will go on turning no matter what we do. Will two days make that much difference?' Albert seemed to be talking to himself. 'There hasn't been a declaration of war yet.'

We looked at each other and smiled sheepishly. I gave Albert a slap on the back and we were off.

At 1.30 a.m. we were dressed, equipped and roped up, holding our ice axes in one hand and coiled ropes and lanterns in the other. Our pockets were stuffed with chocolates and prunes; our woollen caps were pulled over our ears and down to our eyebrows and snow goggles dangled round our necks.

'Ready?' asked Albert.

'Yes, Chief.' My tremulous voice showed fear and intense eagerness.

'Let's go, then.'

We were blasted by the polar cold as we opened the door. Once over the shock, we stood wonderstruck by the spectacle. The enormous Argentières Glacier shimmered softly in the moonlight. We could only guess at the long parallel zebra stripes formed by crevasses. In front of them rose the chain of needle-shaped peaks amongst which emerged the perfect pyramid of the Verte and from the unfathomed depths of the night surged the voices of the icy windswept spaces. Silent and still, we stood side by side. Albert was the first to stir.

'It's time.'

As always, the start-up was awkward. We stumbled and tripped on the moraine, had difficulty keeping our distance and got entangled in the safety rope. The candle that flickered through the cracked burnt-mica windows of the lantern cast ghostly shadows and lit everything except what was wanted, making each step guesswork. We began to thaw out and then to sweat under the multiple layers of sweaters and jackets. Our hearts were beating fast and we felt queasy but, as our muscles warmed up and our eyes became accustomed to the dark, things fell into place. We became exhilarated and our hearts lifted in a rhythmic melody that was echoed by the cadence of our steps.

When we reached the glacier we fixed crampons on our boots and walked briskly over the crusty ice, always wary of the unexpected appearance of deep crevasses whose murky depths would suddenly gape up at us. The crampons crunched reassuringly at each step. We guided ourselves by the spire of the Verte, which was silhouetted, all white, against the starry sky and which seemed to be beckoning us from its 4,122-metre height.

After crossing the glacier we started the interminable climb up the snowy slopes at a slow, even pace. Dawn surprised us as we came up against the enormous Bergschrand at the foot of the Grand Corridor. We paused to eat. I wasn't hungry; the mere thought of food revolted me.

'Never mind. You've got to force yourself. This is the last meal you'll get until we reach the top,' admonished Albert.

The Couturier Corridor, a 1,200-metre wall of raw ice

without rocks or fissures, rose vertically above us and slightly to our left. It went up so steeply we had to crane our necks back to see the top.

I panicked. 'Is that the way we go?'

'Not exactly, but almost. Look over there. We're going to tackle the right-hand side.'

We had first to get across a yawning abyss before we began to scale the icy wall. We cut precarious steps into the ice with our axes and hammered in pitons which gave us an illusion of safety. We progressed step by step – almost inch by inch. After the initial cold had almost frozen our hands, the scorching sun beat down on us singeing our eyes in spite of the dark snow goggles.

The following hours were an endless grasping for rocks, a careful groping to detect the rotten snow covering the icy sheet which would crumble treacherously under our feet. Sometimes showers of stones loosened by the heat flew by, whistling and ricochetting, and we would plaster ourselves against the wall under almost non-existent rocky spurs. We took turns leading at each rope length, securing each other. Our throats were parched with thirst and when our energy sagged, we rubbed snow over our faces and necks and dug into our pockets for a prune, a sugar cube, or a half-melted square of chocolate. At four in the afternoon we set foot on the summit. We had made it – the climb we had planned and dreamed about for four years! Our fatigue evaporated and we laughed, slapped each other on the back and cried for joy like children.

We sat down to contemplate the panorama that unrolled below us and were filled with a sense of wonder and peace. To the east the limpid air allowed us to see the Swiss Alps extending to infinity; to the south we could see Mont Rose made of sheer ice; in the foreground rose the chain of splendid peaks which dominated the Argentières Glacier while to the west we perceived the incomparable Dru. The blinding light of the afternoon sun chiselled out the jumble of ice and rock. Our contemplation was occasionally disturbed by the bursting birth of an avalanche.

'At least here we are not in danger of anything falling on our heads, except maybe droppings from a jackdaw and that doesn't hurt,' said Albert.

Our eyes kept returning to the vertical ice wall we had just scaled. It plunged steeply down to the glacier which smouldered like fire below. Over to the west lay the Chamonix Valley; we could distinguish the roads, the villages and the silver ribbon of the River Arve which threaded through its centre. Time stood still.

Then we realised it was necessary to begin our preparations for the night. We found a ledge just below the summit and settled in snugly. Only the peaks of Mont Rose on one side and Mont Blanc on the other still caught the rays of the sun; one after the other, they too melted into the dark.

As night crept up from the valley, the riot of oranges, reds and yellows of the sky toned down to violets. We could still make out the peak of the Dru silhouetted in black against the last traces of purple light. One by one the familiar friendly stars lit up while down in the valley the lights of man speckled the blackness. Far away, the halo of Geneva glowed and to its right a garland of lights glimmered on the edge of the lake. Lausanne.

I squirmed in my sleeping-bag for a while but was then pervaded by a sense of well being and warmth due to the mugs of boiling tea we had drunk before turning in. Suddenly we heard the ever-stirring voice of the mountains – the sound of the wind hissing around the peaks, on the sharp edged rocks, over the icy ferns. The sound merged with the rustle from the abyss into a murmur, so low as to be almost inaudible. The mountain streams took up the resonance and made the echoes of the night sing endlessly with a shrill crystalline vibration; from time to time a loosened stone would rebound off the ice with the clear high peal of chimes, and an animal, aroused by danger or nightmare, would let out a cry amplified by the cold.

Deep-down inside my sleeping-bag I was worn out, but could not relax. I was full of aches and pains but, more than that, with an ill-defined malaise. I could not dismiss a feeling of foreboding that my life was about to be turned upside down. At present I was comfortably cocooned in my own little world: living in Paris, my beautiful city, interested in my medical studies, loving Françoise of the smiling green eyes, occupied with the Boy Scouts, feeling pride in my new motor bike and climbing mountains whenever I could with Albert. I felt that when we stood on the crest of the summit tomorrow, I would be on the brink between peace and war, between a quiet existence and adventure.

'Do you feel that this is our last climb?' Albert had asked during the night as if he also had a similar premonition, and I had been seized by anguish. All night we fought the sleep which could be fatal at this altitude and glacial temperature. We brewed tea on a small kerosene stove, told each other stories and sang; the light from the candle-lantern dangling from a piton stuck in the snow above our heads gave a glow of false intimacy.

Nights are short in August and even more so at 4,000 metres; soon we saw the sky brighten, and fill with colour again. We were frozen stiff and had a hard time worming out of our sleeping-bags before stretching and standing up straight. We drank a last pot of tea.

We were burning with fever, the fever of fatigue, impatience, and fear of the dangerous descent before us. As day broke, we revived in the sun's warmth. We stripped off the encumbering layers of woollens, slung our rucksacks on our backs and refastened our crampons tightly. I planted a piton into the ice and engaged a snap hook through which I passed the sixty-metre rappel rope doubled. I stepped to the edge and threw it out horizontally so it would not catch or cling to a spur on the wall; the rope unrolled with a swish and hit the wall with a dry snap. We were all set!

All around us, the magnificent play of light on the snow and ice unfurled, but we were blind now to its beauty and had forgotten last night's exhilaration. With lumps in our throats, our eyes filled with tears and we faced each other.

At last, Albert spoke. 'Well, it's all over.'

'*Merde! Merde! Merde!*' Filled with despair, I could find nothing else to say.

Albert and I held each other tightly and without another word he passed the rope over his shoulder and stepped out into space. I followed.

Far below, smoke swirled from the chimney of the Couvercle shelter which was identifiable by the slab of stone projecting over it. We had taken the first step back to the world of men . . . the first step to war.

I

Poor France . . .

There was no more singing inside the bus; the cadets of the First Company of the St Maixent Military School, their noses glued to the windows, looked out aghast. The bus was heading north towards the Loire, where the front line was believed to be, pushing upstream against the current of the French nation in flight. Old and young, men and women, children, dogs, horses and pigs . . . a terrorised population which had lost all common sense and was heading 'south', a word that, for some strange reason, had become synonymous with safety.

Everyone had taken 'home' with them. Carts piled high with mattresses, chairs and kitchen pots were drawn by donkeys, horses, oxen, men and women; wheelbarrows, bicycles and prams loaded with bundles, which had been haphazardly lashed down, zigzagged down the road while thousands of people, encumbered by hastily tied bags and packages, plodded unsteadily on. Here, a little girl carried a rooster in her arms, its legs pointing to the sky; there, an old peasant with a thick moustache and velvet jacket bore a very old woman on his back . . . a pathetic convoy *en route* to the end of the war, but incapable of going beyond the next village.

The cars, overstuffed with passengers, suitcases, boxes and birdcages crawled along slowly, looking like giant turtles under the mattresses that were piled on their roofs. They rapidly overheated or ran out of petrol, and little puffs of steam rose from their bonnets before they finally expired. Their owners, who had taken more than they could carry, now had more things to worry about before abandoning their vehicles on the roadside.

Buses and trucks were stuck in the human tide. Here and there, shabby deserters shouted stupidities. People who heard

them were not convinced, but became just a little more
demoralised.

The two battalions from St Maixent had left at dawn. Fifty
Paris city buses, which had been requisitioned much in the same
way as had the taxis at the Battle of the Marne in 1914, had
arrived from God-knows-where. They had been repainted olive
green and were lined up in battle formation in the school yard,
looking very official and warlike. The expedition had been
organised at the last minute to save France's 'honour' when
everything else had gone to hell.

It was the end of a long, tedious road for me. Since the
outbreak of war I had felt an increasing indignation and worry.

The gloomy mobilisation, the anti-patriotic demonstrations
of the French Communist Party, the disastrous 'phoney war'
had shocked me. While the French were feasting and frolicking,
while political and military leaders were quibbling and quar-
reling, Poland had been smashed, Norway and Denmark
enslaved, and Finland forced to capitulate.

On 10 May 1940 the thunderbolt struck: the Wehrmacht
invaded Belgium, Holland and Luxembourg, and stormed into
the Ardennes. Only then did a stunned world learn about such
things as parachute troops, dive bombers, the '5th column', and
the levelling capacity of Guderian's ultramodern tanks. Above
all it came to know the flash-flood of a huge army, which was
young, disciplined, fanatic and motivated. Then came the
overall defeat, the crumbling of the Allied Forces and the escape
from Dunkirk, followed by the German parade through the
deserted streets of Paris and through the Arc de Triomphe . . .
Poor France!

I now felt a strong determination to join the fighting. I didn't
know exactly why. I certainly could not stop the tide that was
rolling over Europe, but it was a strong gut-feeling. There were,
of course, many noble reasons and strong reactions to the latest
developments which I could wave like banners. I loved France
unconditionally and felt somehow responsible for the disaster,
but deep within myself I felt less patriotic motivations. I had a
total disregard for danger, a basic need to prove myself, to find
my limits of endurance. I felt an obscure attraction to the
adventure that the war was offering me, simultaneously hideous

and exciting, which gave me an opportunity to shake up my nice but humdrum existence. For these various good and not so good reasons I had decided that this was to be 'my war', that I must now dive headlong into it. As a medical student I was eligible for the Medical Corps, so to forestall being drafted into a relatively safe unit, I volunteered for the Infantry, hoping to transfer later to the Air Force.

In February 1940 I was admitted to St Maixent Officers Training School for Infantry and Tank Units, situated near Poitiers, south-west of Paris, where I was taught the arts of war.

On 18 June the German advance units reached the Loire and staked out their lines to regroup. It was then that the two infantry battalions from St Maixent were sent to join the cadets from the famous cavalry school of Saumur to try a last-ditch defence 150 kilometres from there. We were fully aware that this was a hopeless mission, but we had all smarted with shame at France's downfall and were now ready to fight to the last man.

The day before leaving we prepared ourselves feverishly, almost joyously, for combat. We were issued battle uniforms, ammunition, first-aid kits, food rations – all the little trinkets of the good soldier going off to war. Because of the early departure we received orders to sleep fully dressed, with our gear at our bedsides. That evening, when the lights were extinguished, we were offered a memorable send-off by those who stayed behind. The old school bugler gave us a rare and strictly forbidden recital, a call to taps *en fantoche*, usually reserved for gala occasions. It was an unforgettable serenade.

The old veteran, his chest covered with medals, planted himself in the centre of the court, legs apart, fist on hip, and rendered an improvisation on the regimental theme. He embroidered on the melodies, making thousands of variations, producing unknown harmonies and made the old bugle sing clearly, joyously and nostalgically. The clear notes drowned themselves in the dark, ending in a final farewell which was full of peace, sweetness and desperate resignation, melting in a slow diminuendo into the silence of the night: 'Goodbye, men, goodbye. Soon you'll be free, soon you'll be free.'

The young warriors, even the sophisticated ones, were surprised and touched to the quick, and wept like children in the dark; not many slept that night. The smell of leather, gun grease and naphthalene pervaded the dormitories, and the moonbeams which stole in through the window played on the gun barrels producing flickering metallic reflections.

I dozed and thought about the next day when we would become acquainted with the war for which we had so assiduously trained. Some would be killed, others wounded and many maimed for life. Strange that I, who had so eagerly awaited 'my war', had never stopped to think of its consequences before. Now I was afraid of being afraid.

From the window of the old Paris city bus, I watched the collapse of my beloved country. As we pressed on through the mob we were often insulted, because we were going against the acquiescence of the general public, and the crowd took our young courage as a reproach. But the worst, alas, were not civilians. Very rarely a voice of encouragement was heard: 'Go get 'em, boys. Bravo!'

Suddenly, out of nowhere or from hell, a fighter squadron appeared, attacking the long line on the road. From their wings they spat machine-gun bullets and on their tails were half a dozen light bombers which released a rosary of strung-out little bombs.

They were flying in a wedge like geese over a field, but so low they were almost skimming the defenceless human stream, so that the pilots could see with their naked eyes the faces of their victims and the results of their butchery. The roar of the engines, the rattle of the machine-guns and the bombs, dropping with deadly precision on the road and exploding into fire and iron, dispersed the crowd in all directions: some into ditches, some under trucks and cars, some letting themselves fall on the spot, spreadeagled, as if wanting to melt into the pavement.

As inexperienced students we froze. When we realised what was happening, some of us scrambled out of the buses and unsuccessfully opened fire on the enemy planes, but most remained inside; several were grazed by bullets and shrapnel and cut by shards from the windows. The attack lasted only a few seconds but had seemed an eternity.

An eerie silence reigned, broken finally by a hideous clamour:

curses, children's howls, wild screams. There were wounded and dead bodies, upturned vehicles, gutted suitcases strewn everywhere. Wild-eyed, distraught survivors got up slowly, hesitantly, looking around incredulously. Then came the cries for help from the wounded and from families searching for each other mixed with the sobbing of lost children.

I was shocked by the suddenness and savagery of the raid. Joined by my fellow cadets, I stood deathly pale and trembling, impotently raging and cursing at the sky. The glorious heroes of this feat were pilots of the Italian Air Force whose noble country, after seeing France conquered, had declared war on her a few days previously.

After a while, help arrived and the convoy moved slowly on but this experience remained forever etched in my mind.

Because of their intense emotional impact the events of the following hours, days and weeks were to leave me only kaleidoscopic memories like disconnected dreamlike sequences.

Why were we sitting next to a shack in the middle of an open field? There were ten of us and all we had was one machine-gun and a thimbleful of ammunition. Other small groups of cadets were scattered 150 metres to either side of us.

Why had we been ordered to take position fifteen kilometres south of the Loire? Why? Why were we not using the river as a natural defence line? How were we to stop the Germans? Why was it assumed that they would pass by us on this small country lane?

The lieutenant, however, had been adamant. The Germans were everywhere! Furthermore, those were his orders and it was not up to anyone to question them. Besides, France's honour would be saved.

The exodus had dried up long ago. Occasionally, small scattered groups of fleeing French soldiers dragged down the road heading south. Most of them had thrown their guns into the nettles. They were dressed in slovenly fashion and went bare-chested because of the heat. They carried only their wine flasks and some food and personal items bundled in blankets; some were drunk; all were completely demoralised. Seeing the small group from St Maixent, they shouted at us provocatively, trying to justify their own desertion.

We heard them shout that they had been betrayed and abandoned by their officers; they claimed that German parachutists were all around killing everyone, and that some were even disguised in nuns' habits or French uniforms. They told us that the Germans' armoured cars were invincible and that their tanks crushed everything in their path. 'You are crazy to stay here,' they shouted. 'Throw away your arms and join us. What's the good of fighting?'

In the distance, the cannons were thundering intermittently like a summer storm.

Evening was falling when our lieutenant showed up.

'Pack up, take everything, we're leaving. We're going back to the school.'

'What, without fighting?'

'Without fighting.' The lieutenant's eyes were sombre and his jaw was set. He looked at me thoughtfully and asked me if I knew how to ride a motorcycle. When I said yes he ordered me to ride to the Second Battalion which was positioned by the Loire, near Saumur. I was to hand the commanding officer an envelope containing orders to withdraw.

'Be careful,' he added. 'Things seem to be hot over there.'

I found an infantry unit which had taken up position in a small village on the banks of the Loire and asked for the Second Battalion, but I was told they had not waited for orders. They had folded up a while ago.

From a height overlooking the picturesque town of Gennes, I surveyed the Loire, my eyes following her slow, lazy course. The scorching summer had dried up her waters, and long sand banks had emerged, spread like thin fingers cutting up the river.

I could see German units on the opposite side in front of the bridge which spanned the river. A French cavalry platoon held the south bank. Two 47mm anti-tank cannon and four machine-gun nests had been placed to protect the bridge.

'Is this all you have?' I asked.

'It's more than enough. They'll never cross! Not this bridge!'

I was far from convinced, but wanted to be obliging. 'Bravo! Can I lend you a hand?'

'Sure! But where is your regiment?'

I tried to explain. 'It's gone. In any case, I am here.'

'Bien. Put your motorcycle away and come over here. We can use anyone.'

Impregnable! The bridge was impregnable!

The party started half an hour later. First there was a rain of mortar shells which fell as precisely as if thrown by an invisible hand and which produced a strange noise like the gargle of a flushing lavatory which burgeoned and ended in a blazing rocket of fire. A few minutes later the sky seemed to be tearing itself apart in a long stream. Dive bombers! Stridently shrieking Stukas attacked, falling like falcons out of the sky. I watched them, wild-eyed with terror, and threw myself on the ground even before they dropped their bombs, blocking my ears to the infernal noise. The bombs exploded in a terrible paroxysm. Bits of stone, iron and assorted fragments fell everywhere. When I finally lifted my head, everything around me was burning or smoking. The cannon lay overturned; the machine-guns had been pulverised. Here and there, munitions continued to explode. Bloody bodies littered the road and a few survivors wandered about in a trance. The wounded were baying at death.

I had only one idea . . . to flee this hell. The motorcycle!

In a daze I stumbled to the low wall where I had sheltered her. She was intact! I pushed her to a clear spot, started the engine and, carefully evading the piles of scraps, rode slowly away.

Fifty metres up the road, as I was gathering speed, doom caught up with me. A stray mortar shell exploded almost directly overhead. The motorcycle vanished in the blast and the first thing I heard when I came to was the rumble of the German tanks peacefully crossing the bridge.

Impregnable, my eye!

The French doctor at the German field hospital where I came back to life was making his rounds, accompanied by a German officer. Once a week the wounded who had recovered sufficiently were chosen to be sent to a prisoner-of-war camp (in Germany, no doubt). Today was one of those days.

'This one', said the doctor nodding his head convincingly, 'is not yet transferable. Look!' He lifted my bandages with a dramatic gesture, and I produced several groans to achieve the desired effect. Appearances were in my favour. There was nothing wrong with me . . . nothing of importance anyway. I was slightly damaged all over. I pissed blood, had several internal injuries, was black and blue, a bit burned, a bit deaf, and had been riddled with small bits of shrapnel.

'Postponed until next week,' said the German.

Bending over me, the doctor put his ear on my chest and managed to whisper rapidly, 'I can't help you any more. Get away if you can.'

The flesh was weak, but my spirit was willing. As a matter of fact, my spirit was high. I had finally experienced war. I had 'my wound' which officially stamped me a hero. I was not seriously incapacitated and, to cap it all, I had not been scared . . . not much, anyway. Propelled by fear of deportation and by sheer willpower I was up and about two days later.

Through the window I had watched a group of Senegalese skirmishers playing a game that resembled Petanque, which was very popular in southern France; they seemed to be singularly adept. Suddenly I had an inspiration. I went to the courtyard and spoke to an enlisted officer who was leaning against a tree watching his men play.

'Tell me, sergeant, are you content here?'

'Hmm.' The man didn't want to commit himself.

'I mean, content enough to stay here doing nothing but playing with pebbles and waiting to be deported.'

'But what can we do?'

'Do you know what the Boche do to the Senegalese whom they capture?'

'Oh, one hears so many strange stories.'

'One also hears true stories. For instance, I have heard that they massacred many, machine-gunned some and crushed others under their tank tracks.'

The sergeant turned grey. 'Is that really true?'

'Where there's smoke there's fire. These rumours are so persistent there must be some truth to them; the Boche are capable of anything! Can you think of any reason why it couldn't happen to you?'

'Well, I –'

'One reason,' I insisted.

'Well, no, not really.'

'Well then, listen to me, I have an idea . . .' I took the sergeant aside.

If anyone had been watching he would have seen us shake hands a few minutes later. The next day he would have seen three African Petanque players practising their stone shots into an empty can, supervised by the sergeant, and the following day he would have seen them innocently standing about the entrance court with their musettes full of stones and accompanied by me, who just happened to be there.

The field hospital was installed in what had been an old boarding school. Every day, at 10.00 a.m. on the dot, a German colonel arrived for inspection.

On this day, exactly on schedule, the entrance barrier lifted, the guards presented arms and the colonel's Mercedes Benz solemnly entered the court, circled slowly and stopped at the front entrance. The chauffeur left the motor running, ran round the car, opened the back door and stood stiffly at attention while the colonel stepped down.

At precisely this moment, I gave an imperceptible signal. The four Senegalese dipped into their satchels and brought down the two Germans with stone throws to their heads. For good measure, they threw a few more salvos and the Germans were out of commission for good.

We raced towards the car and I quickly grabbed the revolver from the colonel's holster while the sergeant did the same with the chauffeur's. I took the wheel, the sergeant got in beside me, and the other happy Petanque players took the back seat. The car lurched forward and crashed full speed through the entrance barrier, throwing the guard up in the air. I drove up the street like a bat out of hell.

Nine hours and 240 kilometres later we found ourselves at the edge of a forest waiting for night to cross over to the French front line – if it could be called a front line, since the Germans had engulfed the countryside leaving only small pockets of resistance to be cleaned up later.

We had driven along shady side roads and had kept the car as long as the petrol had lasted. Afterwards, it had been foot-slogging all the way. Nobody paid the slightest attention to us; having seen the exodus, everyone was completely blasé, even the Germans, who evidently had other fish to fry. The war had left its taint in the most out-of-the-way places: abandoned weapons, abandoned uniforms and abandoned dead. We salvaged a machine-gun and some ammunition, mostly for the feeling of protection it gave us rather than with any special purpose in mind.

The sun was low on the horizon when we heard a sound that had lately become only too familiar – the rumbling of motors and the grinding of tracks. It seemed to be a German tank reconnaissance unit heading south, followed by several troop transports.

The convoy stopped 100 metres from where we were sitting. Wearing helmets and battle uniforms, the soldiers descended, their weapons at the ready. After a brief huddle, the tanks arrayed themselves in battle formation and started to advance slowly, giving shelter to the infantry.

'Maybe they are getting ready to attack,' I said, perplexed. 'Perhaps we are nearer the French lines than we had supposed.'

A burst from an automatic weapon rang out somewhere far to the left. It didn't seem to faze the Germans, who, bent forward, were advancing at a fast trot. Then a command was bellowed and something very bizarre happened. Simultaneously, they straightened up and began to sing – a warrior's song, a victory song, rhythmic, irresistible, in counterpoint to the roaring of the motors. It was really something to see – an incredible hallucination of flaming triumphant youth shining with glory as they marched to battle! It was idiotic! But then, who was fickle victory smiling on?

I unshouldered my machine-gun and the sergeant, who was kneeling next to me, took out the magazine and fixed the rear side-adjusters. I lay flat with the butt of the gun tight against my shoulder, my hand on the grip and finger on the trigger. I had a full view of the Germans in my sights, straight ahead of me at a distance of sixty metres. I should have fired immediately – should have – but I was sweating bullets, couldn't breathe, was paralysed.

The sergeant fumed at me.

I took a long breath and held it, closed my eyes and, as a shiver shook me, pressed the trigger, releasing a deafening burst. Through tears I saw several young men spin round and fall. Gritting my teeth and clutching the gun, I started to shoot in long bursts, sweeping the German column and leaving a trail of dead and wounded. Crazily I continued to press the trigger long after I had run out of ammunition. The survivors started to regroup and return my fire, while I lay oblivious next to the useless gun, crying my heart out. It was the first time I had killed.

Eventually, I pulled myself together. Leaving my gun behind, I joined the others, who had slipped quietly into the woods. As night fell, we reached the French positions, which had been near. It was all over; we were safe!

Two days later, quartered beneath tall fragrant pines, I met my lieutenant.

'Mission accomplished, sir.'

'It's you! Where the hell have you been? I thought you were lost.'

'I was, sir, but now I'm back and I have brought you a sergeant, three Senegalese skirmishers from the Colonial Army, a tall story and a Croix de Guerre.'

'I see the Senegalese, no doubt I shall have to listen to your story, but what about the Croix de Guerre?'

'Why, the one you are going to get for me, sir.'

I had heard of General de Gaulle's call to arms. He proclaimed that France had lost the battle but hadn't lost the war. I was itching to go to England to carry on the fighting.

We were then located less than 100 kilometres from La Rochelle. I had found a motorcycle at a nearby farm and got hold of some petrol so I discussed the matter with the lieutenant and asked him to come with me. He refused.

'I am a career officer! My duty is here with my men . . . and above all my duty is to obey.' However, he agreed I was doing the right thing and wished me luck.

Fate decided otherwise. I arrived at La Rochelle just in time to see the last boat sail. I had missed it by fifteen minutes at the most. Full of misery, I returned to my unit. The lieutenant received me with a compassionate look.

'It didn't work out?'

'No, sir.'

We never spoke of it again.

During the scorching July of 1940 the battalion was quartered in Le Vernet, a peaceful village on the outskirts of Vichy. Some of the men slept in barns, others in tents in an orchard next to a fireworks factory. We had been assigned as Honour Guard to Marshal Pétain, head of the French state. Every morning, before going to his office in the Hotel du Parc, he inspected the daily guard, which presented arms.

Today was the turn of my Company. The old man passed slowly, scrutinising each one of the cadets; he had the look of a child in his limpid blue eyes. He looked endearing in his Homburg hat, little round celluloid collar and double-breasted black suit, which gave him the air of a peasant in his Sunday best. For a moment, I was touched by this old man who tried so hard to symbolise France, but then I recalled the betrayals and outrages that were committed every day in his name or on his orders.

The St Maixent school term was coming to an end. It was about time. The weather was unbearably hot, the men were exhausted, unoccupied and had had more than enough of this stupid life.

The final exams were welcomed, even though they felt the commissioning of officers in a disbanded defeated army to be highly redundant. The final assembly after the exams was filled with excitement as each fledgling officer was permitted to choose his final assignment, in accordance with his standing in the examinations.

I was sixth in my class but couldn't get what I really wanted – the Alpine Corps – so I chose the Colonial Troops. In Africa I might get a chance to escape the Vichy regime and join an English or Free French unit.

Leaning over the railing of the SS *Ville d'Alger*, a cadet officer of the Colonial Infantry, second in command of the repatriation of the Senegalese detachment 304-V, I stood proudly wearing my black kepi, adorned with a gold anchor. As was traditional, I waved farewell to the Church of Notre Dame de la Garde, while I watched the buildings of the old port of Marseilles fade into the distance.

It was the first time I had ever left France other than on brief vacations, and I had the dire feeling that this time it would be for a long time, if not for ever. Ahead of me lay the unknown, full of marvels and adventure, perhaps, but my thoughts kept going back to my beloved country, to sweet Françoise of the green eyes, the dimples, and the foxy little teeth; and to my friends. I relived the past year's events, which flashed by in colourful images, emerging from the greyness like a range of mountains rising out of a sea of clouds.

The last weeks before my departure had been strange. A month ago, having just received my beautiful new stripes, I had been sent to the camp of Rivesaltes, a few kilometres from Perpignan, to join the Colonial Troops which were being sent back home to Africa. As soon as I had passed through the big entrance gate crowned by a huge gold anchor, I was engulfed in the world of the colonial army.

Defeat had also left its footprints here. The Senegalese, who had witnessed it all, didn't look at their officers with the same eyes anymore. They had lost much of their respect for the shamefully defeated mother country. The officers, old hands who had lived in the colonies off and on for years, reminisced endlessly, telling incessant stories of Africa, the bush, the jungle; of Indochina with its pestilent deltas, of bridges they had built, of justice they had meted out, of women they had possessed. Now on their way back there they were well aware that things had changed; that their world would never be the same again. Thus, the idle talk became nostalgic, for their horizons had become narrow and cloudy.

In France, everything was going to pot. Her liberties had been abolished, the Constitution mocked and political squabbles had reached a new high. While Germany was digesting her triumph, consolidating her grip on the country and enslaving Alsace-Lorraine, Britain had announced her determination to fight on to victory – at this moment, a somewhat chimeric declaration! In spite of the enormous losses she had suffered, she had broken the back of the Luftwaffe and postponed, perhaps forever, the threatened German landings.

I was more determined than ever to join the fighting.

I took advantage of my free moments and started to search in the bars and crummiest dives of Perpignan for a smuggler who would be willing to take me to Spain. I was too naïve to know that I could have done it perfectly well on my own, but my head was filled with images of a strict border patrol and an omnipresent police. I finally found a man who was willing to do the job and we agreed to meet in a bar in the slummiest part of town on 18 September. The timing was right, since the departure of the convoy to Algiers had been set for the twentieth, and my disappearance had a good chance of passing unnoticed in the hubbub of the preparations for sailing.

It had been raining incessantly. Dressed in mufti, I arrived in Perpignan to find the city flooded. Its three rivers had overflowed. I managed to get to the rendezvous in a flat-bottomed boat, but found the bistro under five feet of water. There was nobody – no smuggler, no message, just nothing! As the flood could last several days and the smuggler would probably not show up, I decided to rejoin my unit having no stomach for the clandestine life and being flat broke besides. Racing against the clock I arrived at the dock in Marseilles just one hour before sailing time. I made up a story about a 'skirt' escapade. My superior officer, being a colonial, appreciated the quality of the excuse and pardoned me, not without a hint of envy.

2

Much Ado About Nothing

In the weeks following the sea voyage, I had the impression of leafing through the illustrations of an exotic travel book. Our first port of call was the swarming and disconcerting and aptly named city Algiers La Blanche where, because we could not pass through the straits of Gibraltar, we were forced to take the train to Casablanca. From there, it was a long cruise towards the sun and an exciting encounter with West Africa – Dakar, Conakri, Abidjan, Cotonou, Douala, Libreville and, finally, Port Gentil.

The Tiralleurs were going home! They celebrated night and day. The continuous tom-tom of the drums pulsated with the throbbing engines, causing the old metal ship and the hearts of all on board to vibrate. At each stopover, a long line of gleeful Tiralleurs, shoes laced around their necks, sporting enormous sunglasses and loaded down with sacks, bags, cases and umbrellas jiggled and bobbed their way down the gangplank to their native land.

Feeling rather rueful, I began the return journey from Port Gentil. Now I could calmly reflect on the options of escape open to me. I had considered jumping ship several times on the way down, especially when the stopover had been near British territory, but had been dissuaded by the risks involved. The police were keeping a sharp look-out and the terrain was totally foreign to me. I would have a two-week leave after landing in Casablanca before proceeding to my new posting in Algeria and it seemed a good opportunity to get away. I pored over naval charts of the Mediterranean in order to make navigational estimates. At the same time, I plagued the officers aboard with leading but random questions. Perplexed, they scratched their heads but answered me patiently. I could hardly tell them my goal was Gibraltar, so I left them to their conjectures. I had considered getting hold of a large vessel somehow, but discarded the idea as impractical because these were under strict police surveillance and too expensive for me, anyway.

Then I had a brainwave – a kayak! A vivid mental image of these canvas-covered canoes shooting down the rapids, skimming the foam of the swirling water, flying with the hellish current, hurdling every peril in the treacherous Isère Gorge above Bourg St Maurice in the French Alps flashed through my mind. It was a brilliant idea and so simple! Although it was not the quickest way of getting there, the kayak was unsinkable, easy to handle and safe.

Between the Algerian town of Nemours and the Spanish Moroccan border there was a tiny fishing village called Port Said, which I thought would be a good launching point. As the crow flies, Gibraltar is about 310 kilometres from there. However, a direct course would be foolhardy at that time of year, so I planned to ply along the African coast as far as was feasible to a spot which lay between Al Hoceima and Tetuan; from there, the crossing of the Straits would involve no more than 100 kilometres of open sea. Following the shoreline would afford me shelter, especially during bad weather, and there would be little chance of being seen by unfriendly eyes, since it was deserted and mountainous. In spite of the fact that it added forty-five kilometres to the crossing, I considered it well worthwhile.

I spent two days in Oran, where I bought an unassembled kayak and sundry supplies. I took the train to Tlemcen and the bus to Port Said, where I had my baggage carried to a beach near the hamlet, dropping broad hints that I would be camping for pleasure for a week. They might have thought it strange since the camping season was over, but then, people sometimes do funny things. I pitched my tent at the edge of the beach, lit a fire for cooking, unpacked, ate and, in spite of the cold, slept like a baby, rocked by the lullaby of the waves.

Next morning I got to work. I assembled the kayak meticulously and then proceeded to try it out, staking out a five-hundred-metre stretch of beach to test my speed. I practised crossing and recrossing the breakers; I learned how to paddle properly, how to right the kayak in case of an upset, how to use the minute sail, how to dress and undress without getting wet and, most important of all, how to manipulate a bedpan on the high sea.

At last I felt ready for departure. I carefully secured my equipment, balancing it evenly and precisely, putting the most important things close at hand. I left enough space to allow me to stretch out fully on the bottom of the kayak. My provisions, packed in waterproof bags and properly tagged, consisted of dried dates, cans of sardines, sea biscuits, several large bars of cooking chocolate, a dozen oranges and sixteen litres of water in rubber bottles. I also carried a few toilet articles, a flashlight with extra batteries, a small repair kit for the kayak, two spare paddles, gloves, sweaters, changes of underwear, a Michelin map of the area and a pocket Bible. Even though I planned to remain within sight of land as much as possible, I had brought along a good army compass and a small homemade log.

At noon I made a final check, swallowed my last meal on solid ground, and took a nap. Afterwards, I stretched and shook the sand carefully off myself because it could become a terrible torment once on board. I looked at the sea which seemed to be lying in wait for me, and then at the kayak, fidgeting impatiently at the edge of the waves like a horse raring to go, and thought of how much I detested the sea. I looked at my watch. It was 5.25 p.m. 3 December, 1940. I embarked, feeling terribly alone.

With a lump in my throat I crossed the breakers and started to paddle diligently, soon finding the right tempo, slow and regular. I had installed the compass on a Cardan joint in front of me which allowed me to keep the course under control. The sunset was disappointing, the sun simply vanished into greyness; but soon Venus, the shepherd's star, lit up low on the horizon, then another star, then two, then thousands. I met up again with my faithful guides: the Big Dipper, the Polar Star, Orion, Cassiopeia, and felt reassured. I set my course by a star; a light breeze caressed my face; the roll of the waves lifted the kayak in rhythm with my breathing. Everything was calm and harmonious; I felt serene and asked God to protect me.

The first night seemed interminable. I paddled fifty minutes out of every hour, but at midnight I took an hour's break to have a snack. I felt completely silly sitting there alone in the vastness of the ocean, munching away inanely at my biscuits. My first goal was the Cape des Trois Fourches in Spanish

Morocco north of Melilla, a run of about 110 kilometres.

At daybreak I was feeling pasty; my eyes were as red as after a night's carousal; my body felt kneaded; my shoulders, arms, thighs and buttocks ached; but I had done it, the night I had so dreaded was over!

The morning haze dissolved and unveiled a stretch of land a few kilometres straight ahead. I rubbed my eyes and fearing I had drastically deviated from my course during the night, corrected it north. An hour later I realised that what I had taken for the Cape were in fact two small islands situated two kilometres from Ras-El-Na. Now I had a point of reference. I was not off course and had covered twenty-eight kilometres without undue strain. I circumnavigated the islands and fixed my sights north-west.

The day was tiringly tedious, but the weather held. I took a few breaks to massage my legs and tried to nap, but when I lay stretched out on the bottom of the kayak I had a tendency to become seasick. The wind freshened in the evening and a steady breeze from the mainland enticed me to sail. The sail was only one metre square and I hoisted it to a small mast which was attached in front of the binnacle and held from the back by two little shrouds. By adjusting the course slightly north, the kayak made quick headway. I delightedly abandoned myself to the sea and stayed awake most of the night, taking advantage of the breeze.

I felt elated when I saw a halo of light illuminating the sky portside on the horizon, exactly where I had calculated Melilla should be. I reefed the sail and paddled towards the glow. Two hours later I was close to land, but then progressively increased the distance from shore as the day brightened. Around 2.00 p.m. I reached the level of the Cape des Trois Fourches, where I was met by a strong west wind and long swells, from which I had been protected up to this point by the Cape. The harbour of Melilla was strategically important and highly guarded, so I made a long detour round the Cape and then changed my course south.

At sundown I paddled into a forlorn little creek and stepped on land, patting myself on the back. I had covered 115 kilometres in forty-eight hours. I quickly pulled the kayak ashore, hid it behind some prickly bushes and dropped on the sand, sighing blissfully. I was worn out, crammed with aches and jammed with stabbing pains in my lower back and my stiff legs could hardly hold me up – I was literally out on my feet. In a word, I had had it! I rapidly reconnoitred the surroundings, assembled the tent in a sequestered spot and sank into a deep sleep.

I awoke at daylight but felt too tired to go on, so I rested and finally got up around 10.00 a.m., gulped down a lot of food, exercised to limber up my joints and swam out into the coldish sea. The area was probably populated and, as I didn't want to expose myself unnecessarily, I took to sea again, feeling renewed and telling myself I must be completely crazy. The weather was sullen but, thank God! the head-on north-west wind had died down. I started up tortuously, but slowly my muscles warmed up and the paddling rhythm was found again.

It wasn't really cold, but I was perpetually wet; everything I touched was clammy and slippery. My skin became spongy exactly where it shouldn't, on my hands, below my buttocks, at my lower back where I leaned on the crossbar of the kayak. Now and then I would change gloves, powdering them with talcum to prevent my hands from blistering; but, as the hours passed, I ended up feeling liquefied by the dankness which was watering down my mettle. Bent forward, I continued to paddle and, little by little, routine took over; I became numb and drowsy losing all notion of time. I was almost surprised when I discovered it was night again and time to eat.

The second stretch which should take me east of Al Hoceima was about eighty kilometres. Having left around noon, I arrived at my destination thirty hours later. I was pooped out, but radiant to see that my scheme had worked; I was more than halfway there! The coast was rocky and desolated. I slept for twelve hours, but then decided to rest for a whole day. I checked the kayak, washed, shaved and walked to a small settlement I had spotted on my way in where I bought marvellous things: eggs, oranges, oil, olives . . . paying in pesetas which I had purchased in Oran. I aroused no suspicion and met no problems. After refilling my water containers, I went back to camp where I turned out a fabulous omelette!

In good fettle but with a queasy stomach, I sallied forth around 9.00 p.m. The weather had cooled off considerably and the swells had deepened. During the afternoon I had watched from the dryness and warmth of my tent a slight shower fall. Although it had stopped by now, the visibility remained poor and there were no stars. I had to orient myself by the compass and the direction of the waves. I wanted to cover at least seventy-five kilometres if my strength held out, because the further westward I could get, the shorter would be the crossing to Gibraltar. I paddled all night, all next day, and the following night. The wind had waned but a dreary drizzle drenched and chilled me to the bone. I was tempted a hundred times to turn back to shore, to wait for better weather; but I kept telling myself how lucky I had been not to have encountered any storms from the north-west, which were so frequent in this area at this time of the year. I set myself goals: one hour more . . . another hour . . . until the next snack . . . (The count of the hours was strictly theoretical as my watch had become water-logged long ago.) I lured myself on by playing tricks like the fools who tickle themselves in order to laugh.

At daybreak I landed on an arid rocky beach, which neverthe-less looked to me like the Garden of Eden. The rain had finally stopped so I set up camp, lit a big fire to dry out my things, had a hot meal and took a long, long rest. Twenty hours later, under a feeble sun but favourable winds, I simultaneously sailed and paddled north to gain speed and cut the hazards of crossing the open sea. I had burned my bridges as I had abandoned my tent, clothing and camping equipment, and had taken only enough water to last forty-eight hours. The lightened kayak dashed merrily ahead. I felt elated, propelled by boundless energy; even the sea seemed to be playing fair with me. I was still tired, but that was nothing compared to the sense of euphoria that filled me now that victory was within reach.

Gradually I set my course to the north-west and twenty hours later I steered a little more towards the west. At sunrise I sighted land on the horizon. Now I felt sure my gamble had paid off. I kept going north and around 10.00 a.m. I saw the land fade away to the left; I had just passed Monte Hacho, at whose foot lay the Spanish harbour of La Ceuta, the northernmost point of Africa. I sailed past the first of the famous columns of Hercules and now ahead of me lay Gibraltar . . . Europe . . . only four-teen kilometres away. I was almost there . . . almost!

I took stock of the situation. A small navigational error would suffice to make me lose my way and end up in Spain, either in Algeciras on the west or San Roque on the east, so I should keep Gibraltar in view. I now had two options: to sail during the night and approach land at sunrise and risk arriving at the coast in broad daylight, or to push on immediately. getting close enough to Gibraltar at day's end to get my bearings before nightfall. A daylight crossing could be very dangerous, as there was bound to be a lot of maritime traffic. Even now, I could see several whisks of smoke on the horizon, but the tiny silver-grey kayak would blend with the colour of the sea and most of the time would be in the canyons formed by the waves. I calculated the chances of not being spotted were more than fair and, even if I were, who would bother to slow down for a small kayak on the rove?

Everything went satisfactorily. I crossed the route of a convoy and saw several other solitary ships but didn't really worry about them as they were too far off to be identified. The swell was now rolling in from the west and pitted against me but, by now, I was the captain of my ship! Towards the end of the afternoon I could make out land and, as I got closer, I started looking for landmarks. There on the left lay Algeciras and Punta de Tarifa, the southern tip of Europe, and there, right there! rising 426 metres above the sea, the second Column of Hercules . . . the massive rock of the apes . . . Gibraltar! I stopped paddling and, popping up and down like a cork in the water, scanned the perimeter for any ship movements, trying to figure out what to do next.

The east shore of the escarpment looked craggy except for a straight stretch of beach below Europe's Point, which was hardly perceptible from my viewpoint. The west side seemed more hospitable. I could see many scattered houses; the terrain was relatively flat; far to the north I could vaguely make out the harbour. I mulled over the layout. The east bank really seemed inaccessible. I feared the entry to the harbour might be heavily protected by nets or other defensive devices but, as I saw nothing alarming, I decided to take a chance.

While I was making up my mind it had become dark, so I started out tensely, very much on guard, guiding myself by compass. On my left the lights of the Spanish coast ended abruptly and the dark area I passed confirmed the whereabouts of Gibraltar. An hour and a half later, the shore was dimly visible, and I sensed, rather than saw, the high mass of the huge rock looming over it. I advanced warily until I saw a jetty constructed of big blocks piled one upon each other. I stopped a metre from it to avoid a collision which could smash the kayak to flinders, slid silently into the water, and – touched bottom! I remained still for a while, unconscious of the cold and the urgency of the situation and let a wave of joy, relief and gratitude wash over me. After eight days and eighteen hours and 355 kilometres, I had made it! I was with friends, the English!

I beached the kayak tenderly and started walking in the dark in search of a sign of life. I bumped into barbed-wire fences and *chevaux-de-frise*, which I bypassed easily. Then I got lost in the dark but found a small path and suddenly ran smack up against a guard post which was next to a depot. The guard was dumbfounded to see a tousled, dripping man who was wildly gesticulating, laughing and repeating with distressing insistence, 'Gibraltar? *Oui?* Gibraltar?'

Half an hour later, I found myself (a little less wet and a little less joyful), facing a Military Police Sergeant, struggling to make myself understood in my entangled English.

'You say you have come from Algeria?'

'Yes, from Algeria. I want to fight with you.'

'You want WHAT?' The sergeant sounded alarmed thinking I meant to attack him. I painfully explained, which alleviated the tension but only confirmed the sergeant's conviction that he was dealing with a lunatic, and the more I reeled off my saga the more incredulous my listeners became. Finally I convinced them to take me back to the landing place, which I had trouble finding. The sight of the kayak shook the unflappable sergeant.

'Maybe he came from Spain . . . It's just around the corner,' ventured someone.

'Maybe he's a spy?'

'Don't be stupid! Why would he look for us then?'

'One never knows with these Frogs.'

Unfortunately it was Saturday night and weekends are sacred to the English. My arrival had shattered the routine but it was absolutely out of the question to disturb an officer with such a crazy story. War or no war, one must wait for Monday! Consequently, I was put in the guardhouse. There I sat in a barred cell, I, who had finally reached what I had thought was the land of the free, the country of the authors of *Habeas Corpus*, of the men I had already envisaged as comrades-at-arms. There I spent the first night, the following day and the night after, but I was too exhaused to get really angry. Instead I slept and slept.

By Monday morning I was slept-out, in good shape and very indignant as I listened to a not very laudatory telephone conversation.

'Yes, sir,' said the military policeman, 'he is a weird charac-ter . . . Looks as if he escaped from a zoo . . . He says he came on a bicycle from the moon, or something like that. Right, sir, I'll send him right over.'

The lieutenant received me with more curiosity than sym-pathy; he was blondish and flabby and regarded me with disgust. As a matter of fact, the officer was disgruntled that morning, which was unfortunate, as his mood matched my growing fury. I had never expected to be greeted with a fanfare, red carpets and flying banners but to be thrown into the clink like a stinking criminal, to be left to rot for a whole weekend without an explanation, a friendly gesture or even a change of clothes, that was too much. I must have looked like a repugnant rat by then. My mental rantings were interrupted by the lieutenant who, having glanced briefly at the file in front of him, asked me with an expression of loathing on his face: 'You say you are French and that you arrived in a kayak proceeding from Port Said in Algeria. You must take us for bloody idiots!'

Holding myself in rein, I answered in a shaky, slightly strangled voice, 'I'm a French officer. I arrived in a kayak from Algeria and it is I who am being taken for an idiot!'

'What about the minefields?'

'What minefields?'

'All the passes are mined, the surrounding areas of the port are mined. Nobody, but nobody, can enter without being piloted through the minefields . . . so your story doesn't hold up.'

I was astounded. 'All the surroundings are mined?'

Suddenly I was seized by retrospective terror; I had con-sidered all possibilities except that one. Of course, the kayak was built of canvas and wood, had practically no draught, and was light as a feather in the water, but my complete ignorance of the minefields sent shivers rippling down my back. To think that I had so happily paddled along. I became outraged. 'Do you realise what you are telling me? You are criminals. I could have been blown up at any time.'

Now it was the lieutenant's turn to gasp. 'This is a bit too much. You have the gall to complain . . . you . . .' He was so shocked that he lost the thread of his speech.

I took the opportunity to counterattack. 'I have told you again and again that after sailing from Algeria and crossing over directly from Spanish Morocco, I went through your shitty minefields, supposing they are really there, and the hardest part of the expedition was finding your stupid guards! So much for the impregnability of your famous fortress! I asked to be taken to the authorities and all you were able to dream up was to throw me in jail! Can't you see that if I had any underhand reason to enter this hole, I would have hardly taken the trouble to find your unfindable guard, that if my story wasn't true I could have very well invented a better scenario? I could have easily slipped in from Spain and not gone through all this rigmarole, and I certainly wouldn't have trumpeted my arrival. You might be thankful for the great service I have done you!'

'What would that be . . . if you please?'

'Thanks to me you have realised in time that crossing your minefields is as dangerous as crossing a public square!'

The officer was visibly shaken and looked troubled. Sarcastically, I consoled him. 'I won't tell anyone. Anyway, I'm sure any enemy wanting to conquer your rock would hardly storm it with a few men in kayaks.'

We finally started talking, but the conversation quickly turned into a deaf man's dialogue. I explained with (almost) infinite patience that I had come because I wanted to enrol in a British fighting unit, preferably the RAF, although the commandos, parachutists or the Free French would do. The lieutenant repeated, also with (almost) infinite patience, that at this stage England wasn't interested in unspecialised, unqualified recruits. It was true that the RAF was short of trained pilots, but it was bursting with hordes of volunteers; transport from Gibraltar was in short supply and overloaded; and in England, or any of her dominions, the army lacked everything and could hardly take care of the needs of the men already under arms.

'Look,' he concluded, 'even here the guards have nothing but shot-guns to fend off the enemy at this vital naval base.'

'Perhaps you could mobilise the apes with cudgels,' I jested, but I was deeply shocked and remained silent for a long while. 'Then, must I go back?' There was such despair in my voice that the lieutenant, in spite of his irascible temper, was touched.

'Listen to me. Here I can do nothing for you.'

'Perhaps your superiors?'

'No, they have other things on their minds; I don't think they could do anything for you. There's a war on, you know. I'll make you a proposition. We shall make a quick security check on you and if everything is cleared I'll send you to our Secret Service man in Tangiers, who should be able to give you a temporary rating until the situation gets better.'

I stayed a few days longer in jail, but this time the door was left open, while the investigation washed me clean of any suspicion of infamy. Then a nice young man came to fetch me and escorted me on the ferry to Tangiers. I left Gibraltar without regret and also without having seen anything of the oldest and smallest colony in the world.

In Tangiers I was discreetly deposited at the Minzah Hotel which was like something out of a Moroccan travel poster; gold-braided doorman, a flamboyant Moorish lobby right out of the *Thousand and One Nights*; a spotless, benevolent barman; enticing ladies perched on high stools; and a crystalline swimming-pool under gently undulating palms. A meeting had been arranged with a Mr González, probably a local someone in the British Intelligence Service.

Everything was splendid, even Mr González, who was as superbly British as his name was not; a Savile Row tailored suit, creased in the right places, and bulging pockets stuffed with voluminous objects; ostentatious handkerchief drooping from his breast pocket and another crumpled one peeping out of his shirtsleeve; unpolished shoes; smelling of Egyptian tobacco and lavender toilet water, he babbled in an Oxford-accented speech interspersed with aristocratic stutterings and splutterings. In strong contrast, from an anthropological point of view and probably to his great chagrin, González' physical appearance

was without a doubt Mediterranean: stocky, of olive complexion, heavy eyebrows, coal-black eyes, and with hairy tufts that
grew out of his nose and ears.

The historic interview lasted ten minutes at the most. (My
watch was still on the blink.) I tried briefly to tell the story of my
life, to make Mr González sympathise with my hopes, but I was
cut short by a limp gesture of Mr González' hand.

'I know, I know . . . I know all about you. I've read your
dossier . . . very interesting . . . very, really . . . Shocking business, indeed . . . Unfortunately, at the moment I regret infinitely
to have to tell you that I wouldn't know what to do with you.
Our team is complete . . . with real professionals . . . but perhaps . . . we could use you . . .'

'That would be great! How?'

'Well, go back to where you came from; then proceed to your
assignment.'

'And then?'

'Well, then wait for us to contact you.'

I produced a long whistle which sounded like air escaping
from a collapsing tyre. In one full sweep I had been deflated.
Suddenly I was filled with rage. 'Do you think I'm crazy or
something? A nut, maybe?'

'But no, no, not at all. You must realise that any day now
North Africa will become a very important theatre of military
operations. It will then be very important to have informants on
the spot who can give us precise strategic information. Do you
follow me, my dear chap?'

'I follow you very well . . . and what happens between now
and then?'

'You must establish yourself solidly, get to know everything
in your region, and wait.'

'Wait for what?'

'Wait to be contacted and questioned, of course.'

I was sweating cold and had become as white as a sheet: I felt
like vomiting as I got up slowly. 'I'm going', I said quietly.

'Do you need anything? Do you have enough money?' asked
Mr González with condescending solicitude.

'No, thanks. I spent almost all I had on the kayak and its
equipment, but . . .'

'Perhaps I can help you out.'

'No! Well, maybe . . . I don't want your money. All you can do for me is to pay for the orange juice I just drank in your charming company and help me return to Algeria. It really would be the last straw to be arrested while going back to the fold!'

A few hours later a car took me to a Godforsaken place at the foot of the Beni Iznassèn mountains on the Algerian border. The local intelligence agent was waiting for me and passed me over the frontier without any difficulty. I had the impression of having stormed an open door; after all the hassle of the harrowing kayak trip, the terrestrial route seemed so simple. I chewed my resentment at the way I had been fobbed off by the British all the way back to Algiers, where I arrived the following morning.

I had a fabulous alibi ready, but I didn't even get to tell it as no one gave enough of a damn to ask. The staff seemed much more annoyed at having to find an assignment for me as a new reserve cadet than bothered about my absence. I spent a week hanging around and waiting for orders until they finally found a niche for me in the Fifteenth RTS in Phillipeville. To ease my conscience, I put a small ad in the local paper, the *Dispatch d'Algiers*, giving my new address as had been agreed upon with Mr González. There it was . . . finished . . . all that effort and heartache . . . all that ado about nothing!

3

A Long Vacation

I landed in Phillipeville on a beautiful sunny morning in January 1941. It was a lovely little town situated east of the province of Kabylie on the Mediterranean shore. Its port was the outlet for nearby Constantine, which seemed to be the main reason for its existence. The main street was flanked by small stores and flowed like a small stream between two runaway hills before plunging into the port where high cranes were silhouetted against a luminous sky. The houses were painted in light pastel colours, had louvered shutters and flat red-tiled roofs which conjured up the Midi region of France. Phillipeville had its 'Sous-prefecture' with cast-iron balconies and a war memorial – a soldier in full battle uniform brandishing an 1886 model of a Lebel gun. There was a sparsely-flowering central square shaded by tall enormous palms; a kiosk with a bandstand stood in the centre. Around the square were the cathedral, the Sunday pastry shop and the sidewalk cafés, furnished with cane chairs and marble-top tables – naturally, there was the public urinal. This was the neighbourhood of the noteworthy, somebodies, the élite of the town.

The public benches, the street lamps, the wall posters, the architectural style, the iron grilles around the tree trunks – everything recalled France, everything – but all with a difference that was just enough for one to feel elsewhere. There were the street noises which sounded different, the smell of the burned fat of the 'beignets', the rich and heavy scents which wafted out of the shops, the cries of the brown-skinned merchants who chanted in a strange guttural language; there were the little donkeys stumbling under piles of straw baskets, the fezes of the passers-by and their jellabas, whose long coloured tatters fluttered in the wind. Everywhere the play of light and colours gave this little corner of France an air of what it really was – a little North African city.

The barracks which housed the First and Second Companies of the First Battalion of the Fifteenth Regiment de Tirailleurs Senegalais were perched high on one of the hills overlooking the town. Long before arriving at the military post one was greeted on the steep road by the calls of bugles telling the story of the daily life of the Battalion.

Sweating and panting, I presented myself before my superior officer, Captain Verdier of the Infanterie Coloniale. He was an awkward-looking fellow with very short skinny legs and an enormous chest surmounted by an oversized head. He sported thick eyebrows and a bushy moustache over a thick, vulgar mouth. His steel-rimmed dark glasses scarcely disguised his evasive look. I felt slightly irritated by the captain's silent inspection, as I waited stiffly at attention for any sign of life.

Finally, emitting a long sigh, Verdier spoke with a grating, exhausted voice. 'One more!'

'Yes, sir.' I was really happy that the silence had been broken and felt full of goodwill. 'One more what, sir?'

'One more officer cadet. I've already had two others to put up with lately and now you! Headquarters must think I am running their kindergarten. What do they suppose I am to do with all these greenhorns? It took me fourteen years in this army to get my first stripes and all these novices who know practically nothing have become officers in less than a year. Hell!'

'Yes, sir, but – '

'But what?'

'Well, sir, greenhorn or not, at least I have something that you have not got in spite of your long years of service!'

'What's that?'

'Well, sir, I have the Croix de Guerre!'

This was the beginning of a spontaneous mutual antipathy.

I was received cordially by my other fellow officers who were lodged in the stuffy quarters below the town, as well as by the Commander of the Battalion, a congenial old fogey who seemed saturated with Pernod. All these glorious warriors spent happy, peaceful days in the small town, whose inhabitants asked nothing of them but that the defeat be forgotten. Nobody wanted to remember what had happened over there in France the previous spring. On the other hand, everyone appreciated the blessings to business and recreation dispensed by the

Fifteenth RTS. There were the band concerts in the bandstand on
Saturday afternoons, the ceremonies in front of the war memorial monument, the parades on national holidays, the regimental ball and the general sleeping around of the officers with young
girls which occasionally led to marriage – sometimes happy, but
always flattering to local society.

I installed myself in my quarters in the attic over the central
aisle of the barracks, a place reserved for officers who didn't
lodge in town. It was a small double room furnished with the
refined taste reserved by the French army for its installations, but
this shabby setting was brightened by a window between the two
beds which gave out on to the rooftops and provided an extraordinary view of the sea, a dazzle of sunlight and colours.

The other occupant, who had been alerted to my arrival, soon
appeared. He was Cadet Officer Yves de Launay, an ex-alumnus
of St Maixent. He was thin and gangly, had straight unruly hair
which made one think he had just got out of bed, arched
eyebrows placed high on his forehead which gave him an air of
perpetual astonishment, a long sinuous nose, too large a mouth,
long teeth and protruding ears – he wasn't exactly handsome but
he had a golden look which sparkled with humour, and the aura
that emanated from him was all warmth, intelligence and class.
One immediately perceived an innate authority which generated
respect.

Yves and I quickly became inseparable friends; one was rarely
seen without the other. Captain Verdier was too absorbed in his
personal problems to take an active part in company life and
contented himself with riding at the front in parades, signing
punishment orders, and occasionally giving hell to his subordi-
nates, who could not have cared less. A triumvirate consisting of
Yves, me and another greenhorn, Cadet Officer Arnaud, quickly
took matters in hand and things changed rapidly. Rooms were
repainted; new uniforms which the Supply Corps had been
keeping for the next war were issued; drilling and theoretical
infantry exercises were cut to a minimum and replaced by
training sessions in the stadium, shooting practice, and long treks
to the nearby mountains. I became military champion of both the
1,000-metre and the 1,500-metre running competitions and this
honour, which reflected glory on the company, somewhat eased
the tension between myself and the captain.

At first, I had been disconcerted by my soldiers' black faces and had had a hard time distinguishing one from the other. Mostly, I was intimidated by this confrontation with a strange new world. Now, slowly, I began to know my men, to learn to recognise them, to appreciate their warmth and simplicity. I tried to learn their language, Bambara. This primitive tongue had been the lingua-franca of the Mali and Senegalese pedlars, whose itineraries covered a large section of West Africa. It was used by the colonial troops to allow a minimum of communication amongst the numerous tribes which were foreign to each other. When I ventured into Bambara, I was greeted with howls of happy laughter at my simple jokes and enormous *faux pas*.

I found a solid guide to my men in my orderly, Mamadou Coulibali, a tall, thin, catlike Mossi from the High Volta. His skin was relatively fair, his features fine, his almond-shaped eyes glittered with malice and the tribal scar beneath his cheekbone added another dimple to his smile. He spoke in a hesitant, fluted voice and, as soon as he started talking, his head would oscillate from left to right. He seemed not to know what to do with his hands, which fluttered in all directions. Mamadou knew everybody and everything and could take care of any situation. He took over the management of 'his lieutenant', taking meticulous care of my wardrobe as well as waking me up a quarter of an hour before reveille with a steaming cup of *café-au-lait* and a ration biscuit. He made himself indispensable, taking bouquets to the ladies, escorting me in town, and rendering a thousand and one services with infinite good will. He answered my most incongruous questions about Africa, its tribes, their morals, loves and beliefs.

Realising my interest and affection, my troops adopted me. I had proof of this the day I found out I had been given a name, Bele-Bele-Bah, which meant 'big goat'. At first I found my new name a bit ridiculous, but it was explained to me that, on the contrary, it was extremely affectionate, flattering and respectful. Not being able to verify this, I was glad to believe it.

By relentless insistence I had succeeded in being officially charged with the organisation of the long treks. Soon the surrounding villagers got used to seeing the Tirailleurs of the Fifteenth RTS file through the countryside preceded by a group of scouts and followed by heavily loaded pack mules. It was a long procession of black men wearing red chechias and light beige uniforms. At the beginning, the people fled, terrorised at the approach of troops armed to the teeth, but now they welcomed them noisily, offering water and shouting encouragement. France's image was enhanced and everyone was happy! Even Verdier, who had been congratulated by Headquarters, started to ride ahead of his troops as they passed through Phillipeville upon their return. The hikes, originally one or two days in length, were increased up to eleven days and covered 450km, a great feat for these heavily loaded soldiers in such mountainous country.

I never tired of contemplating the high scorched mountains of Kabylie, where the heat from the burning sun released strong resinous scents from the scraggly vegetation. Then too there were the bivouacs, where, lying on my back, I observed the dazzling trajectories of shooting stars while the moon, whose course measured the length of the break, flooded the desolate landscape with a blue-ish light.

A ray of sunlight filtered into my and Yves' rather arid social life the Sunday Yves met the de Sonis, a young couple belonging to the Papal nobility. They were cultured, sporty, fun-loving people, blond, tanned and handsome. She was in the full bloom of her thirties and looked kindly on the world with a bemused expression. They were very modern and led a fast and luxurious existence with complete disregard for public opinion, a fact which incensed the gossips but inspired many with troubled dreams. Their apartment was a veritable haven of well-being. There were books everywhere, deep comfortable sofas, artistic lighting, and splendid modern paintings.

Yves and I quickly became habitués of their circle of friends and there I met Sylvianne. She was eighteen years old; she had golden highlights in her hair; she had the hips of a boy coupled with the narrowest waist I had ever seen; she was long-limbed with muscled thighs and shapely calves; she had a face of classical beauty with well-defined features and high cheekbones; she had a mouth which smiled ever so promisingly; she was gay, cuddlesome, and coquettish; she was an imp!

'You shall see', said Jacques de Sonis, who had noticed how

smitten I was. 'This little one improves when she is undressed. She has a perfect body – a real Nefertiti.' I agreed enthusiastically, wondering how the hell my friend could know. I plunged into the *Petit Larousse* at the first opportunity to find out what a Nefertiti was and was quite thrilled by what I discovered. When the moment arrived, I realised how right my friend had been.

Whenever we were off duty, my friends and I threw ourselves delightedly into a heedless, happy-go-lucky existence. There were afternoons on the beach swimming in the clear tepid sea, horseback rides, sailing regattas, picnics on the rocks, evenings of long conversations where, sipping whisky, all and nothing was discussed. Sometimes there was dancing to the nasal sound of an old phonograph which produced languorous, romantic melodies. Then Sylvianne, the imp, became an ardent young woman, desirable and desired. There were those other miraculous nights when beautiful Sylvianne and I lay stretched out naked on the fine sand, satiated with pleasure, silently marvelling at our joy as we gazed up at the starry sky and listened to the breaking waves.

During those months, which for me had been like a long holiday, the world had not ceased turning. In fact, the world had more or less turned upside down. Like a river of incandescent lava the war was spreading. In France, matters had gone from bad to worse; in Egypt, Rommel had pushed the English back and was 180km from Alexandria; Germany, having subdued Yugoslavia, Greece and Crete, had now turned its attention toward Russia, where the Wehrmacht was advancing in giant leaps – Smolensk, Leningrad, Sebastopol, Moscow; Japan had annexed French Indo-China and was starting preparations for the future Pacific war. The Allies, it was true, had had a meagre success in Syria but, above all, the resolution of the American Congress to approve the lend-lease of arms, ships and ammunition to England gave the first pale hope to the free world.

Late one night in August 1941 I found myself sitting on a hill overlooking Phillipeville. I was slightly tipsy, having just left my birthday party, and was feeling vigorous and intoxicated by Sylvianne's kisses. As I looked down on the lights of the town which seemed to drown themselves in the sea, I started to add

up my annual self-reckoning and came to the sobering conclusion that I didn't feel at all proud of myself. Since my arrival
in January I had more or less closed my mind to the rumblings
of war. However, these last months I had begun to feel more
and more concerned and increasingly guilty about wallowing in
carefree pleasures. My duty quite evidently lay elsewhere;
nevertheless, I had not done anything about it.

I had had no news from the English, notwithstanding Mr
González' pretty promises, so I had to admit that they had
apparently washed their hands of me.

I felt frustrated that my incredible kayak trip had led to
nothing, although I was also immensely relieved, as the idea of
spying on my compatriots displeased me.

I came to the conclusion that I would have to start from
scratch to get out of this checkmate and do what I really wanted
to do – fight for my country! It became imperative that I join a
fighting unit, either French or English. This fact assumed the
importance of a revelation. I shook off my inertia, overcame the
feeling of nausea which invaded me at the idea of resuming
action once again, and started to look for a solution. I went to
Algiers, Constantine, Bone, talked to all kinds of people – all in
vain. It was a total impasse.

The gods, however, were watching over me. One night,
Biche, Jacques' wife, who had been watching my efforts with
apparent indifference, took me aside and calmly declared, 'My
dear Alec, I think I have found what you are looking for. Would
you be interested in a place in a small boat making a run for
Gibraltar from Algiers?'

I was so completely astounded that I started to babble
incoherently.

'Splendid,' she continued as if she had understood what I
hadn't been able to say. 'I have a friend in Algiers who lives with
a young medical student who is quite a remarkable fellow. He
has decided to join the Free French Forces in London. He and a
friend have just bought a solidly built motor boat and are
looking for a third companion. Thus, I have been thinking – '

'Thinking?'

'I've been thinking that this might interest you, so I told my
friend you would be in Algiers in a week's time.'

For an answer I took her in my arms and showered her with

random kisses. My heart was heavy at the idea of Gibraltar all over again, but perhaps the situation had changed. Besides, did I have any other solution?

A veiled telephone conversation to Algiers confirmed Biche's proposal and I made an appointment. I requested leave from the military authorities, pretending that I wanted to register at the medical school in Algiers and, as the new academic year was just starting, permission was quickly granted, since registration would lead to my legal demobilisation. I put my affairs in order, paid my bills, and gave a royal present to a tearful, uncomprehending Mamadou. I took leave of my fellow officers and men, who gave me a formidable tom-tom as they escorted me to the barracks' gate. I left without looking back and for a long distance could hear the undying chant – Bele-Bele-Bah, Bele-Bele-Bah. After a sleepless night on a moonlit terrace, I tore myself away from Sylvianne. At dawn on 1 October I took the puffing little train to Algiers.

The rue Michelet was Algiers' widest and busiest street and descended gradually towards the post office, the university and the port. It was crowded with a noisy, bustling mob – there were the pied-noirs dressed in light trousers and short-sleeved shirts, all sorts of Arabs wearing fezes, turbans, chechias and embroidered skullcaps; hawkers shouted their wares; the little shoeshine boys squatted at the edge of the sidewalk beating the flat side of their brushes against their small wooden boxes, drumming up customers; overflowing trolley-buses glided silently through the heavy traffic. The scent of North Africa was everywhere – oranges, charcoal, fritters, spices – it smelt good! The sun, warm even though it was autumn, made the colours sing and gave the street a festive air.

After registering as a second-year medical student, I went to the rendezvous. I rang the bell of a house in the Mustapha quarter. The door was opened by a tall, beautiful girl, Christianne Portolano. I stepped into a cool, tastefully arranged apartment. A few minutes later a man appeared, planted himself in the doorway with his legs slightly apart and scrutinised me. Then he broke into a smile and advanced holding out his hand in a welcoming gesture.

'I'm happy you are here. I'm Jean-François Coggia. Your friend, Biche de Sonis, who is usually so reserved, spoke to

Christianne about you in such glowing terms that we have been wondering what kind of a bird would show up.'

We installed ourselves comfortably and started to talk. I introduced myself and told of my medical studies, my war and my sea escapade. Coggia had the rare gift of listening well. Then he in turn talked about himself. He was a pied-noir born in Algiers of Corsican parents, was in his fourth year of medical school and was an accomplished athlete. He spoke in a grainy voice with an inimitable Algerian accent and seemed to amuse himself by stressing the pied-noir expressions. His high forehead and short, chestnut-coloured hair emphasised his tiny protruding ears. His eyes were so transparent that they seemed green, but were in fact a golden hazel and reflected thousands of little lights. Suddenly he became tense and serious and explained that he had had enough of sitting on the sidelines while real men were fighting for fundamental principles such as liberty, country and human dignity. He was able to say all this without sounding pompous or ridiculous even for a minute.

His plan was very simple. He and a friend had bought a small fishing vessel capable of taking them to Gibraltar in any kind of weather; from there, they would try to reach London. Like all local fishing-boats, it was pointed and decked at both ends, with a rudder and tiller aft, and a cabin in the middle for the engine, which was worn and battered but in good condition and thoroughly overhauled. The fuel and water supplies had been doubled, and the keel and sides of the boat had been reinforced. A compass and navigational charts were ready; Coggia had even learned to use a sextant, a superfluous but reassuring luxury! The boat was mounted on a trailer and hidden in a warehouse in a small place called Aïn-Taya, ready to be taken to the huge deserted beach at Fort de L'Eau. Half a dozen men would be standing by to lower it from the trailer and push it down a steep dune and across the thirty-metre-wide beach at high tide into the sea.

'It should be,' he said, 'an easy task.'

I was enthusiastic, asked pertinent questions and gave advice gathered from my own experiences as we excitedly discussed the project far into the night. I finally spent the rest of the night on the sofa.

After inspecting the boat and the beach, I met our third

shipmate in a bistro. Eduardo Chorat was a stocky man with an old monkey face which was constantly changing expression and was furrowed by a million lines. His jaw was square, his thin lips looked like a slash in his face and his steel grey eyes gave him an implacable look of determination, but there was a strange sadness in them. Chorat had been a rich Catalan businessman from the region of Barcelona, who had been swept up in the Spanish Civil War. Although he was not a Communist, not even a Socialist, his liberal ideas had led him to join the Republican ranks and after the Civil War he had taken refuge in Algiers, but now he felt tagged as a revolutionary and sensed danger. He thought his duty lay in pursuing his ideals and wanted to engage in the battle against Nazism.

We divided the work for everything had to be ready by the following evening as our departure, weather permitting, was scheduled for the day after at sundown. Chorat was put in charge of putting the trailer on the beach. He was to take wooden blocks of all sizes, rollers, sticks to serve as levers, long lines and ropes, and was to hide all this among the reeds in the dunes and set a watchman to guard the place. Coggia would get the meteorological report and bring the battery and navigational instruments. I was charged with procuring food, medicine and other necessary supplies.

Next day, a small group gathered at the arranged hour on the beach. There was a pale Coggia, a determined Chorat, and me, enthusiastic but slightly nervous, besides a group of half a dozen friends who had come to lend a hand. Four of them were Spanish workers in a nearby circus, experts in putting up the big tent; one was a physical education teacher who resembled a good-natured orang-utan; another, a taciturn red-crested fellow whom nobody seemed to know. They had all arrived separately as agreed. Everything was calm and deserted.

The sun went down in a blaze and the men got to work. In a few minutes they had lowered the vessel from the trailer on to the rollers and the great moment had arrived.

'Ho', hissed the chief of the circus gang, who had assumed command. Everyone arched their backs and shoved. Catastrophe! The boat was too heavy. The rollers sank into the sand. We attached ropes and tugged and pulled with all our strength. 'Ho!' This time the boat moved – one inch. This was the beginning of a hellish struggle. Frantically we tried improvised levers and a truck jack found in the trailer; we put boards under the rollers; we greased the keel.

Four hours later, hysteria and rage had taken over. I insisted we take a break, drink something, and mull the situation over. The moon had come out and the little waves which came to die at the edge of the beach sounded like little dogs lapping up their soup, but the angry men were far from being sensitive to beauty. We took up the gruelling fight which had become a battle of will and intelligence against an idiotic brute mass, but the idea of throwing in the towel never occurred to any one of us.

During the night, I learned a diversity of insults, injuries and blasphemies in several Iberian dialects. The boat advanced slowly. The closer it got to the edge of the water the better the wet sand allowed the rollers to move and the boat finally moved into the water at 5:00 a.m., just as the sky was beginning to pale. A unanimous cry of relief arose. We embarked quickly thinking that, even though we were behind schedule, we could be out of sight of the coastguard by the time day had broken completely.

It had taken us almost twelve hours to get there.

The battery was connected and Coggia pressed the starter with a solemn gesture. Nothing! Not a sound! The motor didn't respond. He tried again . . . and again . . . and again . . . Mad with anxiety, he searched for what could be wrong. He found nothing.

'Don't we have a crank somewhere?' I shouted.

We found one and Chorat, in exasperation, started to turn the handle, while Coggia operated the controls and I started to row to get the boat away from the beach; Chorat ran out of breath and I took over, then Coggia. We held a brief war council and finally had to accept that the battery was dead. We considered rowing to Gibraltar but discarded the idea as insane. The small sail which the boat carried was completely inadequate. The boat would be very obvious in a few minutes so, with rage and bitterness in our hearts, we decided to postpone departure. We sank a grapnel, tied the boat up, and went back to Algiers. All of us were exhausted and looked like sleepwalkers as we staggered to the bus station. Christianne was terror stricken to see Jean-François and I looking like two zombies collapse without a word of explanation, dead to the world.

We awoke at 2:00 p.m., ate a bite and ran to the nearest garage to find that the diagnosis had been correct. The battery was dead! Coggia was appalled. He had neglected to have it checked and since there was no time to have it recharged, we bought a new one with our last sous. We had arranged to meet at the boat at 8:00 p.m. Each of us was to arrive separately except for Coggia and I, who had to carry the heavy battery suspended from an iron bar. It was a black night and only the glimmer of the stars allowed us to make out the narrow road. A man had been posted since early afternoon to warn us of impending danger.

When we were about 100 metres from our goal, Coggia whistled three notes softly. Nothing! He whistled more loudly. Nothing!

'Everything must be all right,' said Coggia, 'otherwise we would have been warned. Let's go.' We started walking again, taking care to make as little noise as possible. Again we stopped and Coggia whistled. Suddenly we were caught in the beams of half a dozen flashlights.

A voice out of the night ordered, 'Police! Freeze!' We were immediately overpowered by strong men, thrown to the ground and handcuffed behind our backs.

Fear flooded through me. My bones felt liquefied as I got up with great difficulty while my legs trembled so that I could hardly keep myself upright. To cap it all I realised that in my panic I had wet my pants. Coggia, what could be seen of him, didn't look much better. A group of men surrounded us, some in uniform and others, apparently, plainclothesmen.

'Put them with the others and get back to the hide-out,' ordered the same voice as before. The police marched us about 100 metres away from the beach, where we found Chorat and two of the others handcuffed, sitting on the ground under guard and ignoring each other. Several minutes passed. I could hear only the waves and the wind blowing through the rushes.

I was gradually calming down. I breathed deeply to gather my wits about me and got hold of myself. My mind was racing. 'I must get away now. Afterwards it will be too late. I shall be locked up.' I looked at the five or six guards who seemed to be completely relaxed as they smoked and chatted quietly. It was now or never. I bounded up as if triggered by an outside force and started to run. Hampered because they were unable to leave the other prisoners alone, the police reacted belatedly. One of them finally fired in the air to alert the others. I had a slight advantage but was having a hard time running with my hands handcuffed behind my back. Fear shortened my breath; my pulse was hammering in my ears while my limp legs made me stagger. After running about 100 metres I came to a ploughed field and hesitated. There were bushes and reeds some 200 metres further on that might afford some cover, but the terrain between was uneven and disastrously brightened by the moon, which had just risen.

Someone shouted, 'Stop or I will shoot!' There was a single shot – then two – then three. The one who had fired had not stopped running and I could hear the panting of my pursuer. I suddenly felt very calm as if frozen inside and began to reason: 'If they continue running while shooting, they have very little chance of hitting me. If they stop to shoot they will lose ground and I already have about a twenty metre lead.' My mind reeled: 'Funny that those ridiculous firecrackers should represent a deadly danger.'

Crack! Crack! Two 'ridiculous firecrackers' brought me back to reality. Realising I had lost precious time, I leaped into the field with a desperate hoarse cry, ran a few paces on the soft earth, caught my foot on something, catapulted forward, fell flat on my face and blacked out. A few seconds later I came to, pervaded by an uncontrollable fear that made me want to cry, to vomit, to die.

Two breathless policemen with guns in their hands bent over me. 'Get up, you sonofabitch! Move! Fast!'

As I didn't move fast enough, one man kicked me hard in the belly. I moaned and heard myself say, 'Bastard!' For answer I got another kick, this time in the face, which laid me out again.

'Stop!' the second policeman intervened. 'What's the good of all that? He hasn't done anything to you.' He put his arms under my armpits and got me up. 'Come on. Let's go. Stop being stupid.' They marched me back to the group.

The policeman who seemed to be in charge told me, 'Well, your attempt to flee is certainly an admission of guilt.'

'Admission nothing,' I shot back. 'All I admit is that I had no wish to be arrested, much less taken in.'

The Chief beamed his flashlight on me. 'You are in fine shape! Just tell me, the boat down on the beach – is it yours?'

'Which boat?'

'Which boat! Which boat! And those people, do you know them?'

'I can't even see them. How do I know?'

'Put the light on them.' One by one the livid faces of my friends were lit up.

'Never seen them before in my life.'

'What were you doing with the battery?'

'What battery?''

'You were carrying it with one of those men when you were arrested.'

'You must have made some mistake in the dark. I wasn't carrying anything. I was alone.'

'Well, then, we're wasting time. Load them up. Let's go.'

Coggia and I were taken to the Maison Carrée Gendarmerie. The others were taken elsewhere. A sleepy, fatherly looking sergeant held a brief interrogation.

'Too bad, all this. I'm simply doing my duty. We'll see about all this in the morning. Go and wash yourself; one can hardly see your face for all that blood. We'll call a doctor, if necessary.'

Slowly, I washed in cold water.My face and forehead had deep cuts and bruises; my nose looked broken and was terribly painful; but what I most wanted in the world right now was to be left alone. I was worn out! They took me to my cell and the metal door slammed shut with a prolonged vibrating sound that hit me in the gut. It was a sound I never forgot.

The days and weeks followed in a haze. Nothing seemed to touch me. Every point of contact with ordinary life had been lost. I felt like an outside observer of my own life. They transferred me to the Mobile Brigade on the rue d'Isly. There I stagnated in a dirty crowded cellar, completely cut off from the outside world, oblivious to the cold, the repugnant food and the openly practised promiscuity. I refused to acknowledge my surroundings fearing they might sap my tenacity and courage. I thought my plight couldn't last long so I slept and waited. I was taken upstairs several times for interrogation, but retreated into an obstinate silence, which earned me a lot of blows and insults. Finally I was called before the Commissaire Superieur, M. Achiary. He was a broadbacked pudgy man with blond sauerkraut hair and a crafty look. He studied me for a long time, no doubt to make an impression. I was standing in front of the desk and turned towards the window. From there I could see the glimmering flat sea with a slight mist on the blurred horizon, a sign that autumn was well advanced.

'No luck, eh? You see the splendid weather and beautiful sea.'

I sighed deeply without turning. 'Oh, yes, no luck, really!'

'You'd be in Gibraltar already in this weather.'

I pulled myself together. 'Gibraltar? Who should be in Gibraltar?'

'You, my friend. Your sigh was a dead giveaway.'

'Giveaway? Stop trying to bugger me. One can certainly regret being in a stinking black hole, seeing only dirty cops who are in the pay of the Boche, without leaving for Gibraltar or the moon.'

The big chief turned red. 'You, my dear fellow, will present your apologies to me this instant or – '

'Or what?'

The policeman got up and walked around his desk. He quickly slapped me back and forth across the face. I stood there struck dumb. 'I'm waiting to hear your apology.' Everything about Achiary was menacing.

'*Merde!*'

The cop raised his fist but then lowered it. 'All right, you have guts. I'm with you and those who want a free France. You must understand this stinking job makes me play a double game.'

'You certainly are damned gifted at it, sir.'

'Now, between friends, how about Gibraltar?'

'Friends? Humph. I'd hate to have enemies then! Gibraltar, that's nothing but a figment of your imagination.'

A beautiful friendship had been nipped in the bud. I was literally kicked back to my cellar.

Three days later I was sent to the Admiralty Prison in the port of Algiers – thus I became a non-paying guest of the Marine Nationale Française. I was cordially received by the second-in-command, a square alcoholic Breton. The regulation utensils were issued to me: bowl, spoon, a piece of soap and a strip of rag called a towel. I was escorted to a small common room already inhabited by a dozen sailors.

Meanwhile, I had learned that Chorat was at the Barberousse Prison and that Coggia had been set free on parole. Coggia was of Corsican descent, as was the case with a large number of the French civil servants: cops, customs officers, judges, tax collectors, station masters, prison wardens, non-commissioned officers. This clique had closed ranks to help one of their own. I was happy for Coggia but couldn't help feeling slightly disappointed in my friend.

It was a long holiday – a bit special, but nevertheless a holiday. For almost a month I led a peaceful uninterrupted life. My days were spent reading stimulating comic books, sunbathing, doing benign drudgery and holding long happy conversations with my fellow unfortunates.

One day, inspired by a driving need for freedom, I got the devil in me. I edged my way to the end of the jetty, took off my clothes at the foot of a small lighthouse and plunged into the water. This was strictly improvised. Since it was the lunch hour the Admiralty seemed completely quiet and deserted. Unluckily, someone noted my absence, someone else had seen me slink away towards the lighthouse, so another one went out to look for me and found the pot of gold at the end of the rainbow – the little heap of my clothes. A quarter of an hour later, as I was swimming swiftly towards the other shore, I was fished out, dripping and sheepish, by a small navy boat. For appearances' sake, I was put in the guardhouse, but four days later I rejoined my mates and resumed my exciting daily schedule, only now they kept an eye on me.

Two gendarmes came to fetch me one beautiful mid-November morning. They took me to Constantine, where I stayed just long enough to become infested with crabs and lice. Then they took me in successive stages to Bizerte, the seat of the Marine Court which was to investigate my case. During the long train trip I stood in chains, nose glued to the window, as I watched part of Algeria and Tunisia pass by. I was polite and docile but kept waiting constantly for a chance to escape, which unfortunately never came.

There was a sign over a heavy grey gate that read Marine

Nationale Fort Ain-Roumi. This old fort, which was located in
the vicinity of Bizerte, was built on a height and overlooked the
sea. It was surrounded by a high stone wall capped with pieces
of broken glass and three lines of barbed wire. My guards and I
stepped into a stone courtyard closed at the end by a flat low
building with barred windows. Two noncommissioned officers
came out to greet us.

'Who's he?' asked one.

'He is an officer of the Infanterie Coloniale accused of an
abortive attempt to join the British Forces.'

'Officer! From the Infanterie Coloniale! Well, well, well,' and
he let out a peal of vicious laughter. 'And a Gaullist! Wonderful! We'll teach this Gaullist officer a good lesson here.'

Such a perfectly matched pair was rare. One was fat, short
and sweaty; the other tall, thin and pale. Both were repellently
filthy physically, but the expression on their faces was even
worse. The fat one had a piggish round head, small eyes set too
close together, mean and depraved. The bony one had a small
head with a stringy neck knotted by his Adam's apple; his face
had blurred features; his big bulbous lashless eyes were the
colour of an oyster; his wet half-open lips were set in a
perpetually dissatisfied grin. This pair, so dissimilar physically,
made a perfect match in cruelty and viciousness.

Once the formalities of booking me in were over, the
gendarmes took affectionate leave of me. I almost felt sorry for
their departure; now I felt just a little more abandoned and
miserable.

Fatso approached me. 'Unpack your things and strip! Quick!'

'But –'

'Don't but me! Do what you are told!'

'But –'

'Last warning! Unpack and strip!'

'But –'

The violent blow of a cudgel landed on my back. I had not
seen Skinny creep up behind me. Furiously, I turned around.

'What's with you?'

A hail of blows and kicks from both descended upon me. I
shut up. They confiscated my things, left me with a minimum of
clothes, and also took away my belt and shoe laces.

'Follow us,' said Fatso. 'Solitary confinement for you for

refusing to obey. In any case, our orders are to put you in solitary until the investigation of your case is finished.'

'What investigation?'

'Shut up! Come on and follow us!'

I shuffled slowly in my laceless shoes. We walked around several buildings and finally went into a kind of blockhouse hidden away at the end of another small courtyard. It was an old munition dump transformed into underground cell quarters.

'You'll be installed like a king, you'll see!' Fatso laughed sarcastically. I turned to look at the sky as if I might never see it again. They pushed me forward and I went down and down again on a narrow spiral staircase that apparently sank into the bowels of the earth. Fatso opened a metal door which moved soundlessly on its hinges and we entered a hall where one could see six wide-open doors that led into unoccupied cells. It was 21 November. The long holiday was over; I had just entered the world of the rats.

4

The World Of The Rats

Fatso pointed towards a cell, jabbed me in the back and shoved me in. The door slammed shut with a chilling thud. For a fleeting second a ray of light stole in through the crack below – then, absolute darkness . . . I heard the outside door close and stood with dangling arms and droning ears, buried alive in the centre of the earth.

I groped for the cement block I had seen in the cell while they were pushing me in and, feeling as if I carried the weight of the world on my shoulders, I sank into oblivion.

A good while elapsed before I surfaced to an absurd, incoherent void in which there was nothing to cling to. The silence was all-encompassing, like being packed in cotton wool, and this was augmented by the hallucination of a persistent deep humming in my ears.

I could taste fear seeping insidiously into my very being. I tried to make sounds but they were meaningless, since they were self-produced and were immediately swallowed by the immense silence.

Frenzied, I started to howl. I howled like a beast at my enemy, the door; I howled out my terror, my desperation, my frustration, my rage; I howled out my soul; I howled until I could howl no more! Silence . . .

Collapsing on to the cement block again, I fainted. This time, when I came to, I had to make a supreme effort to pick up the threads of my existence. The terror and frustration gave way to blind fury and I hurled myself at that damned door as if it were the cause of my plight. As a man possessed I started to hammer with my fists and kick with my feet, even knocking my head against that unfeeling sheet of steel. I was past screaming, but kept battering away at it, making it ring like a gong until I was so exhausted I slid to the floor in a heap.

Suddenly a ray of what to me seemed blinding light filtered in under the door and I heard a peal of derisive laughter.

'Well, you bastard, are you through making a racket? Soon you'll be tamed. In a week's time you'll be eating out of my hand; in a month you'll be stark raving mad. You have it coming to you, you stinking Gaullist!' A last guffaw, then silence and darkness.

I was bruised and emptied but a little glimmer of reason stirred in my mind and revived my nerve. 'Of course he is right,' I thought. 'If I don't want to go completely insane I must quickly learn to control myself.' I began to reason: 'My life is not in danger. I will probably be out of this hole soon. I'd better be in good shape when that day comes. I must find some kind of formula which can stimulate human life.' Suddenly convinced I was on the right track, I fell into a deep sleep, much like a soldier the night before battle, and was only awakened by the 'soup ceremony'.

This ritual took place twice a day. First there was the slight click which denoted the drawing of the bolt to the entrance door; then the snap of the light switch in the hall which threw a beam of summer light under the cell door; then footsteps and the metallic scraping of the soup pot being dragged across the floor; the clink of the lock after which my door swung in silently. Then, miraculously, the whole outside world erupted into my cell, a world of life and humans, even when personified by two such miserable specimens as the guards, acccompanied by a naval prisoner who served the soup.

The filthy sloppy guards stared at me mockingly as if to say, 'We hope you are learning your lesson, you bastard. This is what you get for playing the good little soldier.' However, not a word was uttered as the rule of silence was strictly enforced.

I held out my messtin while something was dished out from the steaming pot with a mammoth soup ladle. At the same time, I was given a chunk of dark bread. I raced to the cement block to deposit my booty, raced back to deposit the contents of my slop jar into a second huge pot on rollers, raced to the faucet installed on one of the walls to refill my water jug, and then, back to my ratlike existence until the next ritual.

I tried several times to question my jailers: 'What day is today? . . . Is it morning or evening? . . . How's the weather out

there? . . . What's going on in the world?' but I was met by a
stone wall of ironic silence, and finally desisted when I understood that this was part of the 'treatment'.

'God damn it, why?' I was filled with anger. 'What for? . . .
What does it accomplish? . . .' but I kept my questions to
myself.

I organised my life. I explored every nook and cranny of my
domain by running my hands over the walls and found the
dimensions of the cell to be about two and a half metres long,
one metre twenty centimetres wide and two metres ten centimetres high. The cement block which served as a bed occupied
most of the space. On top of it rested an amorphous mattress
stuffed with putrid straw and two rough heavy blankets which
stank of chlorine. At the foot of it stood a wooden bucket with a
lid and a rope handle which served as a toilet. These extrava-
gant facilities were complemented by a coverless army messtin
and a heavy metal spoon.

The steel door set in a metal frame was as smooth as glass,
except for a barred opening closed from the outside by a solidly
bolted shutter. The walls felt scabrous but there were no cracks
or fissures except for a small hole about ten centimetres deep in
one corner near the floor. Stuck into the wall to the right of the
door, there was one twisted rusty nail. It was the only incongruous element in the cell and, since it broke the oppressive
uniformity, it became a vaguely tangible symbol of hope. I
found nothing of interest when I groped over the floor.

I then decided it was of importance to recover my sense of
time. I arbitrarily decreed the next soup ritual to be morning
and the following to be night, etc, etc. Having created my
'mornings' and my 'nights', I kept the time straight by rolling up
the mattress in the morning and unrolling it at night.

I felt a basic need to orientate myself in a dark and silent
world. I was often invaded by anxiety when I awoke because I
was unable to place myself in time or space and found it even
harder to begin again to pull the threads of my life together. As
my eyes and ears were of practically no use to me, my senses of
touch and smell prevented me from dissolving into nothingness.
Through touch, I had placed myself into a concrete environment and now odours took the place of light. I could tell where I
was by the intensity of the stench of the slop jar. I carefully put

aside a prune-sized piece of bread ration to place next to my mattress where I could perceive its aroma with singular clarity.

The two meals were the focal points of my day. The soup was made of three basic elements: vegetable scraps, stalks, peelings and leaves which, if sufficiently boiled, become perfectly palatable to a starving man; noodles or dried beans which, if they were good were, alas, not plentiful except on holidays when I sometimes found as much as a dozen chickpeas or a small handful of mixed pebbles and lentils (I was wild about lentils). Meat or fish bones appeared very rarely; these I gnawed on and sucked dry before leaving them aside for my 'manual arts'. Of course, there was also bread, a chunk of more or less 150 grammes per meal, greyish in colour, sour in taste, sticky in consistency and with a crust that shone as if varnished. It dried out very rapidly, becoming deeply furrowed; it was foul . . . but it was bread! As I chewed this substance, I reflected on how bread regained its primordial value in catastrophic situations; even revolting bread became food, strength . . . the bread of life!

I swallowed my soup right away so as not to lose its beneficial heat, but it was very important to me to drink it reverently, with complete consciousness of each and every swallow. I tried to identify the paltry vegetables that made up my pittance. The flavour of each morsel invoked a glowing daydream. I could see the sunny bustling markets; I could see the shop windows of the charcuterie on the rue La Fontaine in Paris; I could see the sea with the trawlers discharging their catch; I could see and see . . . The repugnant brew opened the doors to the world outside and, after the meal was finished, I would sit completely still, momentarily sated and comforted.

Then, remembering my daily chores, I would wash my bowl and get to work.

From the depths of darkness I cried out to God. When I had finished praying, the darkness and silence were even deeper and my heart was more forsaken. I sulked and ate out my heart in bitterness. As I delved deeper into myself, I realised my behaviour was not only sacrilegious but also stupid. Who was I to demand or even merit an immediate response from God when the rest of the world was being scourged by blood and fire? I felt abashed by the arrogance of my prayer.

Suddenly I felt as if illuminated from within and I grasped my head in shame and started to weep. However, I was not crying out of self-pity now and I felt I had crossed a barrier. After a time, I stopped crying and sat very still as if listening; I felt unshackled from myself and my spirit was swept away by an irresistible current and then a prayer gushed forth. I was astonished at the words and sentences that issued from my mouth as if formed by themselves; it was like reading from a text, but one I had written!

'Thank you, God, for giving me this experience, since, for the first time, I begin to understand what loneliness, fear and misery are; thus I can begin to understand all those whose life is made up of these, no matter why they suffer or who they may be; they have now become my brothers. I pray for my wartorn country and for all those who love her and are suffering, fighting and dying for her. I pray for . . .' For the first time in my life I had forgotten about myself.

Total darkness ceased to exist for now I had found one more reason to endure.

After prayer came physical education. It took me some time to dream up exercises that could be adapted to the limited space, the dark and my undernourished condition, but I limbered up quickly and ended feeling vigorous and spry. I soon stopped bruising myself against the walls of my cell.

After thirty minutes of gym I stripped and washed myself from head to toe, waited to dry off and dressed. In spite of the dampness I felt warm and clean (strictly psychological, since I had no soap, no towel and no change of clothing). Then I had my morning coffee-less coffee-break. I had previously saved half my bread ration and sat on the cement block savouring it with delight.

Afterwards I chose a favourite book to read. I struggled to recall it to the letter. It was extremely difficult to go step by step without skimming to the end or letting my thoughts stray, but strict discipline allowed me to reach a point where I had the impression I was really reading, turning the pages, becoming excited by the story and even being surprised by the turns the plot took.

Not only was this a wonderful way to pass the time but it also represented a victory over the dark and the bastards outside.

As this mental exercise was very taxing and put me under a

great deal of stress I relaxed by taking up my 'manual arts'. I decided to transform my spoon into both a tool and a weapon. It was a massive, well-hollowed-out, friendly spoon made of an alloy of pewter and iron and the solidly built handle tapered at the end into a spatula. I ground the edges of it against the border of the cement bunk until they became razor sharp; I worked over the tapered end until I had a cross between a double-edged knife and a cabinet-maker's chisel. It amused and reassured me to be the owner of such a fine arm but, fearing the guards might nose around the cell or frisk me, I enlarged the little hole in the corner to stash it away. A weapon . . . a tool . . . a secret place . . . I had ceased to be a rat and was turning into a man again.

I arduously pulled the nail from the wall and sharpened its point. This was the pursuit of art for art's sake, as I had no real use for it until my socks gave out. Then I selected a big fishbone from my collection and after many fruitless attempts, succeeded in piercing an eye in the new needle with my trusty nail. I sculpted a meat bone into the shape of an egg, picked at my blanket until I unravelled several long threads and darned.

After some weeks I was amazed at how accustomed I was becoming to living in the dark; I didn't even think about it any more. My reflexes had become slightly lopsided – for instance, I closed my eyes to lace up my shoes and to pee into the pot.

The lack of light didn't interfere with my long 'walks'; it took exactly two and a half steps to cover the length of the cell. The procedure was: one step, another, a half-step to turn, one step, another, a half-step to turn. Slow and prudent at first, my pace accelerated and became automatic to such a point that I could maintain it at a fast clip without counting my steps or running into the walls. Only one precaution was still necessary – to remember never to turn in the same direction in order to avoid giddiness, which could cause me to fall down. My promenades made me feel higher than a kite and I let my imagination soar; I stopped only when so exhausted I had to sit down, but these hikes were so exhilarating that I took as many as possible.

One of my favourite pastimes was building a boat. This kept me busy day after day for many weeks. What a marvellous sailing-boat I had projected in my mind; it was a tough, elegant sea-going ketch! Although I was not a sea lover, I had often sailed during my summer vacations; I had even done a month's apprenticeship as ship's boy on a tartan that plied between Genoa and Barcelona, so I had a hazy idea of what a sailing-boat should be like.

Then I would sit poring over my imaginary blueprints on my imaginary drawing-board: the hull, the rigging, the specifications of the sails, and the layout of the interior. Each detail was subject to acute reflection to be argued about with myself as to its merits: engine or no engine, which type of steering, location of the ballast, which kind of construction material, the shape of the keel, the respective heights of the masts, the plan for the galley, the installation of the cabins and the placement of the holds. The more I thought, the more problems presented themselves to be solved. At last, one exciting day, the plans were finished! I could visualise my ship down to the last bolt and screw. In spite of all the erasures and modifications, I could 'read' the blueprints as if they were spread in front of me on a brightly lit table.

Now I started building the boat; I set up the cradle; I prepared the sub-assemblies; I laid up building materials; I stocked up on fittings ... The moment arrived when I could admire a copper-sheeted, painted hull, well stayed. As I launched it I was scared stiff, but it slipped down the ways smoothly into the water. I quickly finished the interior, rigged the sails, filled the water and diesel tanks and laid in supplies for life on board ship.

To top it off, I invited Françoise to accompany me on the maiden voyage! One sunny morning off we sailed into the wild blue yonder and into ... disaster! From the moment this charming creature stepped aboard, I lost interest in my magnificent ship. I tried to keep on reminding myself about manoeuvering the boat, but, instead, I thought only about manoeuvering myself into Seventh Heaven ... When I came back to earth I realised all this was leading up to no good so, regretfully, I threw Françoise overboard and continued my voyage alone. But the spell had been broken. I found myself bored stiff on my phantom boat so I cast her aside without even having christened her.

I started to build my dream house, but as my ignorance on this subject was total, I had more problems than I could handle.

Just as I was about to give up this project, too, other more important events captured my attention.

I had been so busy of late that I had completely forgotten to keep track of time.

I had continued to throw my jailers off balance, always appearing smiling and in fine fettle. They had frequently ransacked my cell in search of a clue to this riddle, but always beat a mumbling mystified retreat.

My nights were dreamless as I was tired from my bustling days and I was awakened only by the pungent scent of the dishwater soup.

I had my ups and downs. Several times, for no special reason, I sank into a bottomless stupor when nothing worked. I forsook my promenades, my books, my prayers and plunged into despair. I slept endlessly plagued by nightmares from which I awoke soaked in tears, unable to get up to receive my soup or empty my bucket, to the rapture of the guards, who were looking forward to my eventual breakdown.

Then, for no rhyme or reason, my fortitude returned as mysteriously as it had disappeared and I resumed a full and active life.

Three or four times I became violently ill with fever, diarrhoea and migraine headaches. Then I would drift off to sleep awaking completely restored a few days later to a carefree life in my enviable resort.

Christmas and New Year came. I had never before lived the birth of Christ with such reverent awe; never before had I had such expectations for the New Year – things could hardly get any worse than they already were.

On these two holidays the prison administration offered us a banquet: dried dates, chicken, noodles, chickpeas, all arranged on a splendid platter. Best of all, the two bastards had gone on holiday! Their replacements were two cheerful young guards who, while mute as trouts, still gave me a friendly smile and a pat on the back when I wished them a Merry Christmas.

Enriched by this human contact, I retired to celebrate the feast in my way. I evoked sweet memories of past years full of happiness, which brightened many of the following days.

One morning I rebelled! Struck by the conviction that my lot was unacceptable, I decided that, unless I took matters into my own hands, God and man would soon forget that I existed. It was fantastic that while the guards had been trying to annihilate me through madness, I had, thanks to God, drawn strength and riches from my tribulations, but now it was enough! In this frame of mind and serenely composed, I confronted the two bastards the day after New Year.

'I want to see the warden.'

'You what?'

'I want to see the warden.' I didn't raise my voice, but they knocked me about, manhandled me back into the cell and slammed the door, cursing me all the while.

At the next meal, I repeated my request tenaciously. 'I want to see the warden.'

Again – jeering, curses and threats.

'I want to see the warden. If I don't see him by tomorrow, you'll be sorry!' The scene of the previous day was replayed, but the guards seemed upset when they left.

When they brought me my food the next day I calmly announced, 'I'm going on hunger strike until I see the warden.' With this pronouncement I flung the boiling soup into Fatso's face, emptied the slop jar over Skinny's head, kicked the big soup pot over and scurried back into my rat hole. Livid with fury and trickling filth, the guards drew their revolvers, which only made them look more ridiculous. Their helper, who was laughing so much the tears were rolling down his face, earned himself a vindictive kick in the rear. I was petrified, but nothing happened! Once more the door banged shut. The guards were too stunned to insult me.

Shaken, I sat down. With one blow I had changed the course of my life and was now past the point of no return. I reassured myself that, unless they killed me, they could not worsen my predicament. Reliving the incident, I could not help laughing joyously at the ludicrous picture my mind presented. I paced back and forth spouting brilliant arguments until I slumped from fatigue and hunger. I lay down determined to see things through and awaited the consequences that surely would not tarry. I slept so heavily I didn't even hear the fatigue party cleaning up the mess in the hall.

A click ... a light ... the bastards stood beside a sailor

holding a steaming bowl of soup and a piece of bread. 'Are you going to eat now?'

'*Merde!*'

The door slammed shut and I returned to sleep and self-assurance. This scenario was re-enacted eleven times, like a well choreographed ballet. I was starting to lose strength, but was adamant in my decision not to give in.

Upon the arrival of the twelfth bowl of soup, the act changed. The two neatly dressed, smiling, boot-licking bastards flanked a corpulent new man who, from the little I could distinguish against the light, had a square head, salt-and-pepper moustache, clear eyes and crimson, fleshy lips. Dressed in a navy blue suit adorned with gold buttons and the ribbon of the Legion d'Honneur, he held himself straight as if on a parade ground, from which I deduced he must be a career naval officer.

A harsh voice rang out clearly: 'Well . . .'

Fatso, grovelling, intervened, 'Yes, sir, that's him.'

'I have won,' I thought. 'He is a naval officer.'

'You wanted to see me?'

I felt disconcerted by the sensation of being back in the world of questions and answers, of light and sound; I was at a loss for words. I spoke up: 'Yes, sir, I want to know the time and the date.'

A long silence fell. The warden, regarding his acolytes with puzzlement, asked, 'Is he crazy or what?'

'No, sir, I don't think so, but he is a sly one. I wouldn't put anything past him.'

'Is that all you have to ask?' The warden was irritated and perplexed. 'Did you bring me all the way down here just for that?'

I had carefully plotted my strategy. I must be polite, respectful and, above all, well bred.

'Oh no, sir. But just to know the time and date, to me would be marvellous! For you it's normal. Don't look so perturbed! Perhaps it seems normal to you to isolate another human being from any contact with normality, to put him into a stinking black hole where he can hear nothing, see nothing, has nothing to connect him to reality. Or perhaps you are afraid that if you answer my first question you will be obliged to answer all? Why this gratuitous cruelty that can only drive a man insane? I have not been condemned. A judge has not yet heard my case. Can you rest without a qualm when persecuting someone whose only crime has been a desire to fight for the freedom of our country while the Marine Nationale, the so-called 'royal one', has found nothing better to do than hide itself away in its ports and shoot at its allies and is content to fawn over the Boche! Your silence confirms my accusations, while I have been reduced to the only method of defence remaining to me: continuing my hunger strike to the bitter end! I'm going into my eighth day and I make you responsible for the foreseeable results.'

I had emptied the sack of my grievances and run out of breath as well . . .

The warden had listened, rubbing his brow with his suntanned paw. 'Well, to begin with, I myself do not know why you are here.'

'So, now you're trying to wash your hands of me. Is that it? Well, it isn't going to be that easy. Tell me, who gave you orders to torture me? Who?'

The warden blanched. 'Now, you shut up. I'm at the end of my patience. That's quite enough. If you want to play a military game, I can give as good as I get. It is I who will cut off your rations for the next forty-eight hours as punishment for insubordination. Back to your cell you go. We shall see afterwards.'

White with anger, I obeyed orders. The two smirking bastards were just getting ready to close the door when the warden stopped them.

'Just a minute.' Then he said to me, 'Today is 9 January, 1942 and it is exactly 10.17 a.m.'

The door slammed.

I sensed something had changed although I couldn't put my finger on it exactly. The only thing that was unaltered was the gnawing in my stomach; I really was starving to death.

A few hours later the door opened to admit a brand new nice-looking young guard. 'Orders from the warden: you are to be transferred one floor up. There you will have a cell with a window. You will also have a light and you will be allowed to converse with the other prisoners. You will be confined there for a fortnight to get used to normal prison living again; then you will be transferred to ground level and allowed to exercise in the courtyard and have normal privileges. Come on, let's go! It's 12.33 p.m. Can I give you a hand?' he asked smilingly.

I wanted to throw my arms around this guardian angel but, incapable of jumping with joy because I was so feeble, I broke down. I was so emotionally stirred up that I was near tears and my head was spinning. Pulling myself together I struggled to my feet, took a last look at my kingdom, my home, my hell. Leaving behind my nail, my spoon, my dreams, I walked forth.

Staggering slightly, I followed the guard up the stairway – out of Hell into Purgatory!

My new home was identical to the old, but light and air poured in through the now open window. The walls had been white-washed, the mattress and bedspread were spanking new, everything was spotless, and I got a double ration of soup. As the door was being closed, I heard a voice cry out, 'Guard?'

'Yes?'

'Is that him?'

'Yes.'

'Give him this.'

I saw a hand come out between the bars of the cell across the hall holding a piece of bread.

'I thank you for this,' said the young guard. He handed the bread to me and closed the door. I literally fell on the food; I tried to control myself because I knew that if I ate too fast, I was sure to be sick.

A voice across the aisle broke the silence. 'Are you all right? Do you feel better?'

'And how!' I responded slightly out of breath. 'Thank you for the bread . . . My name is Alec.'

Two bearded faces appeared at the openings of the two cells across from mine. 'I'm Jean,' said one.

'I'm Eduardo,' said the second, with a marked Spanish accent.

'I'm Heinz,' said a third muffled voice from behind a closed shutter.

'I'm a captain in the Merchant Marine and a Gaullist!' said Jean.

'Gaullist, my eye!' spoke up Eduardo teasingly. 'Why don't you admit you're nothing but a smuggler? Now me, I'm something nobody can deny, I'm a Spaniard.'

I squinted, looked again, rubbed my eyes and looked again. Lo and behold! There, in the cell across from mine, long-haired and bearded, grinning from ear to ear, was my friend Chorat!

He winked at me and said in an undertone, 'We were better off in Algiers, don't you agree?'

'I'm condemned to death,' said a smothered German-accented voice from behind the closed shutter.

'Oh him. He's a German spy,' said Jean in a commiserating tone. 'He is just waiting to be exchanged, otherwise . . .'

'Otherwise?'

'Otherwise, bang bang!' concluded Heinz bursting into a peal of laughter.

Eight days later I made my grand entrance into the communal hall on the ground floor. I was in top form again; my eyes were accustomed to the light, I had picked up the rhythm of normal confinement and I was marvellously at ease. I had listened to Jean's hilarious, endless stories and to the Spanish musical offerings of Eduardo, who sang a fiery *paso doble* called 'Mi Jaca' a thousand times a day. I had exercised my power of concentration by playing mental chess games with Heinz, who at long last had found a worthy opponent. I had almost forgotten the nightmare from which I had so recently emerged. I was dressed in clean clothes and had scrubbed myself with Marseilles soap. The barber from the little fort garrison had given me a shave and a haircut. In a word, I was a new man ready to enter a new life.

5

Blind Justice

On the morning of 7 May 1942, the corridors of the Bizarte Courthouse were swarming with people. Maître Vinciguerra, Coggia's lawyer, led a small group, including me, to the Marine Court. He was Corsican, of course, and considered the prima donna of the Tunisian bar. Resembling a Roman proconsul, he ploughed through the crowd, his black satin gown, bedangled with many decorations, floating around him, revealing a stately paunch. Behind him strode his assistant, carrying his master's briefcase. Coggia, looking rested and self-assured and dressed with simple elegance, accompanied us. As had been agreed, he had obediently appeared a few days earlier to join the group of prisoners at Fort Ain-Roumi, and had regaled everyone with his ample repertoire of anecdotes about the outside world.

In contrast, I made a pitiful showing. I was pale, handcuffed and led like a dog on a leash by a gendarme. I was also accompanied by my lawyer, Maître Sorroquère, a timid, subservient fellow who eked out a living defending small-time crooks. He had been assigned as a state defender for me, as I had no money to pay for a lawyer. Sorroquère bore no decorations and carried his own battered briefcase.

All of us entered a dark panelled room furnished with some benches and a long mahogany table covered with green baize, surmounted by an enormous portrait of Marshal Pétain. We took our places, and waited . . .

A blaring roll of drums announced the arrival of the court. A door opened and then seven officers in full regalia, preceded by an honour guard of six marines, marched in and took their assigned places at the table. I was amazed at the turnout of VIPs – seven officers and a midshipman totalling twenty-eight stripes! All had long, glum, frowning faces, especially the prosecuting attorney, who looked like a bilious shark and was muttering to himself as he waved a folded newspaper. I asked my lawyer what all the fuss was about.

Maître Sorroquère dolefully replied, 'The French Antilles, Martinique and Guadeloupe have just rallied around General de Gaulle and, to top it off, the British and Gaullists took the Port of Diego Suarez yesterday. I am willing to bet that the entire island of Madagascar will go over to the Free French before long. For us this spells disaster! They are going to throw the book at us!' The guard of honour, after presenting arms, marched out. Everything was ready for the kill.

The accusations were implacable, the interrogations superficial and biased. Coggia's face flushed with embarrassment at the florid defence presented by his big-time lawyer. The lawyer painted him as a sacrificial lamb, led astray by a Jewish–Communist–Gaullist–British henchman, namely me. I was really taking it on the chin. After a while I didn't know where the next blow would come from. Between the indictments of the prosecutor and the accusations of Coggia's lawyer, which echoed and corroborated each other, I was lost. When Maître Sorroquère stood up I felt a surge of hope, which quickly vanished. The lawyer made a whining plea full of sentimental platitudes. It was bad – worse than bad – it was nauseating! I tried to stop him but there was no way. The little lawyer continued to the bitter end.

The court adjourned and half an hour later the verdict was in! Coggia, due to his family's excellent connections, his handsome face and his fabulous defence, drew a minimum sentence. On the other hand I had Articles 75 and 76 of some code or other invoked against me; I was found guilty of being a deserter, of being an officer who had tried to join an enemy army during wartime, of having aggravated my offence by forcibly resisting arrest and trying to escape, of having led an innocent Coggia astray. I was condemned to military degradation, deprivation of civil rights and eighteen years' hard labour.

With the season's first heat wave at the end of May, I arrived at the Tunis Central Prison after a detour through the penal colony of Tiboursouk, a small hellhole where I had been sent by mistake. Now I was suddenly faced with the overwhelming fact that I had plunged into the hardcore world of crime. The prison was a city within a city – a maelstrom of men of all origins – Arabs, Italians, Greeks, Blacks, Maltese, French, Chinese, Spaniards . . . Here they all became members of the great prison fraternity. They mingled, banded together and murdered each other in accordance with their origins, individual interests, grudges or affinities, all of which led to the formation of terrifying gangs.

Upon arrival I was put in 'quarantine'. All newcomers, regardless of their crimes, had to go through a two-week period of 'mutation', which would transform them into fully fledged prisoners, a status that would stick to them for the rest of their stay. I was included in a 'class' of about one hundred new inmates; together, we were put through the meat grinder.

The first day we had to scrub ourselves with black soap, we were disinfected, deloused, shaved, sheared, showered, smeared with kerosene and left to sleep naked on the cement floor. On the second day, by far the more colourful of the two, we went through the administrative formalities. At daybreak we were given morsels of bread, bowls of 'coffee' and uniforms which were threadbare sacks with black and white horizontal stripes. These were not only torn, scratchy and stank of sulphur, but had also been cut to fit the average sized Tunisian, which presented unsolvable problems for those classified as 'large' by their tailors – the tall and the fat. When I stood up the lower hem of my shirt hung just to the upper part of my penis, producing a most singular effect.

The prisoners were then shackled six to a row. Having been classified as an especially dangerous convict because of the length of my sentence, I was put in the front line with my arms cross-chained to my two adjacent companions, which was awkward and raised the damn shirt even higher! Heavily guarded, we were marched out of the prison and down the middle of the main streets of Tunis, blocking the traffic along the way, to the Anthropometric Bureau, a good half-hour's jaunt.

An ape-like man who was grinning broadly and seemed to be enchanted with the outing marched on my left. I had heard that this fellow had barehandedly killed a dozen people; when asked how it felt, he always answered that he had enjoyed it thoroughly. A puny little Arab, pale and pitiful enough to inspire any passer-by to give him a bowl of gruel, trotted on my right. This inoffensive looking creature had a record of rapes, tortures and sadistic assaults leading to the deaths of his victims who had all been under fourteen years of age. Neither of them had been sentenced to terms of eighteen years, which made me reflect on the seriousness of my offence!

This parade seemed to be a well-established ritual, as all the families had turned up and were crowding the pavements. The women were shrieking, screaming, crying and wringing their hands. Occasionally some would rush out and throw themselves around their men's necks, covering them with kisses; children darted in and out of the ranks trying to pass letters, money and small packages of drugs and other goodies. The harassed guards tried unsuccessfully to maintain a semblance of order, but no one got really upset, as this chaos seemed to be standard procedure. Although I was at first embarrassed to be leading a parade with my penis waving in the breeze, even I ended up consoling myself with the fact that no one knew me but when a beautiful young woman blushingly gazed at me with barely concealed interest, I felt vaguely stirred.

After several days of indoctrination, I was called to the warden's office. There I encountered a small well groomed man who looked at me kindly through steel-rimmed spectacles. On the desk I glimpsed my own face staring back at me from the cover of a folder.

The warden spoke in a smooth voice: 'You're in for eighteen years.'

'Yes, sir.'

'Eighteen years is a long time.'

'Oh yes, sir.'

'I don't want to talk politics but I must say the court certainly was rough on you.'

I agreed politely.

'Well, we shall try to make your stay as bearable as possible. The first reports on you are favourable. You will be transferred to a normal detention block tomorrow. Afterwards, if your conduct is satisfactory, we may offer you work. If you accept and continue to behave well, you can earn a lot of privileges, step by step, which will make your life a little easier. I don't consider you a run-of-the-mill criminal and I shall see to it that you are always treated correctly.'

As promised, I was transferred to a ward the next morning. It was a vast high-ceilinged room holding about 150 men paying for their crimes by wasting their lives at a desperately slow rhythm – five, ten, twenty years . . .

As I entered I was met by a deafening silence and I felt nailed to the door by the hundreds of eyes converging on me. A stocky man pushed through the crowd. Although he was dressed in prison garb and his head was shaven, he seemed somehow to be different from all the rest. He held out his hand to me and asked quietly: 'Who are you?'

'A newcomer.'

'How long are you in for?'

'Eighteen years.'

'What for?'

'For being a Gaullist.' An approving murmur rumbled through the ward. 'And you?'

A voice answered from the crowd, 'He is a priest.'

'Are you really a priest?'

'Well, I was . . . Come on, I must introduce you to the Chiefs.' The men made way for us as we started to move but then the priest said, 'Put down your things and wait for me here.'

As I waited, a bright young Arab came and crouched next to me. 'Do you know what the families are here?'

'Not yet.'

'Then let me explain. Nobody can survive here by himself. Everyone belongs to a "family" ruled by a Chief who must be obeyed as if he were your own father. Everything you have is owned in common; those who receive packages or money to buy things at the canteen must share with their family. If any member is attacked, robbed or molested the other members must defend him and –' He was interrupted by the priest's return.

'Come on, they're waiting for you. Did Ali explain how the system works?'

'Yes, a little, but . . .'

'OK then. They're going to ask you some questions and then they'll decide which family will adopt you for the time being.

Later, if you want to, or if the family wants you to, you can change. Well, you'll see. Let's not keep them waiting.'

There in a corner sat the eight Family Chiefs. I introduced myself and the interrogation began.

'Do you receive parcels?'

'Do you have any money?'

'Are you Jewish?'

'How old are you?'

'Are you an officer?'

Everything was carefully considered and, at long last, one of the paterfamiliae stood up and said, 'I'll take him on trial if that's all right with the rest of you.' The others agreed. Thus I became a member of the Noble Hearts Family to which, by some strange coincidence, the priest and Ali also belonged.

All the families had names that would have been most suitable for Masonic lodges or sports clubs. They were called 'The Red Lions', 'The Aces', 'The Golden Arrows'. The Jews were known as 'The Sons of Abraham', while the sticky-fingered were appropriately united as members of the community of 'Ali Baba'. Each clan had a clearly defined territory in which their belongings were stacked against the wall and there the members slept and shared their meals. The Chief's authority was absolute: it was he who administered the members' few belongings, ordered food from the canteen, distributed the daily chores and presided over the Mutual Aid Society which could cover anything from protecting a menaced member to helping a wife or child in need.

This social structure made it possible to lead a relatively normal life. Sometimes, on birthdays and other important dates, one family would invite another to a feast. These were joyous occasions and laughter resounded far into the night, as all gathered, as if around a campfire to sing, tell jokes and perform.

Then there were the 'Kif' parties. 'Kif' was the local name for marijuana. These took a lot of forethought as the setting had to be carefully prepared to obtain the drug's maximum effect, and special sweets and tongue-tickling appetisers had to be provided.

It was a fantastic sight! The men sprawled in a circle, staring haggardly at the flickering flame of the smoking oil lamps, which were made from a wick placed in an ordinary tin can; the little heaps of dates, the honey-dripping Arabic candy, the crystallised fruit and the Kif at arm's reach. The Chief meticulously rolled the joints and then took a deep drag before he passed them on. The parties began with an over-excited exhilaration and peaked at a stage of hysterical laughter, where everything and anything became irresistibly funny. Then, as night deepened, the men would sink into the ghostly shadows of their dreams, the orgy of hallucination melting into reality until one by one, like the oil lamps, their consciousness would be snuffed out and swallowed up by nothingness.

During the day, the prisoners killed time as best they could. A side door opened on to a small courtyard surrounded by a six-metre-high chain-link mesh fence, where we were allowed to walk, play soccer and sun ourselves for two hours in the morning and two in the afternoon. This was the contact point with the outside world; messages, money, small packages crammed with drugs and photographs often came flying over the wall, which must have given on to a street.

The guards rarely went into the wards or interfered with the lives of the prisoners. The only security measures consisted of a weekly frisking of the prisoners and a routine search of their quarters and the courtyard which, needless to say, produced no results.

There was supposed to be a small network of informers known about by the senior prisoners who, however, never talked about it. Living daily side by side with the men who had become my companions, I lost sight of the fact that they were all, in one way or another, hardened criminals: murderers, sadists, swindlers, habitual second offenders who had reaped severe punishments. Behind the innocuous façade ran a hideously vicious undercurrent which periodically erupted into violence amongst the men or the families: adolescents sexually abused; blackmail that led to suicide; bloody vendettas; all sorts of crimes would surface at any moment in this world, supposedly dedicated to law, order and contrition. In the mornings it was not rare to find a mysteriously murdered body lying on the floor, and I, who tended to look at the world through Boy Scout glasses, quickly realised the hard facts of my present life.

One morning, a young boy, the beloved concubine of my

powerful Family Chief, was found to be missing. He had been kidnapped and had literally disappeared into the bosom of another family. Had he gone willingly or had he been torn away from the arms of his lover? The answer itself was irrelevant as the forsaken family was *ipso facto* dishonoured and each of its members felt personally cuckolded. It was a very grave matter. The priest spent his entire day in ineffective secret negotiations, but everyone held fast. During the day bargaining continued as secret deals were made by chiefs of the different families, forming and reforming alliances invisible to the guards, and most of the prisoners had no concept of what was going on. As night fell the tension mounted; the men, absorbed in their thoughts, became dangerously quiet. When the lights were switched off the ward was engulfed in a deadly silence. Here and there an oil lamp gave a puddle of light and lit men's faces with a wan glimmer. The men stood at opposite ends of the room, according to the alliances concluded during the afternoon. Between them lay a black stretch of no man's land; neutrality was out of the question!

The offended Chief stepped out of the ranks and advanced like a Homeric figure to take his stance in front of the assembled enemy. He hurled abuse and threats at them and in the same breath demanded the return of his beloved. I suddenly became aware that everyone was armed and ready to fight – some held iron bars unearthed from God-knows-where; some held glass bottles; some had fixed forks to the ends of short sticks; others even held knives. Many had shirts or pants wrapped around their left forearm so as better to fend off blows; almost all were bare-chested in order to be less encumbered.

Fear stirred in me as I watched the expressions of excitement on their faces at the prospect of battle. The accused Chief answered in no uncertain terms; he cursed and mocked those who were sticking their noses in his business. Suddenly, at an imperceptible signal, the two sides threw themselves simultaneously at each other in a cacophony of howls, yelps and roars, hitting out blindly at anyone in the semi-darkness, which only added to the confusion. Not knowing the men well enough to distinguish friend from foe, I was swept along and hit out in every direction hoping to fend off blows. Soon I got a gash on my left cheek and I finally caught a blow on the head which put me *hors de combat*.

When I regained consciousness the brawl was over. The acrid stench of burning mattresses and bedding set on fire by over-turned oil lamps penetrated my nostrils and made me choke. Peering through watering eyes, I saw the floor strewn with bodies. The guards, reinforced by a squad of gendarmes, had quickly intervened, pushing the men to the far end of the room and forcing them to strip before channelling them into the courtyard and then into a special detention block. The balance sheet read: twenty wounded and three dead – the betrayed Chief, the boy in question and the priest.

The next day, the weight of the law descended on the culprits, adding to the already long sentences accumulated by some. I was surprised at how the warden's lightning bolts fell on those really guilty and acquired great respect for the warden's intelligence network. I mourned the priest, even though I had found out that a passion for abusing little girls had led my friend to prison. He had been my friend and I felt that the man's present behaviour had been spurred by contrition and profound despair, as if attempting to buy back a mite of Grace by helping those around him.

After the riot the inmates were scattered throughout the prison. I was shifted to another ward, an exact replica of the first.

I was called to the warden's office. The warden told me, 'I am very pleased with you. You've stood up well during these crucial three months, so I have a job for you. How about it?'

I accepted enthusiastically and, from one day to the next, my lifestyle changed completely as I was transferred to a room where twenty of the prison élite were lodged. There were actually beds, a table, benches and shelving; it was like a palace to me. I was assigned as accountant to the Admission Office; as such I had to keep inventories of the personal effects of incoming and outgoing prisoners, as well as a running account of their money and canteen bills. It was dull, tedious work, but carried with it many fringe benefits. From my work table I could see the entrance court, the main gate through which cars and trucks came and went, and a postern to the right which opened a hundred times a day and afforded me a flashing glance of a wide central avenue. From there it was only a short step to dreams of escape. My job allowed me to talk with many new and released prisoners, who provided valuable information.

For administrative reasons, such as checking over the canteen and getting papers signed, I was allowed to roam freely through the penitentiary, thus making many useful contacts. The Admission Office was a good place to get to know the guards well, render them small favours and establish cordial relations. 'Necessity makes strange bedfellows.'

A point of civil law, which stated that any prisoner acquitted be immediately released at the end of his hearing, became of prime importance to me. When the court sat in night sessions at the Palace of Justice, a guard and I were on duty to take care of discharge formalities. For the first time I could envision possibilities of escape. I became happy and hopeful.

The prison compound covered several city blocks. Slowly I got to know my way around the enormous penal colony with its population of several thousand inmates, and its facilities which included kitchen, bakery, disinfection centre, showers, laundry, forge, carpentry and infirmary. These were staffed by the prisoners themselves which made the prison autonomous.

The wards, alternating with exercise courts, were spaced around a large quadrangle. In the centre were several atriums surrounded by shaded corridors. The administration building and the warden's private quarters were at the entrance court. The high security blocks were at the back. In the first of these blocks, special cases, such as political prisoners, were isolated. They were lodged two to a cell which gave on to a central hall where a guard was stationed during the day. I was overjoyed to find Coggia there, who was finishing his short sentence, as well as many other friends from my brief stay at Tirboursouk. I also ran into three Englishmen who had been arrested for espionage. One of them was reputed to be a big wheel in the British Secret Service.

The sultry summer heat had given way to the wetness of autumn. It was the end of October, 1942. Things were happening fast out in the world. I had heard the worrying reports about Rommel's blazing advance into Egypt and then learned of his retreat before the Eighth Army, which had pulled itself together, made a stand, and won the battle of El Alamein on 23 October, opening the way into Libya and Tunisia. Rumours of an Allied invasion of North Africa spread like wildfire and excited the imagination of my group.

I began to work on my escape slowly and carefully. I didn't want to leave Coggia behind, but this presented a difficult problem as he was locked up in the high security block, while I slept in the special workers' room. I found out that there was no night guard for the political prisoners, so I only needed to find a way to open the armoured door to the hall, as well as Coggia's own cell door. I had observed the cluster of keys hanging from the guard's belt; they didn't look impossible to duplicate, but I had to be sure which were the right keys.

My room mate, Emile, worked in the forge. Alsatian by birth and a confirmed Communist, he was serving time for his political activities. While not agreeing with his philosophy, I nevertheless admired him for his idealism, efficiency and discretion. During one of our lengthy conversations I stopped beating around the bush and asked outright if Emile would help me escape. Emile showed no surprise.

'I'll have to think it over. I would really like to but I can't afford to have extra time added to my sentence for aiding and abetting an escape.'

A few days later Emile brought the subject up again. 'I'll help you. Listen carefully, this is what you must do . . .'

I had become very friendly with Felix, a fat Tunisian who also worked in the Admission Office. He was a very rich man whose passion for horse betting had landed him in prison. He had cheated at the racetrack by bribing the jockeys and manipulating the odds, and had been caught redhanded. When I asked him for a favour he was more than happy to oblige.

M. Richard, the guard who held the keys to Coggia's cell block, laid the precious bunch on the table in the office one day. At my signal Felix diverted the guard's attention and kept him engrossed by telling him of fabulous betting opportunities, while I, as per Emile's instructions, pressed the two necessary keys between two pieces of soap to get their impressions. Afterwards Felix, who had been watching me, asked anxiously, 'Exactly what are you up to? Why the keys? You are not planning to escape, are you?'

I laughed nervously. 'Want to come along?'

'Me? Are you crazy? You know I'd never do anything like

that! But if you need any more help, just let me know.' He was excited at the thought of being allowed to participate in a Grand Adventure and his eyes sparkled.

My plan was simple. Felix often ordered meals for himself from the best restaurants in Tunis, so on a night when I would be on duty Felix would invent an excuse to order a special gourmet dinner which I would share with the guard. I would take advantage of any chance to leave and would release Coggia. Together we would overpower the guard, take his key to the gate, change into street clothes, which I would have hidden inside the office. We would then calmly walk through the entrance court, chatting as if we were talking with the warden, to fool the guard outside, and out the door we would go! Child's play, if all went well . . .

A few days later, Emile appeared with the most bizarre object – a two-ended key on a steel rod, six centimetres long, with a cross-bar to make it easier to turn in the lock – a little masterpiece! The long awaited moment arrived when the secretary received a schedule of hearings for men accused of serious offences which almost certainly would cause the court to sit far into the night. I bustled busily about, alerted Coggia, mobilised Felix, reviewed each and every phase of the plan and cleared the decks for action.

On 8 November, 1942, the eve of our planned departure, news broke . . . The Americans had landed! When? Where? Gradually the facts emerged from the jumble of contradictory news reports. Operation Torch – objective, to push Rommel and the Italians into the sea – had begun. 100,000 British and American soldiers were on Algerian and Moroccan beaches. The French Vichy authorities wavered between the disgraceful and the ridiculous, and finally opted for both! The opposition to the invaders was minimal and the official attitude was absurd. The noble Marine Nationale Française opposed the landings and, once more, took a beating. The Army and the general population were undecided but later sided with the victors, when everything was over. This does not mean to say that there were not any truly brave Frenchmen, but they were too few and too disorganised to play an effective role. The time to prove their valour was yet to come.

The prison was boiling with excitement. My group and I were chafing at the bit. We followed the news hour by hour, expecting to be liberated at any moment. Suddenly our hopes were dashed as the situation took a turn for the worse. From 9–11 November German troops retaliated by occupying the so-called Free Zone of France in violation of all signed treaties. Simultaneously, planes and ships, which encountered no resistance, occupied all Tunisian airfields and the port of Bizerte, to prevent the Afrika Korps being cut off from their supply lines or attacked from the rear. A parachute regiment, based in Italy, flew two battalions to Tunis and a third one, as well as an engineering battalion, to Bizerte. This action took French Headquarters by surprise. My friends and I had been dreaming of freedom, now we suddenly found ourselves in imminent danger, trapped in prison.

I requested an immediate interview with the warden and insisted that Major Dick Jones, the head of the English prisoners, be present. We found the warden, his face pale and set, nervously playing with a ruler. He listened to us without saying a word.

After a seemingly endless silence, he reacted. 'You must understand that I am only a cog in the machine, a simple civil servant. I cannot make the decision you are asking of me. I must consult higher authorities. On the other hand, I don't want to be guilty of handing over French patriots or British agents to the Germans. If by 5.00 p.m. I still haven't received authorisation to release you, I will take a decision.'

'What if the answer is "No"?'

'Well, then I'll take the responsibility. You have my word on it.'

By sheer chance, I was put into the same cell as Coggia in the high security block.

'Do you realise, Jean-François, that I have the keys in my pocket to get us out and here we are like sitting ducks. All our plans have gone up in smoke. What if the warden doesn't keep his word?'

After waiting for half an agonising day – with false rumours flying and setting everyone's nerves on edge – the warden, as good as his word, sent M. Moreau with his decision. Apparently no one had wanted the responsibility of our release.

'The warden has given me orders to release you tonight. You

are to remain calm to avoid suspicion on the part of the
personnel that anything extraordinary is afoot. The last thing
you need is to be picked up by the police on your way out. As
soon as it gets dark we'll get everything moving.'

The 'Lights Out' hour was moved forward slightly and, at
8.00 p.m., three Englishmen and about fifteen Frenchmen were
gathered in the Admission Office. Felix had worked miracles.
He had assembled everyone's belongings in little heaps and had
the necessary release papers ready to be signed. Everyone
changed into street clothes. The warden arrived.

'Is everything ready? Good. One more thing . . . I'll probably
be dismissed tomorrow. I would appreciate your signing this
document I have prepared which acknowledges that, for patriotic and humane reasons, I have set you free of my own
volition.' Everyone signed enthusiastically.

The great moment had arrived. 'Let's get out of here',
someone said impatiently.

'Follow me,' said M. Moreau. As we filed out, each man in
turn shook the warden's hand with all respect. Here was a man,
a real Frenchman.

M. Moreau escorted the group to the postern and then the
jailbirds took flight in inconspicuous flocks of two or three.
Awaiting my turn with Coggia, I suddenly began to shake with
suppressed laughter.

'What's come over you?' asked Coggia.

'It's just that . . . just that it's so funny,' I puffed. 'When have
you ever heard of convicts being secretly escorted through the
main gate by the head guard with the warden's blessing, when,
at the same time, they were carrying the keys to the damn place
in their pockets?'

6

The Apprenticeship

At exactly eleven o'clock, after the flight from prison, Coggia and I arrived at a house in the heart of the Medina, the Arabian quarter, where we had made an appointment with Dick Jones. We entered a courtyard surrounded by rooms screened by beaded curtains; in the centre a fountain warbled peacefully. Wearing an impeccable floating jellaba, a red chechia and embroidered mules, Dick welcomed us, smiling at our astonishment as he led us into one of the rooms. There we found Dick's two companions from the prison. We all sat down on fluffy cushions which were scattered here and there on the floor, and a servant placed small cups of thick Arabian coffee on the low brass tables.

Major Dick Jones of British Intelligence seemed perfectly at ease in his Tunisian attire. Up to then I had never looked closely at him but I now began to look him over, starting at his pink pate surrounded by flamboyant red hair and protruding ears. His physical aspect was most misleading – he was small, frail and nervous as a lizard, which he tried to hide behind a nonchalant façade; in spite of his efforts to appear candid, his cold darting eyes belied his doll-like face and infantile mouth; his words, pronounced in a contained falsetto, deserved serious attention – a real stick of dynamite in gift wrapping.

I knew that Dick had been born of English parents in Cairo and that he had lived there most of his life, but not much else. It was said that he was fluent in all the Arab dialects spoken from Egypt to Morocco, that he could cite the Koran by heart, that he had such a deep knowledge of Islam that he could pass as an Arab anywhere.

He had arrived in Tunis a year ago, accompanied by Arthur Wilding and Alan Caldwell, two very typical Englishmen. Arthur had brown hair and sported an RAF moustache; his taste for good living had made him sprout a tummy and he spoke abominable French punctured by ear-splitting guffaws. The only conspicuous thing about Alan, a faded blond, was that he was so inconspicuous that he could fade into any background. The trio had been arrested and locked up a few months earlier by French military security.

Dick said, 'Pretty house, don't you think? We have three safe houses like this one in the Medina where we can count on many sympathisers. You'll get to know them later, *inshallah*, if we can work together. I suppose that, since you were imprisoned for Gaullist activities, you might be eager to collaborate with the British Intelligence Services while killing time until the Allies get to Tunis.'

Jean-François' and my reply was a vehement yes.

'Then the first step in the agenda is to get the green light on you from Security. You must give Arthur all the pertinent information on yourselves. While waiting for your clearance from Malta – yes, that's where we get our orders – I shall give you a mission which, although not top secret, nevertheless is very urgent for us. Later you'll get more sensitive assignments because we need liaison agents to work with the military. All our agents are organised into individual cells which have no connection with each other, for security reasons. We co-ordinate their missions as well as those of a few of the Resistance groups. Odette, one of our agents, already knows you.'

'How?'

'She was also interned at Fort Ain-Roumi, so I know all about Alec's long vacation.'

I blushed and squirmed on my pillow.

Dick's tone changed as he started to give us specific instructions. Coggia, who had relatives in Tunis, was charged with locating some more safe houses and left to get on with this immediately, after leaving his uncle's telephone number as an emergency contact. Then Dick spoke to me.

'Listen carefully. We know that the Germans have landed at La Goulette, Bizerte, Ferryville and several airports, but we don't know how many or which units. All I want right now from you is a report on the Tunis–Bizerte sector, but I want to know everything! You are to drop a daily report in the letter box at the big café, Chez Max, on the Avenue France before 8.00 p.m. every evening. Anyone can show you where it is. Arthur will give you specific instructions. One more thing. Never carry anything in writing; commit everything to memory. You are only useful to us alive so no foolhardiness, please. Good hunting and all the best!'

It turned out to be very good hunting indeed – more of a rabbit race, really. I chased round frenetically during the following days. I covered hundreds of kilometres by bus, bicycle, tram and on foot. I amassed a mountain of information and somehow managed to deliver a report every day at Chez Max, where Odette picked it up. I slept anywhere and lived on beignets, olives and dates, as I had been too embarrassed to admit to Dick that I was almost broke.

I would take the little beige-coloured wooden TGM tram at the Tunis Marine Station every day. Sitting in the jolting carriage, I would watch the shocking pink flamingos fishing near the hazy shores of the Lake of Tunis, pass in front of the ruins of Carthage and arrive forty minutes later at the seaport of La Goulette, which lay in the shadow of windswept palms.

La Goulette was the real port, not Tunis itself. Nose in the air and hands in my pockets, I would stroll around the harbour memorising ships' names, ports of origin and visible cargoes. I was especially interested in those ships unloading troops, military equipment and supplies. By comparing my personal observations with other information gathered through friendly chats with crane operators, truckers and dock hands I could draw accurate conclusions about enemy movements. I would store all this information in my mind by repeating the numbers like an endless litany, so as not to forget anything.

I would walk from La Goulette to the nearby airfield, El Aouina, where I realised that the Germans' air-bridgehead from Sicily grew more important daily. There I saw the famous Junker JU 52s for the first time. They were tri-motor transport planes which appeared to be made of corrugated iron. Mouth agape, I watched the enormous six-motored Messerschmidt ME 323s which could carry up to ten tons. I also took note of the new fighter planes. I memorised the plane numbers, the licence plates of the trucks and the insignias on uniforms. Shivering from the cold, I spent two nights in a shepherd's hut on the edge of the airfield to monitor the number and frequency of the night flights. My head stuffed to bursting with data, I would return to Tunis to summarise them in my report.

I would also go to Bizerte regularly in a dilapidated bus crowded with Arabs, chicken crates and bundles, an hour and a half's harrowing trip. At the port there, I struck up a friendship with one of the pilots whose job it was to guide ships through the canal and channel in the lake to the Admiralty at Ferryville. The pilot, an excitable fellow who loved his Pernod bottle as much as he hated the Germans, made it easy for me to extract information from him about shipping traffic.

From there I would go to Ferryville to find out what was going on at the Admiralty and the Arsenal, then back to Tunis to begin my rounds again. I tried two side excursions west of Bizerte, but got chased away by the Feld-Gendarmerie and didn't judge it prudent to insist.

On the sixth evening I found a message from Dick at Chez Max: 'Meeting tonight, 10.00 p.m.' Exhausted, I plopped down, ordered beer and eggs baked in sand (a house speciality) and reached for a newspaper, to catch up on what had been happening. It was December, 1942. The Free French Zone was now subject to the same laws as the rest of Occupied France. As a consequence, the Gestapo had arrested a large number of important political figures: General Weygand, President Herriot, Paul Reynaud, Georges Mandel. But there was also some good news: Governor General Boisson had come out for de Gaulle and caused the vast French West African colonial empire to become part of Free France. In Tunisia, the situation was confused as Admiral Esteva, his general staff and the officers of the Marine Nationale in Bizerte were still faithful to the Pétain Government and had put themselves under the German boot, but General Barré, along with some of his troops, had rebelled and marched out to join the Anglo–American forces. German forces, composed mostly of parachute battalions, were attacking on all fronts and inflicting heavy losses on the Allies. I was puzzled by this as I knew, first hand, the scarce quantity of materials and troops which had landed in my 'territory' since 11 November. I was still trying to figure this out when Odette tapped me on the shoulder.

'Are you asleep?'

It was 10.00 p.m. on the dot.

Dick was waiting for us at another safe house in the Medina. He looked exhausted too but broke out in a wide grin when he saw us.

'Good for you, Alec. Your reports have been good. Almost all of them have been transmitted to Malta. Yes, Alan has established radio contact. That's really an ace up our sleeve. Security has cleared you. They picked up your track in your Gibraltar – ahem – excursion in December 1940 and only asked me to make sure you are not completely barmy, so you're in. You join us as a lieutenant. Welcome to the club!'

We joined Odette and Alan in the dining-room and continued our conversation while devouring a monumental couscous. I spoke of my doubts concerning the strength of the Germans fighting north-west of Tunis.

'It just doesn't add up, Dick. I think the Germans are pulling the wool over our eyes. I know there aren't as many of them as their attacks have led us to believe. These are out of proportion to the stuff I've seen them land.'

'That coincides with other information which I have, but we can't count on it. We simply can't take the chance,' said Dick. No argument would convince him or the Allied Headquarters to change their minds and this denial of the obvious had dual consequences – on the one hand, believing the enemy to be very powerful, they postponed the offensive against Tunis. When they finally realised that indeed they had been bluffed, it was too late. The winter rains had begun and turned the battlefield into quagmire. They had given the Germans and Italians time to land 250,000 men plus sufficient heavy equipment to reinforce northern Tunisa. It would take the Allies five months of step-by-step fighting to push the Axis into the sea. On the other hand, the heavy losses suffered by the enemy would incapacitate them to defend Sicily, Italy and southern Europe later.

Dick changed the subject. 'Things are really falling into place for us. We have made giant strides this week. I've already told you that Alan has re-established contact with Marie, our codename for Malta, so we should soon be getting explosives, money and other things, including two "pianos".'

'Pianos?'

'Yes, that's what we call our small transmitter-receiver sets.

Our friends in Tunis are co-operating very nicely, but we have a big hole in our organisation. As yet we have almost no contacts in the Bizerte–Ferryville sector and even fewer in the west, from the sea to Mateur and Medjez-el-Bab. Tomorrow I want you and Coggia to go to Bizerte to set up an information network and organise a radio and combat team. You shall have the first available 'piano'. Marie wants an almost hour-by-hour report about German troop and ship movements, as well as what the French Navy is up to. As soon as you are set up, Coggia is to return here because I need him badly.'

Early next morning, Coggia and I were standing in the town square of Bizerte when we heard a siren followed by others and then short blasts of a whistle coming from the ships anchored in the harbour.

'It must be an air-raid drill,' surmised Coggia. But then we saw people running and heard an expanding thunder coming from the north-west – from the sea. Now we could see shining pinpoints in the sky against the sun; these flecks grew and flew in majestic slowness in rows of six.

'My God, look at those planes!' I shouted, shading my eyes. 'There are dozens of them – at least sixty or eighty. It's incredible! Look! Do you think they are German or what?'

Before we could decide, the planes began dropping their bombs. All hell broke loose! Bombs exploded everywhere, houses crumbled, vehicles flew into the air, trees splintered, the earth shook. It went on and on and on. Jean-François and I, lying flat with our heads stuck under a stone bench, thought we would die from fright and pain at the convulsions of the ground. After five interminable minutes, it was finished. The silence was broken only by delayed explosions and the crystalline shattering of falling shards. Little by little, the city came back to anguished life, filled with cries and moans. Weaving like drunkards from the cataclysm, Coggia and I got up and saw others moving about.

'Air drill – humph!' I mumbled.

'It was the Americans,' Coggia replied quietly.

Bizerte had turned into a crackling hell. A quarter of the town had been levelled in a few minutes. Buildings, including the town hall, were in flames, and cinders were flying. The dead and wounded sprawled everywhere.

'There must be something we can do to help,' said Coggia. 'You know your way around here. Where's the nearest hospital?'

'I don't know, but there's a neighbourhood clinic nearby. Let's look for it.'

Approximately a block up one of the streets, we saw a Red Cross flag flying over an open doorway. We entered a courtyard formed by low buildings roofed with corrugated Duralite. Many of the wounded were huddling in corners as the stretchers, lined up willy-nilly in the courtyard, were all occupied. A brown-haired woman dressed in a blood-and-earth-stained uniform was moving rapidly among the injured. Coggia and I approached as she bent over a stretcher.

She looked up, pushed her hair back, and shot at us, 'What are you doing here? This is not a show, you know.'

'We are both medical students. How can we help?' Coggia asked simply.

Mollified, she made amends. 'Forgive my bad temper. It's just that . . . just look over there. It's impossible to cope with. There's just too much to be done.' She turned to Coggia. 'Why don't you help my husband? He is inside in minor surgery. And you,' she pointed at me, 'give me a hand.'

We worked frantically, but the more we took care of, the more were brought in. As darkness fell, we continued working by gas and candlelight. We heard that the main hospital had been hit and that the Army was setting up a field hospital outside Bizerte, but no one seemed to know exactly where. Finally, ambulances began to evacuate the most serious cases, but all the beds in the clinic were still occupied. At 2.00 a.m. the four of us collapsed, looking for the first time into each other's faces.

'I'm Dr Duvergier, Jean Duvergier. I'm a French civilian doctor in charge of this clinic.'

'I'm Françoise, his wife. Thanks for all your help, but, my God, what happened?'

We were too exhausted to wash or eat. While one of us stayed on duty, the rest of us wrapped ourselves in blankets and lay down in a corner of the floor.

The following days were hell on earth. The British and the Americans alternately bombed three-quarters of the town.

Miraculously, the clinic remained intact, surrounded by scorched ruins, rubble and twisted iron beams. At first the civilians had taken refuge in olive groves on the nearby hills, but finally they had given up and fled with whatever they had left stuffed in small sacks.

Coggia and I remained with the Duvergiers, filled with admiration for this couple who had worked unceasingly, given first aid, performed operations with the meagre means at their disposal and saved hundreds of lives. He was splendid as he operated imperturbably, bent in concentration over the patients during the bombings and improvising with whatever was at hand. She was a charmer – she smiled, she bantered, she was infinitely gentle. Both were exemplary in dedication and courage.

At last it was over. The town was empty. Corpses rotted in the ruins; millions of rats, carrying with them the spectre of cholera, had invaded Bizerte; the clinic was out of food, medicines and surgical supplies. There was no water or electricity; there was nothing left to do but leave.

Coggia left first. He got hold of a bicycle and pedalled to Ferryville to catch a bus to Tunis and make his report to Dick Jones. An Admiralty car came to take the Duvergiers to the provisional headquarters set up by the Navy outside Bizerte, so I rode along to take a look before going to install myself in Ferryville.

I simply could not understand what had happened. A beautiful city had been laid to waste. Thousands of civilians, including women and children, had been killed. Why? It was true that a few of the installations had been demolished, but the canal, the channel, the port, the submarine base, the arsenal, the Admiralty and the shipbuilding yards in Ferryville were intact. After a while, we crossed the bridge spanning the canal – it was also intact.

The detour proved to be more than worthwhile. The Marine Nationale had regrouped in what had been an old abandoned munitions dump, carved into the limestone cliffs on the south shore of the canal. Approximately 400 naval officers and their families had been lodged in immense thirty-metre-long caves, which had been furnished with iron beds and some tables and chairs. It was a real troglodyte city. Everything was, of course, shipshape. There was an administrative centre, kitchen, infirmary, latrines and dormitories which held about fifty people each. The Duvergiers and I reported in and were billeted.

I was assigned to Cave Number Four and took possession of a narrow bed which seemed snug and cosy to me after sleepless nights on the floor of the clinic. A five-striped officer sat on the bed next to mine. On the other side, the bed was occupied by a sporty-looking junior officer.

I found everyone with their nerves on edge, which was normal after several days of idle isolated existence. People were having heated arguments about the Bizerte bombings, but the subject which really made tempers flare concerned the latest news from France. That very morning, in Toulon, the French Navy had scuttled itself in order not to fall into German hands. Why hadn't they rallied to the Allied forces in North Africa instead? In a few moments France had lost the mightiest fleet she had had in the last 180 years! 135 splendid ships – 230,000 tons – were lying on the bottom of Toulon harbour. Only three submarines had managed to slip quietly away to North Africa. This was the worst disaster since Trafalgar! On top of all this, most of the officers were not only proud of this feat but were almost congratulating themselves because the Marine Nationale was still 'unconquered'. To me all this was absurd – really idiotic.

Sitting among the dry-docked sailors looking as the sun set behind the ruined city, I thought of France. What now? France was apparently finished! Yet somehow I felt a surge of hope. I knew there was already a different spirit among some of the people and I was to be proved right. They would eventually rise against the oppressors. Out of the ashes, like the Phoenix, France was to be born again in the most unlikely places – in the heart of Africa, in London, in the Libyan and Egyptian Deserts, in France itself. Suddenly I felt proud to be a part of the Great Resurgence.

As soon as it was dark everyone went to bed. The caverns had a festive air about them from the illumination provided by hundreds of candles.

'Good night,' said my neighbour, crawling into bed.

'Good night, sir.'

'Tell me. Haven't we met before? I have a funny feeling I have seen your face somewhere before and I never forget a face.'

'Frankly, sir, I don't think so. I have no recollection of you.'

'This bothers me, I always remember faces. We should chat a bit tomorrow. Maybe it will come to me. I'm certain I have seen you before.'

'It would be an honour, sir.'

I had no idea who the man could be. I noticed that my other neighbour was poring over a paper by the light of a candle held in his hand. He seemed perplexed and was muttering to himself.

'Is something wrong?' I asked amiably.

'It's this paper. Admiral Herrien, my boss, has asked me to explain the contents of this very important document to him, but the whole thing is in German and I can't make head or tail of it. I've never studied German.'

'I think it would be better to concentrate on English, anyhow. It'll probably be more useful to you in the near future. Maybe I can help you, I speak German.'

'You do? What luck? Here, what does it say?'

I took a quick look. 'Are you kidding?'

'Not at all, I assure you. What does it say?'

'It's a circular from the German High Command for the Director of Health addressed to the forces arriving in Tunis. It has precise instructions for the sanitary teams and medical staff telling them never to forget to wash their hands with potassium permanganate after going to the toilet, to avoid contamination.'

The young officer gaped at me. 'You've got to be joking.'

'Not at all, I assure you. But it must be an important document because it is marked "Highly Confidential".' We both burst into laughter.

'What are you doing here?' asked the young officer.

'Oh, nothing really. I'm just a medical student who found shelter here for the night.'

'Does that mean you have nothing urgent to do?'

'Not right now, no.'

'How would you feel about helping us out as a translator-interpreter for Admiral Herrien?'

'Of course, with great pleasure. Who's Admiral Herrien?'

'Admiral Herrien is the Chief of the Health Service. He is

based in Ferryville but since the arrival of the Germans he's been lost in a fog. He has to attend German High Command meetings in order to co-ordinate some of his activities with theirs and he doesn't understand a word of German.'

'I'm yours if you need me, but right now I'm bushed. Good night.'

'Thanks,' said the other.

'Oh, by the way, who's the high-ranking guy next to me?'

'Him? He is the President of the Marine Court in Bizerte. Why?'

'No reason, really. It's just that he is sure he has met me before, and I . . . I don't remember him at all.'

Next morning, as I was seeing the Duvergiers off, I saw the Commander waving and coming towards me. There was no escape.

'I've been looking for you.'

'Me too, sir. I wanted to say goodbye to you,' I said, lying brazenly. 'I'm ready to leave and wanted to wish you all the best.'

'Yes, yes. Well and good. I wanted to tell you that I finally remembered where we met.' My blood froze. 'Don't you remember the Fourteenth of July Marine Court Ball? That's where I saw you. I told you; I never forget a face.'

'You do have a formidable memory, sir,' I said, beating a hasty retreat.

Once installed in the Admiralty, I had it made. I had been appointed as personal translator-interpreter to Admiral Herrien. I was lodged in the military hospital and given permission to buy myself an outfit at the commissary. I put together a sort of bastard uniform: riding breeches, leggings, regulation shirt, and a navy reefer on which I sewed a Red Cross band. Dressed in this get-up I could pass for anything – doctor, navy officer, civilian – anything. I was given a desk at the Secretariat of the Admiralty where all sorts of confidential papers passed through my hands. I was issued a pass to the Admiralty, the hospital and all the navy installations; a safe conduct pass valid twenty-four hours a day; a priority card, and – best of all – an *Ausweis* from the German Kommandatur. I pasted my photograph on all these documents and sealed them officially. Now that I had a legal status, I looked for two apartments in the modern quarter of Ferryville. My requirements were very specific: they had to be located in a large building with various exits so that, in case of a police raid, the occupants would have those crucial extra minutes for a quick getaway; they had to be on the top floor with access to a roof terrace for the installation of a radio antenna; they had to have a window opening on to the street to control the comings and goings of the goniometric (spy) cars; last, but not least, they had to have no snoopy neighbours. Normally this would have been an impossible task, but times were not normal. Many civil servants and military families had left town so I had much to choose from.

As the German teacher of the local Lycée had fled one step ahead of the Germans, I was pressed into service to replace him. It was agony to be teaching a subject in which I was scarcely better than my teenage students.

Now that I had been equipped, documented, lodged, ratified and registered, I could finally start organising an intelligence network to register and report the movements of all ships – this was my top priority. Since my friend, the ships' pilot in Bizerte, had disappeared I had to make a new contact there as well as one at the airfield. This was not too difficult and soon I was drowning in so much information that it was risky to transmit it to Dick. I needed a radio urgently.

One day, while checking out one of the apartments, I ran into one of my students in front of the elevator, a girl named Thérèse. She had very long, strongly muscled legs, which made her pliable as a reed, dark eyes that flashed with joy and malice and wavy black hair that fell below her shoulders. Although I had considered her to be flatchested in the classroom, I suddenly became aware that she had all the necessary assets to make a man dream.

'*Bonsoir, monsieur.*' It always set me aback to be addressed as Monsieur by youngsters who were almost my own age and I felt myself blush like an idiot.

'*Bonsoir*, Kangaroo.' This was the nickname I had given her when I learned she was a champion hurdle racer.

'So, Monsieur, is this where she lives?'

'Who? What? Where?' I was embarrassed. It took me several seconds to catch her meaning. I began to explain somewhat defensively, 'I have some friends who asked me to check on their apartment while they're away on a trip.'

'Oh really? How nice of you. What floor is this apartment on?'

'The seventh.'

'What a coincidence. That's where I'm going.'

We got off the elevator on the seventh floor together and descended from Seventh Heaven two hours later. She was beautiful, suntanned and warm; she was wonderful. I was badly smitten.

'I adore you, Thérèse!'

'Next time we'll do it in German. That way we can combine the practical with the sublime, OK?' There were plenty of next times and, with practice, we became better and better.

Thérèse, the daughter of a naval officer, was contemptuous of her father and his fellow officers for collaborating with the Germans. Apart from being lovers, she and I became fast friends. I trusted her implicitly and confided in her. Thus, Thérèse became the leader of a daring team of young girls who called themselves 'The Kangaroos'. They were a most picturesque liaison unit crisscrossing the whole region on foot, by bicycle, in their papas' cars, on boyfriends' motor bikes, carrying messages and packages and taking incredible risks.

The Admiral had me accompany him everywhere: inspection tours, hospital visits, meetings with the German High Command and even to a meeting with Admiral Esteva of the Marine Nationale where, God knows, my services as translator were hardly necessary. There were numerous German naval officers in the Admiralty, so I became a diligent wastepaper basket fan; I sifted through the trash every night and it usually yielded some interesting titbits of information for 'Marie'. My daily visits to the hospital allowed me to make a rough calculation of the number of German wounded, to talk to them and to identify the units they belonged to from their insignia.

One of the Kangaroos worked at the largest photography shop in town and was able to provide me with copies of all the photos taken by the Germans. As each member of the network brought a new volunteer, it grew so rapidly that soon I had to split it into individual cells, to avoid total collapse in case of betrayal.

One day Alan turned up carrying a small leather suitcase. When I opened it I found neatly folded shirts and underwear. However, when these were taken out there was a false wooden bottom on a hinge and below it was the 'piano' – big knurled buttons, chrome contacts, luminous dials mounted on an ebonite plate. On the left was the receiver and on the right the sender, recognisable by the Morse key. On one side of the radio were metres of neatly coiled electric wire, while on the inside top of the false bottom there was a complicated diagram showing the frequencies for day and night transmitting. Little boxes closed with elastic bands held the crystals and the contact tips. It was truly a jewel!

Alan installed the radio and began to give operating instructions. To avoid being spotted, the sender had a very short range. The signal was to be relayed by a system of mirrors which served as amplifying antennae and were to be installed at about a hundred metres from the radio. Thus, in case we were discovered, we risked losing only the antennae, which would not be a major catastrophe. The broadcast was limited to three minutes on one frequency. If the message was longer it was necessary to change frequencies. We should be ready to change our location at the drop of a hat . . . easier said than done.

Aline, one of the Kangaroos, produced a fiancé who had been trained as a naval radio operator. He was a lanky, sleepy-looking fellow called Marc and was nicknamed 'The Marmot' on the spot. Even Alan said he was the best radio operator he had ever met. Another operator was recruited a few days later and briefed by Alan. It took three days to complete the installations and establish contact with Malta. 'Marie' answered and we introduced ourselves. Ferryville had become part of the intelligence network, with communication on a twenty-four-hour basis. Alan left regretfully, as he had found the Kangaroos to be a lot of fun.

The team had its share of sleepless nights and jitters, but slowly we all settled down. When we received the second 'piano' it was a cinch. Sometimes we saw an occasional small plane circling over where the antennae had been placed, but the look-out was very efficient and we were able to stop transmitting before we could be pinpointed. A Kangaroo patrolled the neighbourhood during transmissions and would warn us immediately by telephone when she saw the revolving antennae on the roof of a 'goniocar'. The only victims of Operation Radio were Thérèse and I who, now that both apartments were continually occupied, had no place of our own.

Another of the Kangaroos, a fat accommodating girl called Julie, was put in charge of coding the messages. When in prison Coggia and I had whiled away the time by inventing an unbreakable cipher. The letters were tossed, reshuffled and muddled until even a cat could not find her kittens in the tangle. All that was necessary for coding or decoding was a cross-ruled piece of paper and infinite patience, and Julie had plenty of that. Even Malta thought the system crazy enough to approve it.

The network had become so horrifyingly efficient that the group stood in awe of the destructive power which we wielded. The moment a ship or convoy left the Ferryville harbour Malta had all the pertinent information within the hour – the time it took to navigate the lake channel and canal to the sea. The RAF, British submarine and surface naval units would then attack. We also gave Malta plenty of additional targets – planes sitting idle at airfields, munition dumps, camouflaged truck and tank depots. I could evaluate the resulting damage from the long procession of ambulances arriving at the Ferryville hospital. I had good reason to be proud of my team, but it was sickening – all those burned, bleeding, broken people!

The staging area around Ferryville was the supply base for the Southern Axis armies and thus the key to the Western front. I received orders to form a sabotage unit to harass the enemy. I decided to experiment with a small group of men before formalising the operation. I proposed the leadership of the group to a Breton called Karantec, the boatswain in charge of the Admiralty garage. He was a quick tempered forty-year-old man who was not only as brave as a lion but had also had a long naval career which made him totally disciplined. He accepted and was quickly joined by five other marines who had been trained in hand-to-hand combat. By stealing and dealing, they got a small arsenal together – a few cases of hand grenades, a few machine-guns, some ammunition, explosives, revolvers and commando knives. I wanted their début to be spectacular and soon a superb opportunity presented itself.

From time to time the Germans showed off newly arrived military equipment by parading it through the streets of Ferryville. This served a double purpose: it kept the Tunisians in line and the Allied sympathisers in awe. My group always observed these shows with great interest.

One day, a long column came rattling out of the Arsenal door. First came the light armoured vehicles followed by Panzer IIIs and their big brothers, Panzer IVs, a multi-purpose medium weight twenty-five-ton tank; then came the scout cars. After a pause, out came five gigantic tanks the like of which I had never seen before. These were the new Tigers – heavily armoured fifty-six-ton tanks mounted with eight-inch eighty-eight-calibre long cannon. Sent by Hitler to be battle tested, they were remarkably fast and very manoeuverable. They were followed by self-propelled caterpillar cranes, trucks loaded with spare parts, monstrously big tractors towing trailers, special terrain trucks, command and radio cars and, bringing up the rear, enormous tankers. It was a three-ring circus!

My eyes bulged and I was sweating with excitement. The air stank with exhaust fumes and the ground vibrated from the snarling motors and the gnashing tracks. Struck dumb at first, the Tunisians burst into applause and cheers. Ten minutes behind the first contingent came another of similar magnitude. I was preoccupied. I had had no information of a convoy capable of transporting such cargo. Suddenly I did a double-take. One of the armoured cars had a long scratch in front of the gun turret which I was positive I had seen before. Alerted, I began to notice details: an officer leaning out of a turret, adhesive tape over his right eyebrow, broken sun goggles, torn tunic and cap turned backwards, who definitely seemed familiar; a car whose antenna was twisted at an odd angle. There was no doubt – the Germans were trying to put one over. They were parading through town, going to the back door and in the front again. It *was* a three-ring circus!

I quickly sent scouts to find out where the Germans were going to disperse and park their treasures. At four in the afternoon the information began to dribble in. Most of the equipment had gone towards Mateur, but some of the units were parked only a few kilometres away and had been camouflaged under the olive trees growing on the slopes of the neighbouring hills.

One of Thérèse's friends arrived red-faced with excitement an hour later. She had followed one of the units on her boyfriend's motor bike at a respectful distance. They had set up camp on the banks of a small stream south of the lake. There were ten tanks, two of which were Tigers, some trucks and additional equipment.

'That's where we will hit them,' I said, suddenly calm. I sent for Yves Karantec, the boatswain, at the Admiralty garage.

Two hours later our battle plan was ready. A scout had been posted at the site; the men had been called for a briefing; Dick Jones and Malta had been alerted. The group of six assembled at the garage at 10.00 p.m. They were in unmarked battle uniforms and wore tennis shoes to enable them to move silently. They were well supplied with a sub-machine-gun, ammunition and a sackful of hand grenades per man; each one had a flashlight, a commando knife stuck in his belt and a tin of black wax to make up his hands and face. Two of them were issued sticks of explosives with detonators. Our latest report stated that the camp had been made on flat terrain and the vehicles had been parked in a rectangle in the centre of which soldiers were sleeping. A guard had been posted at each corner of the rectangle and the gun turrets had been left open! The plan was to neutralise two of the guards, pitch hand grenades into the tents and tank turrets and plant an explosive charge in the barrel and at the breech of each tank cannon. I looked at my men. They were pale, tight-lipped and resolute. I was sure that, when the time came, they would not flinch.

Karantec arrived driving an ambulance.

'What on earth is that for?' I asked.

'Well, with this we can come and go as we please, don't you think?'

'But . . .' With the Geneva Convention in mind, I hesitated. But, after all, it was an excellent idea! I grinned. 'It's perfect. Let's move.'

As Karantec drove, I clamped my teeth together to keep them from chattering with fear. I felt emptied, cold and like an observer of the action which I myself had initiated. At least my Red Cross band was appropriate for the occasion.

Karantec winked at me. 'I want to thank you, sir. For the first time in a long while I feel proud of my uniform, and I'm not even wearing it! Let's hope everything goes well.'

The scout, drenched from the light rain which had been falling incessantly, was where he should be. 'Everything is as scheduled. Everyone is fast asleep. In my opinion the guards on this side will be easier to get rid of. The gun turrets have been closed because of the rain but can be opened from the outside because the lids have not been bolted shut. The two Tigers are in the centre on the left side.'

'What about the trucks?' I asked.

'They're over there on the right. They're full of sleeping soldiers.'

'And the tankers?'

'Right next to the trucks.'

I addressed my men: 'We hit the trucks, tankers and tents first.' Two men volunteered to take care of the guards and were to signal as soon as the way was clear. 'One more thing. In exactly two minutes, after we start the attack, a green signal flare will go off. Everyone is to withdraw immediately. Let's go. Good luck!'

I knew that things never go as planned in this kind of operation. Mainly, it is the curse of the little things – the village idiot who materialises from nowhere, the irrepressible sneeze, the improbable messtin you step on, all the little things that tripped you up. You had to count on a maximum of foul-ups. He who grasps and reacts fastest will be the winner.

However, on this wet dark night the angels were on our side. A soft whistle let us know the guards were out of commission. We advanced rapidly and silently, took our bearings and dispersed.

Thirty seconds later the sleeping camp was rudely awakened. A shower of hand grenades fell on the tents and trucks. The survivors ran about terror-stricken not knowing from which side they were being attacked and shot blindly in all directions. The second shower of grenades only added to their panic. By this time, each raider had climbed on to a vehicle. The ones on the tanks were trying to open the lids without much success until they found the trick to it; a few lids had been bolted shut and had to be abandoned. On my third try, I opened my tank and dropped a hand grenade inside, climbed on another tank where my first attempt was successful and then looked round. The tankers were in flames as were the trucks next to them; the tanks began to explode; it was as bright as day. The Germans had reacted and were shooting in disorderly profusion. Fortunately they didn't dare throw grenades at their own vehicles, but the situation had definitely become unhealthy for the French. The green flare went up with a hiss, and the raiders slunk away into the dark.

One, two, three, four men reached the ambulance; I joined them. Time was short; the motor was running; any minute the Germans would be upon us. I was about to order the departure when someone shouted, 'Look! There they are.' The last two men came, one carrying the other who had been injured. We all scrambled into the ambulance which lurched forward.

Everything was back to normal as soon as we got to town. By the following morning we had completely covered our tracks – the injured man had been admitted to the hospital as a hit-and-run case; two others with minor injuries had been sent to Coggia in Tunis; the absence of the ambulance had been justified in some way or other; I was at my desk in the Admiralty; Karantec was in his little office in the garage. Only the gleam in our eyes revealed our reclaimed pride in a job well done and the joy and elation of being alive. During the course of the day we heard the result of the operation: one Tiger out of combat, two Panzer IIIs and two Panzer IVs destroyed, two more damaged, eleven trucks and two tractors burned, ten Germans dead and thirty more wounded. We had really kicked the Germans in the rear!

The Germans had begun a frenzied search for the culprits while, undaunted, I looked on wondering where we could hit next. We hit again and again, wherever and whenever possible. We found that constant harassment was more effective than a few high-risk attacks such as the first. Each time we hit the loss in men and materials had demoralising effects on the Germans and Tunisians: bridges crumbled when military convoys passed over; tunnels caved in; rails vanished from the tracks; hundreds of Germans were temporarily out of action due to the effects of powerful laxatives added to their soup cauldrons; officers disappeared without a trace; mail sacks went up in smoke. The commando group was having a ball. Nevertheless we had our ups and downs, our moments of glory and grief, of tears and laughter.

The kidnapping of an American Colonel from the Military

Hospital was one of our more colourful feats. Dressed in hospital whites with a stethoscope dangling over my stomach and escorted by two nurses, I simply went into the ward and rolled him out on a wheeled stretcher. We pretended to be taking him to surgery and neither the guard at the door of the ward nor any of the German hospital staff encountered on the way out paid us the slightest attention. An ambulance waited for us at the entrance; we handled him ever so carefully, put him in and drove away to a secret destination. This caused an uproar! The most surprised of all was the Colonel himself, who had not even been consulted and now found himself snugly ensconced in the bosom of a French family who pampered him for a few months until the liberation of the city. This inspired coup earned me a formidable dressing down from Dick Jones, who found such an action foolhardy and irresponsible – worst of all, I felt the reprimand justified so I accepted it quietly and apologised.

I became worried and jumpy and, try as I would, I could not pull myself out of my depression. I tried to tell myself it was nothing but exhaustion but I became apprehensive. I felt followed and spied upon even though I found nothing to justify this feeling. I became cautious and stayed away from the action.

The Germans had recaptured the hill which controlled the Nedjerda Valley leading to Tunis and had inflicted heavy losses. They had named it Christmas Hill, and were noisily celebrating their victory. Furthermore, my unit had mounted an operation to destroy the German submarine base entrance and this had gone sour. I was really feeling dismal, so I decided to confide in Dick, who listened sympathetically.

'You did the right thing in coming to me. What is happening to you happens to all intelligence agents sooner or later. It's not battle fatigue. It's much more subtle. It's the self-preservation instinct that surfaces from the subconscious when danger is imminent. It's an indefinable feeling, but one should never ignore this kind of premonition. I feel that it is nothing short of a miracle that your network has not been detected yet. You have all been magnificent, but imprudent and crazy.

'It would be thankless of me to reproach you, but you have to understand that things have changed. At first, enemy security was practically non-existent and you literally got away with murder. That's no longer the case, far from it. The police and counter-espionage are now well organised and we have to face the fact that the time of apprenticeship, the time of blind heroics and flamboyant amateurism, is over. Only those who can readjust will survive. For us, a dead agent is worthless and a captured one can pose the worst of dangers. The Allies will certainly get here one day soon, but meanwhile . . .'

Dick, the taciturn, had never said so much before. He fell silent for a moment, sunk in thought, and then continued, 'We have the same problems in Tunis. We haven't let it be known, for obvious reasons, but we have suffered heavy losses lately. Several of our agents have been arrested and tortured. Their networks have been destroyed. A transmitter was seized and the operator killed on the spot. Our codes have been broken and it's getting difficult to maintain contact with 'Marie'. Our logistics are insufficient. We need someone to cross the lines and establish direct contact with our forces. This is a top priority, but it's an impossible dream.'

'Why impossible?'

'Because I'm stuck here. It is extremely risky and I have no one to send.'

'Send me.'

A deep silence followed. The idea had never occurred to Dick before, nor to me, for that matter. Weighing each word, Dick spoke: 'Listen, that's not something which we can decide lightly. We'll have to think it over. It's getting late. Stay here for the night and we will discuss it in the morning. In any case, thanks, old chap.'

Next morning we renewed the discussion. 'Dick, I've thought it over. If you need me I'll stay in Ferryville, but it's very probable I'm already blown. My network would be better off without me. If it's so urgent to contact 'Marie' directly, I'll volunteer, but only on my terms.'

Dick frowned. 'What do you mean by that?'

'I mean that I don't want to cross the Western front into Algeria. The Germans are all over the place, the Arabs are behind them one hundred per cent and they would denounce anyone found pussy-footing around. Even if I succeeded I would waste valuable time trying to convince low level officials of my bona fides.'

'I understand. What about the southern route?'

'To reach the Eighth Army, which is approximately seven hundred kilometres from here, somewhere between Tripoli and the Mareth Fortification Line, I would have to take the coast road, which is probably teeming with German and Italian checkpoints. No thank you! And as for crossing the moving battle line between the two armies in the desert, that would not be sporting; the odds would definitely be against me. Besides, I would have the same problem explaining my presence. The Sidi-Bouzid front, I'm sure you will agree, is out of the question right now.'

'Righto, but what's left?'

'I want to go straight to Malta.'

'How, by sea?'

'Exactly.'

'You are crazy!'

'Yes, but it might just work. They know us in Malta.'

'But how?'

'Let me tell you what I have in mind.'

7

The Galley Slaves

We had rowed all night. Day was breaking and the sun's rays took some of the chill from the air. The frail boat rose and fell with the lazy swells of the sea. The wind, which at first had been unpredictable, was now blowing steadily north-west. Soon we would be able to use the sail. My mate was sound asleep on the bottom of the boat while I slaved at the oars. I was full of aches and pains and queasy after a sleepless night, but felt buoyant because everything had worked out well. We were on our way to Malta.

It had been hard to convince Dick of the feasibility of the project but, once he had agreed, things moved swiftly. While I went to Ferryville to say goodbye and put Coggia in charge of operations, the Tunis network had found a boat that met all my specifications. I recruited a twenty-year-old wheat-blond Norman called Jean-Marie Gueroult to accompany me. Jean-Marie was as strong as an ox and as silent as a carp; he had been in the Merchant Marine but when his ship was sunk he had been stranded in Ferryville where he had become part of our commando group. Because he had taken so many chances his cover had also been blown.

Two days later, I was notified that the boat was ready. Jean-Marie and I went to inspect it that afternoon at a small beach which lay between Korba and Tazerka on Cape Bon. It was what I needed: three and a half metres long, more or less the same size as the boats for rent for Sunday outings in the Bois de Boulogne. An adroit carpenter had quickly decked a metre at both the front and the back, leaving the middle open. A small mast had been placed in the prow and its five-metre-square lateen sail was properly rolled on its pole and securely stored. The cleats had been reinforced, the gunwales raised, the boat's markings effaced and duckboards had been installed to keep provisions and spare parts dry. The rudder was attached by two solid hinges. Two big kitchen pots were tied by their handles to serve as bails; three cement blocks were used as ballast; one pair of spare oars lay in the bottom.

The distance from Cape Bon to Malta, as the crow flies, was 170 nautical miles. We estimated the voyage would take six to seven days, perhaps less if we encountered favourable winds. The real problem was navigational. The north–south projection of the Malta Archipelago was only thirty kilometres so a small steering error would cause us to miss it altogether and get lost somewhere in the middle of the Mediterranean.

We had a sea compass and a homemade log to estimate our sailing speed; sea charts were really of no use to us once we had established our heading and all we had for a guide was an illustrated post-office calendar which had a map of the Mediterranean printed on the back. However, as I had had the opportunity at the Admiralty to study a chart showing the main currents, I hoped I would be able to correct any drifts. Once I was within a forty kilometre radius of Malta I would be able, more or less, to guide myself by the heavy air and sea traffic to be expected around the island. I had decided that, if, after the ninth day, we had not spotted Malta, we would steer south and try to make it to Tripolitania, where the British Eighth Army would be in control. Tripolitania was approximately the same distance from Malta as Cape Bon, so we laid in provisions for fifteen days.

When darkness fell, the four men who had been preparing the boat pushed it from its cradle into the sea. I thanked them warmly and Jean-Marie and I climbed aboard. Ten minutes later we lost sight of the shore and were off into the unknown.

We took turns rowing so the other could rest at the bottom of the boat but the first day was exhausting. We suffered from the sun glare on the water, from blisters, cramps and lack of sleep. As the wind continued to blow steadily, we reinforced the mast with four well-stretched shrouds, hoisted the triangular sail and got the shock of our lives – the sail was crimson, when all we wanted was to be as inconspicuous as possible. We checked our speed and were happy to find it stable at around five kilometres per hour; after twenty-four hours at sea we had covered fifty-nine kilometres! We cruised easily all night but kept a constant watch to avoid keeling over, as the boat was not really a sailing vessel and the slightest mistake might be fatal. We were shaken to our roots at 8.30 next morning when a thin bluish line appeared against the light about thirty degrees off starboard on the horizon.

'Look! Land!' shouted Jean-Marie.

'Are you crazy? That can't possibly be Malta. What other land is there on our course?'

'I don't know, but look! Open your eyes! That is land!'

I had to agree and all kinds of farfetched speculation flashed through my mind: a mirage, clouds at sea level, navigating in circles, anything. We sailed towards the 'land' and the closer we got the more like land it looked. An hour later, it was impossible to doubt. An island rose out of the sea.

Suddenly, from nowhere, a high-speed motor boat zoomed towards us; we saw two plumes of water gushing high in her wake. We could see it was a greyish blue coastguard cutter with a small cannon pointing forward and a heavy machine-gun mounted on the bridge. I was flabbergasted; the spectre of an island and now a coastguard cutter — they were like apparitions from a nightmare. They slowed down a cable's length away and began to circle the rowboat. Gradually, they came closer and stopped dead about thirty metres away, keeping their sputtering motors idling. All of a sudden I saw the flag flying aft: it was green, white and red.

'Oh, my God! They're Italian! Take the sail down quickly. That shows our goodwill and besides it'll cover up the strangeness of our appearance.'

An officer was standing on the bridge looking us over through a pair of binoculars while the three sailors at his side looked at us with scorn. I gave them a friendly wave and Jean-Marie joined me with his handkerchief. Someone spoke to us unintelligibly through a bullhorn. Jean-Marie and I continued our antics and yelled inarticulate sounds expressing friendliness. A miracle happened! The sailors disappeared along with the binoculars. The cutter gave two short siren blasts and left full speed ahead.

Jean-Marie was amazed. 'What happened? Are they blind?'

'Of course not. Stop and think. They see two lousy, shabby men sailing peacefully in a little fishing-boat near their island and naturally think we're from there.'

'What island is this, anyway? What are the Italians doing here?'

I scrutinised my post-office map, but the only thing I could find that might shed some light on the subject was a dot the size of a fly speck lost somewhere between the Tunisian coast and Malta.

'Oh-oh,' I stuttered. 'Now I remember. This must be Pantelleria, a small island belonging to Italy. I suppose it's become strategically important because of the war. I remember there are two or three islands like this one, but they are off our course. But you know what I think is the most fantastic thing of all?'

'What?' Jean-Marie was not very imaginative.

'Well, unless I'm mistaken we've covered a quarter of our route in less than forty hours with very little deviation whatsoever.'

'That's great! What do we do now? Hoist the sail again?'

'No, definitely not! That sail is like a fire engine; you can see it for miles. One visit like this is enough. Let's get away from here as fast as possible . . . but rowing.'

'*Merde!*' grumbled Jean-Marie. 'Sailing was so nice.' He dropped his head woefully but then broke into a smile. 'Did you say we have already come a quarter of the way?'

'More or less.'

'In that case, I'll gladly row the rest of the way to Malta.'

We didn't row quite that far but at the end of the day we were worn out. The weather remained fine so we sailed all night. The wind died down in the morning and the task of rowing a heavily-laden boat became excruciatingly painful under the remorseless sun. Nevertheless, by evening we calculated we had covered 140 kilometres so far and could expect to be near Malta in three more days. The further we advanced, the more I was shaken with metaphysical shivers, as the fear of missing Malta grew proportionally; also, the further we went, the tireder we became and the less inclined we felt about taking the alternative route to North Africa. So far, we had had incredible luck.

The following day the north wind gathered force. The sea became choppy, with froth-fringed white caps which looked like sinister sheep. By the afternoon, it was impossible to row or to keep the course steadily eastward. The sea emptied itself into the boat as it crashed against the hull. To keep the prow heading into the wind and waves, Jean-Marie improvised a sea-anchor from two oars tied crosswise. We took the mast down, secured it lengthwise and used it as a roof beam to form a precarious shelter with the sail. We had been lucky enough to catch the rudder when a brutal wave snatched it away.

By nightfall conditions became hair-raising. The waves swelled out of the dark void and hurled themselves against us with incredible violence. The boat appeared to hesitate and we were sure it would batter itself against the wall of water which rose in front of us. Then the boat would sweep up the wall, traverse a short area of boiling foam and hang briefly suspended between sky and sea. Each time we thought our time had come and our heartbeats and breath stopped. Then the boat would dive down the slate-grey abyss on the other side and the cycle would begin again. The gale, which seemed to rise from the jaws of darkness at the end of the world, howled and whistled with ghastly force. I began to vomit; with each spasm I felt I was being turned inside out like an old sock.

We had tied ourselves to the boat to avoid being washed overboard. On all fours, we tried to bail out the water filling the boat. We could only guess at the level of the water with the aid of a flashlight. Our eyes would meet and we would smile wanly at each other while continuing our futile task. We were flung about but, impervious to our bruises, we frantically kept on scooping, scooping and scooping.

The nightmare went on and on. Day broke in a greenish dawn which seemed to presage the beginning of the end. Low black clouds rushed by in menacing flocks, constantly renewing each other. The sight of the unleashed sea was even more horrible than the blind night struggle. When it was possible to distinguish each other's faces, we were dismayed to see they were drawn, dishevelled, sodden, blue-lipped and wild-eyed.

We had thrown the ballast overboard to lighten the boat which now danced and jiggled but took in less water and held steadier against the waves. The wind raged for sixteen hours, abated during the afternoon, and died around midnight; however, the swells remained high until dawn when the weather, although still morose, became bearable.

Cold and feverish, Jean-Marie and I sprawled on the bottom

of the boat as we continued sluggishly to bail water. Jean-Marie continued to repeat blankly: 'I never would have thought it possible to survive such a storm in such a cockle-shell.'

'But I thought you were the experienced sailor.'

'Sure, but it certainly isn't the same to look down on a storm from the bridge of a thirty-thousand-ton ship as to look up at it from this bathtub.'

We cleaned the boat, lifted the sea-anchor, reset the mast and laid things out to dry, giving the boat the air of a Chinese laundry. We found the food and water reserves to be practically intact so we gave ourselves a treat. Although the boat was very difficult to handle without its ballast, we were back into the old routine – oar, sail, oar, sail – but we were happy to be alive.

During the course of the seventh night we thought we heard the hum of what might have been an aeroplane far to the east on two different occasions. Suddenly, at 10.00 a.m. the next morning we spotted a wisp of smoke on the port side. It must be a ship and heading in our direction! Her trajectory might cross ours. An hour later we could make out she was a warship, but we were puzzled by her zigzagging course – she approached and receded, loomed up and faded away.

I took a guess. 'Maybe she's looking for something.'

'I think she is navigating to dodge submarine torpedoes.'

On each forward pass the ship came a little nearer. By now we could clearly see her superstructure and turrets with their cannons.

'She should detect us soon, but perhaps we should do something to attract her attention, since we keep on disappearing in the trough of the waves. Let's make some smoke signals,' I said.

'What if she is an enemy ship?' worried Jean-Marie.

'And what if she is English?'

'*Merde!*'

'We must take a chance.'

'But, after all, if –'

I jokingly silenced him by splashing him with water. While we had been discussing the matter the destroyer had moved away without noticing us. The two of us were beside ourselves with the jitters and looked about for anything that would burn. We laid a metal sheet on the stern and piled shredded shirts and blankets on it, found dry kitchen matches in a glass bottle, but the ship kept on sailing away from us.

'Maybe she won't come back,' Jean-Marie voiced my thoughts. 'Look! She's getting further and further away.'

'No! I'm sure she'll be back!' It was almost as if she had heard me. She turned round and started back south-east.

'She is going to miss us! Look!'

'No, calm down.'

'But she was north of us before. Now she is going to pass us to the south, but God knows how far away!'

'Look, Jean-Marie, do me a favour.'

'What?'

'Shut up!'

It really did look as if the destroyer was going to pass us by but maybe, just maybe, she was slightly closer this time. A little before she drew level with us Jean-Marie lit the fire, which quickly caught. I dampened the rags, producing thick smoke which the wind dispersed. At the risk of setting the boat on fire, we rashly threw any and everything handy into the flame. Even though the sail was hoisted to attract attention the big ship continued her course blindly, steaming full speed ahead.

'Look! Just look! She's leaving us! She's left us!'

I didn't answer. I was praying. Abruptly, the destroyer veered and swooped down upon us. The engines slowed and she began to make a vast circle around the little craft.

'She has seen us! She has seen us!'

'If you want her to continue to see us you'd better help me push the fire into the sea before we go up in smoke.'

The ship drew nearer, gave two blasts on her sirens and stopped a cable's length away. We saw a lifeboat lowered down her side and – thank God – the Union Jack flew from her halyard!

'They're English! English! They really are!' hooted Jean-Marie, as we jumped up and down and waved our arms.

The lifeboat, manned by four men at the oars and one at the rudder, severed itself from the mother ship and rapidly closed the distance between us. A few metres away, the helmsman shouted, 'Are you English?'

'Hurrah! Hurrah!' I shouted noncommittally.

When the lifeboat came alongside, I could appreciate that it was twice the size of our boat. Without a moment's hesitation, Jean-Marie and I jumped aboard.

Since it looked as if I was going to try to tow our boat, the helmsman ordered, 'Let her go. We cannot take your boat.' I let the rope slip into the sea.

We were taken to the sickbay immediately. We were a sad sight – bearded, sunburned, cut, bruised, staggering . . . The perfect picture of two castaways. Emotionally and physically drained, we sank into a semi-stupor. In the late afternoon, clean and warmly dressed in sailor togs, we were taken before the skipper, who had a hard time swallowing our story.

'From Tunis?'

'Yes, sir, from Cape Bon.'

'In that nutshell?'

'Yes, sir.'

'In seven days?'

'In exactly seven nights and six days and a half.'

'Through the storm?'

'Yes, sir, we went right through the heart of it.'

His Majesty's destroyer had truly been on a rescue mission, which explained her zigzagging. Malta's three deteriorated runways and natural deep sea harbour had made it the key to the defence of Egypt. So long as the Maltese airfields and submarine bases were operational they represented a terrible threat to the supply lines of the Afrika Korps. As a matter of fact, the English had sent three-quarters of Rommel's supplies to the bottom during 1941 and the beginning of 1942. Under these circumstances, Marshal Goering ordered that Malta be levelled. So the island became a prime target for the Luftwaffe and Italian Air Force.

Malta was an easy target, lying only 110 kilometres from the Sicilian air bases, and was bombed as many as eight times a day. Valletta, the capital, was razed to the ground, supply lines were cut and famine became rampant. The British and Maltese bore up very well under the pressure – each day they patched up the runways and each day the RAF fighters flew out to retaliate; they had slowly reinforced their defences and the bombings slackened off while the general picture improved. Each time the air-raid sirens sounded the British planes would take off

.in order not to be sitting ducks. Many were shot down while waiting to land while others simply dropped into the sea for lack of fuel. The Royal Navy kept a constant watch around the island to rescue men and whatever else they could. Thus, Jean-Marie and I had been picked up out of the water. When rescued we were only seventy kilometres from Malta but, had we stayed on our course, we would have passed the island far to the south, a thought that gave me the shivers. Still tired but radiant, we and a dozen other survivors stepped ashore next morning.

Valletta was a vast stretch of ruins – more than 37,000 buildings had been damaged or demolished. All around were carcasses of burnt-out trucks, cars and pieces of planes, both Allied and enemy; as far as the eye could see there were only ruins and more ruins. The general population had been living in grottoes, tunnels and shelters dug into the soft limestone of the island for months on end and were just beginning to emerge, moving into the few still habitable buildings, miraculously left standing.

King's Way, the main street of Valletta, was a disaster area; in spite of this the Security Defence Service was functioning in that neighbourhood. Major Tony Morris, Chief of this important secret service, was absent so I met one of his assistants, a small husky man with greying blond hair, who sat slumped in a chair and spoke slowly. His gestures were those of an exhausted man, but he received Jean-Marie and me courteously.

'Tunis informed us you were coming but, quite frankly, I didn't think you would make it.'

'Frankly, neither did we. We still can't believe we are here.'

'I am especially glad to see you because all the news from Tunis has been bad lately. Their broadcasts are irregular and we are often cut off. Only one transmitter is working and that only intermittently. We believe there has been a wave of arrests, but don't know for sure what is happening.'

'What about Ferryville?' I asked anxiously.

'Well, Ferryville has slowed down, but otherwise seems to be all right. Let's get down to business.'

I gave a report on the situation: problems, means at our disposal, cash, most urgent needs, results obtained, errors committed – I spoke for a long time. The officer, head in hands and eyes closed as if asleep, was concentrating almost painfully; he interrupted me only to ask pointed questions. When I had finished he opened his eyes, straightened up, put his hands flat on the desk and looked me directly in the eyes.

'What you and your companions have done in Tunis is outstanding. Please give me your report in writing so that I will be able to submit it to the Major when he returns and to study all the details and plan accordingly. I'll see you tomorrow to sort things out. Just one more question, would you be willing to go back to Tunisia?'

I caught my breath. 'Tunisia, sir?'

'That's right. You heard me right.'

'If it's an order, yes, I'll go. If not, no, not under any circumstances.'

The next morning, we had a long constructive work session when each point was considered meticulously and an appropriate measure taken. Afterwards I was invited to a cheerful lunch at the Officers' Mess. Once back in the office, the man became serious again.

'Well,' he said.

'Well, sir, it's up to you. If you order me to return to Tunisia, that's it, but what else is open to me? I want only one thing – to fight, but for real. I'm fed up with makeshift jobs, I'm tired of pottering around. I've had my fill of unkept promises, vague improvisations and idle talk.'

'I know how you feel. Calm down and get this into your head – your pottering around, as you put it, has probably harmed the enemy more than anything you could have done by playing the tin soldier. Don't you realise we sank forty-seven ships in December and January and that another twenty were so badly damaged that they will be out of commission for a long time? Do you really think that can be called pottering around? Now I have got that off my chest, if you still say no I'll respect your decision, but I'll be sorry to lose you. We will take the necessary steps to send you off to Cairo and we'll request you be commissioned in the fighting unit of your choice.'

8

The Desert War

At long last I was in Cairo; I was fascinated and let myself be carried along by the boisterous crowds. Long lines of ambulances carrying wounded from the front traversed the city; men in bandages and plaster casts leaned on their canes as they strolled along the streets; revellers on leave still had the drawn faces and the haunted look of battle in their eyes. However, the city itself seemed indifferent to the war raging in the deserts of Tripolitania and Cyrenaica; Cairo was an oasis of bygone luxuries: hot baths; cool beer at the Golf Club, the Cricket Club or the Gezira Tennis Club; opulent nightclubs featuring belly-dancers; and last, but not least, Madame Badia's girls. Cairo's voluptuous setting was the backdrop for innumerable intrigues and rumours of the secret war. Even though Egypt had broken relations with the Axis, she had not declared war; many Egyptians vented their pro-Nazi sympathies loudly; student demonstrators ran through the streets shouting slogans in favour of Rommel; secret agents of the Axis powers moved in the shadows, spying freely and spreading demoralisation.

With my military dossier under my arm, I reported to British Headquarters. The time had come to bid farewell to Jean-Marie, who had already received his commission in the Free French Marines and looked handsomely smug in his new uniform.

'We've come a long way together – Ferryville, Tunis, Pantelleria, Malta, and now Cairo. I hope we'll see each other again in Paris. If not, let's get together at home in Normandy,' Jean-Marie said.

'Of course, Jean-Marie, I'm sure we will.' Alas, we never met again; Jean-Marie died heroically shortly after.

I spent a week waiting for the brass to make up their minds about what to do with me; I had received my pay retroactively and was suddenly flush with money. Perched on a mangy undulating camel led by a guide riding a small donkey, I visited the Pyramid of Cheops; I strolled through the streets and browsed in the thousands of boutiques for hours; I went to the Papyrus Exhibition and to the Cairo Museum to admire the treasure of Tutankhamen. With my elbows propped on the ramparts of the Citadel, I looked down on Cairo covered by a haze which, as it wafted up, seemed to carry the clamour of the city; I had tea lounging leisurely on a rattan chair on the terrace of the famous Shepherd's Hotel. When the cool evening breeze blew off the Nile, I dressed up and went dining and dancing at the Continental Terrace, or went slumming at the Melody Club, where the mood was lively and deceptively romantic, the cuisine refined, the wines French, the reception warm and the girls easy.

One evening I pulled my key out of its pigeonhole and found a note urgently requesting me to go to Headquarters. Next day, with the stroke of a pen, I had become a fully fledged member of the glorious Eighth Army which was very different from what I expected. Besides the British, it was a mixture of Scots, Australians, New Zealanders, Canadians, South Africans, Malaysians, French, Polynesians, a scattering of Poles and Norwegians, plus a few Gabon lumberjacks and deserters from the French Foreign Legion.

I walked on air, my head in the clouds and chest bursting with pride; I felt I had grown six inches; I was jubilant. My orders were carefully folded in my shirt pocket, but I would have preferred to have had them stamped in red letters on my forehead for all the world to see; I was in the Special Air Service. Despite my unorthodox military record and even though I was not British I had been accepted into this élite unit due to the very strong intervention on my behalf by Malta's Security Defence Service.

The major, who had handed me my commission, had the last word: 'It's my opinion that to have gone from Algiers to Gibraltar in a kayak and then from Cape Bon to Malta in a rowboat, and to have mounted the kind of intelligence and sabotage operation you did in Tunisia, you must be completely crazy, perhaps barmy enough to deserve a commission in the SAS. You must have been born under a lucky star! The SAS shock troops have sustained such heavy losses lately that we have eased up on the requirements for new recruits. Don't take this personally, I'm referring to the fact that you are not so well trained for our kind of combat. However, good luck to you, anyway.'

Not so well trained was the understatement of the year. I was sent to a special camp on the outskirts of Heliopolis, where I received rudimentary training in parachute jumping, hand-to-hand combat and desert warfare, and came out twenty days later bruised and bewildered. Along with my marching orders, I received my standard issue kit. I stuffed all the rest of my personal belongings in a dufflebag and left it in charge of the Shepherd's Hotel baggage storage room, which was jam-packed with bags, suitcases and bundles from other officers already fighting in the desert sands, many of whom would never reclaim them.

I met a lot of my new comrades-in-arms at the departure depot. While most of them had been on leave, some were still recovering from their wounds and some were still green – like myself.

After a period of inactivity the war had regained momentum in Tunisia and Tripolitania in mid-January 1943. To the north, the Allied Forces under General Eisenhower were advancing on Tunis; to the south, Rommel, still licking his wounds from the Battle of El Alamein, had entrenched himself, with what was left of his Afrika Korps and the Italian units attached to it, in the Sollum and Halfaya passes near the Libyan border. Leclerc's column, which had marched from Chad through the desert, cleaning out the Italians from the oases along its line of march, had joined up with the Eighth Army; together they were preparing an all-out drive to push Rommel into the sea. By the end of January the front was located on the border of Tripolitania, about 2,400 kilometres west of Cairo by the coastal road.

The long convoy of trucks, jeeps, staff cars, tankers and trailers left Cairo late in the day. We rolled night and day, resting only during the hottest hours. We travelled on a rutted, bumpy, dusty road which bore the scars of past battles. On either side one could see piles of twisted scorched scrap iron, all that remained of the two armies' equipment that had been destroyed there. In some places the route led through partially mined areas; in these, the way was marked by brightly coloured ribbons hanging on poles by day and by lanterns at night.

As new recruits we became brutally acquainted with the desert; we froze by night and broiled in the heat from the moment of sunrise; we were bumped and shaken about like nuts in a bag; our eyes turned red from the dust and sand stirred up by the passage of the heavy vehicles. It took us four days and five nights to reach our destination on the front, where we joined our unit.

The SAS fought a very special type of war. Originally parachute units, they now specialised in hit-and-run raids. They set fuel depots and ammunition dumps on fire, raided airfields and enemy camps in open desert; they slipped in at night, struck, and slunk away to fight again. They were assisted by the Long Range Desert Group (LRDG) whose units lived in the heart of the desert, often far behind enemy lines; like the Bedouins they could survive on a quarter litre of water a day and crisscrossed the unmarked desert wastes almost by instinct alone. They served as scouts and guides for the SAS when it made seemingly impossible incursions deep into enemy territory where the men sometimes stayed away from their bases for weeks and months on end.

I had wanted to be in the thick of the fighting and my wish had been granted beyond my wildest expectations.

I was scared stiff when I realised where I had landed but it was too late to back out now. I fought my first battle against my fellow officers! From the moment of my arrival they had treated me with the greatest arrogance and contempt or, if I were lucky, ignored me completely. These officers had been welded together by combat and were not about to accept a newcomer with so many flaws; French, green, ignorant of desert fighting and an officer just like them!

After two days of being called a Frog and being openly baited, I had had enough. At mess that evening I blew my top. I stood up, banged a bottle on the table, and shouted, 'Shut up!' to a stupefied audience.

'I'll keep this short and sweet. First of all, I want you to know that you are all a bunch of idiots. What would make me happy would be to stave in all your faces one by one, but I realise I'm outnumbered and maybe – just maybe – outclassed. I didn't come to this hell hole at the end of the world to fight the British. Dammit! – we're supposed to be allies. It's not very sporting to condemn a man you don't even know. You can only find out what I am during battle, so until then lay off! I don't know you either but I do know that your conduct towards me does not become fellow officers. I've earned my stripes the same way you have – fighting! If you can't respect me, at least respect them. The only other thing I have to say to all of you high and mighty bastards is *Merde*.'

I sat down white as a sheet in the midst of a deathly silence.

The consequences of this little outburst were various – generally on the positive side. The group commander gave me a first-class dressing down, but ended up by laughing. 'I can't punish you, in any case, for the lack of respect and bad conduct as we're going on a raid tomorrow and that's top priority. But, taking everything into account, I think I rather liked your reaction.' He shook hands with me and the others became progressively more friendly.

The officers were called to a briefing that afternoon. Aerial photographs were passed around and orders given: Departure, 8.00 p.m.; Target, a munition dump and fuel depot circled and marked Number 1 on the photo; Mission, Destroy. The scouts had gone ahead and would meet up with the squad before the attack.

The Jeeps were ready. Their windshields had been removed and two machine-guns mounted, one on the right side of the hood and the other pointing backwards in the rear. Six to eight Jerry cans containing fuel and water had been strapped inside the Jeep in the back, plus three more secured to the hood. There were also guns and rifles, boxes of hand grenades and ammunition and other things necessary for this type of operation.

The men were dressed in khaki shorts, short-sleeved belted tunics, dark sun goggles and kaffiyehs, the typical headdresses worn by the Bedouins; these last were made from a square piece of cloth folded and held in place by black woollen cords. Proper attire and equipment assumed a place of special importance in the desert, where the temperature could vary 65 degrees from night to day, where the sun burned not only the skin but also the eyes, causing acute conjunctivitis, and where sand as fine as talcum powder filtered into everything inflaming the eyes and jamming the gun breeches.

Water was the most precious treasure; each drop was measured. It was used and refiltered and never wasted! In principle, the daily water ration was three litres per man, four litres per vehicle and eight litres per tank, but when water ran short, it was the men who did without as it was impossible to cut the vehicle or tank consumption. Another vital liquid was gasoline, as Rommel had found out to his grief when his lightning thrust into Egypt had ground to a halt due to such a shortage; one of the reasons why the SAS chose to attack fuel depots.

The strike force consisted of fourteen armed Jeeps plus a few general purpose vehicles loaded with spare water, fuel, ammunition, parts and provisions. The new moon dimly lit the way as the expedition left with headlights extinguished. The temperature was glacial and the muffled-up men grumbled and shivered as they waited for day to break. We stopped at dawn; the cars were concealed under camouflage nets and we settled down for the day. The LRDG scouts reported in with detailed information about the target, which was a four-hour drive away. We left around 8.30 p.m. planning to arrive at the target at midnight when we hoped to surprise the enemy asleep. We stopped half a kilometre away.

The first contingents blacked their faces, hands and knees and crept away to neutralise the guards; the others waited. At a signal we simultaneously started up our motors and roared forward. A few minutes later we saw a few of the semi-camouflaged lights of the enemy depot. We snapped on our headlights, ploughed through the barriers and split into three groups: four Jeeps took the central alley which divided the depot from east to west; three Jeeps took the left outskirts laterally parallel to the centre; three others did the same to the right. As we hit the barrier we opened fire and took the enemy completely by surprise; the counter-fire was sporadic and inaccurate.

The first of the four Jeeps speeding down the centre spewed bullets in front of it while the second fired to the left and the third covered the right; the fourth brought up the rear, spraying bullets to the back. The men flung hand grenades into the stacks of munitions placed about twenty metres apart; these exploded behind the Jeeps a few seconds later. The ground shook and the air was rent by the deafening racket and the tremendous force of the explosions. The sky was ablaze with long oblique trails of flame which leapt from stack to stack; garish reds, yellows, blues and greens flared in the sky while chunks of debris rained down. Some of the Jeeps literally had their back ends in the fire; anyone who lagged behind would be caught in the belching furnace. The men, intoxicated, screamed in a frenzy, shooting and hurling grenades incessantly.

From the last Jeep taking the central alley, I could see the two lines of Jeeps taking the parallel routes on either side setting off more and more explosions. When we reached the three-quarters point, we were met by precise strafing; bullets buzzed around us and ricocheted from the metal housing of the Jeeps. I saw a man in the third Jeep raise his arms, turn and reel out on to the road. The leading Jeep succeeded in stemming the enemy fire but the second Jeep, hit, swerved off the alley, crashed into a pile of munition cases and blew up, casting flames which enveloped the following Jeeps. Feeling the tremendous heat of the explosion, I barely had time to shield my face. As we reached the end of the alley we found a small group of crazed Germans who were taking a stand as best they could, but the SAS guns mowed them down in a murderous crossfire finished off by a last rain of grenades, as we gunned our motors and raced away. The last thing I saw were pieces of bodies flying through the air before being swallowed by the burning inferno.

We were rejoined by the others. We could see the fuel depot, located about half a kilometre away, flaming up in thirty metre columns of fire and the blasts from the huge piles of Jerry cans. The men were battle drunk! Flushed by the sight of the apocalypse we had unchained, we shouted and laughed dementedly as we congratulated each other; the euphoria wore off as we looked back at the flaming sky with grave faces. We had lost two vehicles, three men were missing, seven were wounded, but the depots looked totally destroyed! I was singed and half deaf; I was unable to come back to reality. Images of horror and carnage reeled through my mind and, as the convoy drove away, I sank into a dreary numbness, in spite of the jolting cross-country drive.

The next day we licked our wounds, took care of the wounded, patched up the vehicles, replenished the ammunition – in other words, got ready for the next mission. The LRDG scouts reported a small unit of tanks parked in the middle of nowhere apparently out of fuel. The crews had placed their vehicles in a defensive square with the machine-guns and cannon pointing outwards. They were probably Italian M-13/40 tanks.

Proud of having won my spurs with honour, I volunteered to go. 'Let's go get them before someone rescues them. I know tanks; I've already blown up several in Tunis, including one of the famous German Tigers.'

'You did what?' asked the captain, who had evidently not troubled to read my dossier. 'Sorry, my boy,' he continued, 'but you are still green in desert warfare. I can't let you lead such an operation but you can be useful in giving advice to the fellows who are going to do the job.'

The raid was a success and resembled the commando activities of Ferryville: Jeeps parked a short distance away; guards silently knifed; tank crews pulverised by hand grenades; tanks put out of commission forever by grenades thrown into the open turrets; then the fast getaway.

Two nights later we attacked a sizeable convoy of trucks and gasoline tankers escorted by German armoured vehicles. It was an impromptu action – one of the scouting Jeeps had literally run into the convoy and the SAS reacted spontaneously. We buzzed in like hornets on the unsuspecting enemy. The SAS Jeeps dispersed and attacked the convoy from all directions – front, sides and rear – before the Germans realised what had hit them. The escort hesitated, afraid to open fire on their own vehicles, and began circling ineffectually; the tankers tried to move out in order not to be an easy target, but that only worsened the dilemma, as the escort could not guard them at all now. One tanker blew up, then another, then a third. Long tongues of fire licked across the sky and it became bright as day. Both sides had a hard time staying clear of the sprays of flame. The SAS shot continuous bursts of tracer bullets, as if on a practice range, while the Germans, aided by the glare, zeroed in on the SAS.

I saw that two of the Jeeps had been set on fire, saw others whose occupants were slumped over. The withdrawal flare went off but I never saw it. My red-hot machine-gun had jammed and right in front of me, about thirty metres ahead, was a tanker with a trailer in tow. Crazed by the fever of the battle, I had lost all common sense and I steered straight towards the juggernaut. I veered at the last moment and hurled one, then two, hand grenades at it. The conflagration I kindled was phantasmagoric! My Jeep was lifted high into the air, caught by a sheet of fire, and smashed down far away by the blast. Bellowing, I was submerged in pain – in oblivion.

Later, much later, I came back into the world; I couldn't remember anything, I couldn't place myself in either time or space. It was pitch black but I smelt the penetrating odours of ether, alcohol and medicine and sensed the bustle of activity around me, but I could hear only murmurs and muffled sounds. As I became more aware, pain engulfed me in expanding agony and convulsive lacerating spasms. I could not move, but a sudden stab of excruciating pain made me groan. A soft cool hand came to rest on my forehead and a woman's quiet voice said, 'There, there. Don't move. Please don't move. Don't worry. Everything will be all right.'

Several days later – or was it several centuries later? – after an eternity of torment in which I roamed through dreams and nightmares where I alternated between solace and anguish and spiralled into bottomless pits, I emerged into blindness! During my long journey into the dark where I had felt so completely lost, a sweet fresh voice, always the same voice, and a hand, always the same hand, had reassured me. I started to remember and tried to understand – then questioned and questioned.

'Your SAS mates went back to get you. They hauled you through the desert, took care of you and had you flown out on a military plane. No, no, you're not blind forever. The bandages will come off in a few days and you'll be able to see again. Half your body is burned but not too badly. You're battered, but you're only twenty-three. You'll live. Everything is going to be all right.'

I trembled with fear as the bandages were removed. I could see! I could see the blurred figure of a young woman in the twilight of the darkened room. She was beautiful; she had

auburn hair; her smile irradiated the gentleness she had so
prodigiously bestowed upon me during my suffering.

'How lovely you are!'

'Bravo!' came a voice from the shadows and I heard a man
laugh. 'Bravo! You're certainly getting better. The moment a
Frenchman begins to compliment a pretty girl he's well on the
road to recovery.'

Eight days later I was almost well. I still had a gritty pain in
my eyes and was slightly sore, but I had regained my strength
and spent all day daydreaming about rejoining my unit.

One morning I woke up to find a balding pale man standing
at the foot of my bed. His ill-fitting uniform gave him the air of
a somewhat rancid seminarian. It turned out he was a Secret
Service agent. He started to fire questions at me with no
preamble.

'What's your name? Were you in Malta a few weeks ago? Did
you meet with an officer of the Security Defence Service?'

Intrigued but puzzled, I answered all the questions docilely.

'All right. Major Morris is reclaiming you. He needs you
urgently. Are you fit to travel and rejoin the Service?'

'Well, you'll have to ask my doctor about that.'

'He wants you back in Tunis. Will you go?'

'No, never! What's wrong?'

'Come and see me as soon as you are released from the
hospital and I'll explain but, believe me, it's pressing and
serious.'

It was pressing and serious indeed. The two transmitters in
Tunis had been dead for over ten days. The latest news reported
a wave of arrests in the network. It seemed that Dick Jones had
tried to cross the lines into Algeria and had completely vanished. There was no news of him or Coggia, who was supposed
to have accompanied him. Ferryville was transmitting spor-
adically but never answered any of Malta's queries. It was
feared that behind this curtain of silence there might operate a
reign of terror.

Slumped in a chair in front of the seminarian's desk, I had just
finished reading Major Morris's long radio message. While I
played with a small piece of paper folded in four I pondered the
situation. I had found the note among my personal belongings

when I had checked out of the hospital; someone must have slipped it into my pocket before I was flown out. It was from my Commander in the SAS.

I had read and reread the laconic but stirring message: 'Good luck, Alec. The officers and men join me in wishing you a swift recovery and in expressing the hope of having you back among us soon.' Fate had been kind to me in the crazy episode and I felt that, more than anything else, I now belonged to the SAS and wanted to remain a desert fighter. But could I turn my back on my endangered Tunis friends with a clear conscience?

The man on the other side of the desk, who had been watching me silently, snapped me out of my deliberations, 'Well, how about it?'

I straightened up, took a deep breath and said, 'I'll go. I hate this, but I can't refuse. Right now, I'm probably the only one who can renew the contacts and get the network working again. Besides, since the Allies will launch their attack on Tunisia at any moment, they will need all the information they can get. My friends are in trouble and . . . ' I didn't finish the statement; I was thinking about Thérèse.

One of Major Morris's aides came to brief me. Although I was still wobbly I had decided to go as quickly as possible, owing to the seriousness of the situation. They let me rest for two more days while they prepared the details of the mission. I was flown to Tripoli, placed on a Royal Navy PT boat and put ashore in an inflated dinghy under a starry sky the next night. I was back at the beach at Cape Bon only twelve kilometres from the point where Jean-Marie and I had embarked fifty-nine days before. Once more, exactly as in Gibraltar, I was back at the starting point like a pawn in a Parchesi game.

9

Into The Fiery Furnace

Nothing untoward happened on the way and I got off the bus in the centre of Tunis. I was dressed in slacks, a short-sleeved shirt and sneakers and carried only a beachbag bulging with money and new lists of radio frequencies to be used for transmitting to Malta.

I rapidly walked to the rue des Juges in the Arab quarter and rang the doorbell of Dick's house, but there was no answer. I began to pound on the wooden door; I pounded and pounded – still no answer. The shutters were closed and it looked as if the whole house had been abandoned. The same thing happened at the other two safe houses, so I went to Chez Max to try to find out what had been going on but the owner, pretending not to know me, ignored me. Finally one of the waiters surreptitiously whispered to me that neither Madame Odette nor any other of my friends had been seen for the last two weeks.

'Take my advice. You'd better get away from here while the going is good or someone might spot you and start asking a lot of questions. No, sir, don't waste precious time paying the bill. Get the hell out of here.'

The climate in Tunis was definitely unhealthy and there was no point in making myself conspicuous by walking the streets hoping to be contacted by some still-at-large member of the network, so I took the first available bus to Ferryville. I went to the hospital and found my small room there undisturbed. Two hours later I rang the bell at the apartment where we had installed the first radio, but no answer. I went to the second apartment and did the same. Cautiously, the door opened and Marc, the Marmot, looking dishevelled and unkempt, peered out. He turned ashen when he saw me. 'It's you! It's you!'

'Who did you think it was – a ghost? I can't have changed that much in two months.'

'It's just that we were told you were dead.'

Marc finally recovered from the shock and let me in. He tried to tell me how happy he was to see me by repeating my name and slapping me on the back.

'Marmot, listen to me. Where is Coggia?'

Marc's eyes clouded over. He started to stammer and clench and unclench his hands and it took me some time to calm him down to get some sense out of him: Coggia was dead! Twelve days after my departure, Dick Jones had called him to Tunis to accompany him on a trip, as he had received a scrambled together message from Malta telling him I had never reached the island and was probably lost at sea. Therefore, Dick had decided to cross the front lines to Algeria but they had run into a German patrol as they tried to sneak through and the Germans had mowed them down with a sub-machine-gun. Coggia had been literally cut in two as he threw himself over Dick trying to protect him.

I raged silently at Dick's foolishness.

Hadn't we already discarded that route as impossible? Then images of Coggia, my friend, flashed through my mind: our first meeting, our endless arguments which always ended in laughter, our escapades . . . I couldn't believe he was dead.

After a while, I asked about Dick's whereabouts.

'No one knows. Nobody has seen or heard from him. Some say he's in hiding; some say he was taken prisoner; some say he's dead. The two other Englishmen disappeared too.'

I kept asking questions. In Tunis, the Germans had closed in on one of the transmitters, destroyed the radio and killed the operator; the people involved in the network had simply vanished.

In Ferryville, Coggia had not been able to hold things together after I had gone, and after he left the organisation went to pieces. Marmot was still working but the ship pilots gave very little information, the commandos went back home, Karantec went on leave and the second 'piano' went out of order. At the moment, the Ferryville radio was Malta's only source of information in Northern Tunisia and it had really very little to tell.

'And Thérèse?'

Her mother had taken her back to France, to Nice, where

they had some relatives, but how she had grieved and cried when told I was dead. Since her departure, the Marmot had not seen any of the 'Kangaroos' except Aline. And to top it off they were all broke.

I would have to start all over again. I gave Marc some money, a new list of radio frequencies and wrote out a message to be sent to Malta informing them I had arrived safely, would go south the following day, would organise a reception committee to receive the supplies, arms and explosives two Englishmen would be bringing. I signed myself 'Yo-Yo' and when Marc asked me what it meant I told him I was using that codename because I always came back to the same place I had left and felt like a yo-yo on a string. We both agreed Aline should be the one to organise the reception committee at Cape Bon.

'What about the trip south?' asked Marc.

'I think it won't be long before the Allies launch an all-out attack on Tunisia. They'll need all the information they can get about the enemy force on the south and north-west fronts as well as what is happening behind the lines. I'll have to get the layout myself or do you think we could send anyone else?'

'No, you'd only waste time trying to convince someone else. It'll be much quicker if you go.'

'I have a plan, I need two German uniforms, an Army Volkswagen and a companion, who is a mechanic and can share in the driving as I plan to cover 1,000 kilometres.'

Marc suggested a small Alsatian nicknamed 'Fritz' who worked at the Arsenal garage with Karantec and spoke German fluently. I remembered him; he was tough, young and had already been on some commando raids, and I thought it was an excellent choice.

A chauffeur and a lieutenant from General Fritz von Broich's Tenth Panzer Division, alias Fritz and I, left Ferryville the following day at dawn. We were driving a Volkswagen loaded down with cans of fuel and other equipment, in the direction of Tunis, planning to turn south later. Fritz and I got ready in record time. Having resumed my identity as official translator to Admiral Herrien, I had been able to get two uniforms. They had belonged to an officer and a soldier from the Tenth Panzer Division, who had been wounded at the Battle of Thala, a defeat suffered a few days previously by the Germans, and had died at the hospital. I had made a lightning appearance at the Secretariat of the Admiralty; paid a visit to Aline's friends at the photography laboratory to get some official looking photos. I had also renewed a friendship with a draughtsman at the Arsenal's Technical Department, who had artistically tampered with the official seals and photos until I had exactly what I needed: two complete sets of identity papers which would stand up even under close scrutiny. Then I had typed up my own travel orders: Ferryville to Gabes, Gabes to Thala, Thala to Ferryville – reason for the trip and exalted signatures included. The Volkswagen had been lifted from the German parking lot at the Arsenal, passed briefly through the garage where it had been thoroughly checked and then hidden away in a neighbouring villa, where it had been prepared for the long journey.

We had been afraid that the trip would be dangerous and that we would run into many obstacles, but it turned out to be a long boring drive. Everything went smoothly and we were able to replenish our fuel and water supply without difficulty. We had no trouble passing the Feldgendarmerie check points and even managed to camp out under the stars without arousing suspicion.

The road had been bombed, was full of holes, dusty and rutted from the passageway of heavy trucks and tanks. The driving was very uncomfortable and further south became even more so with the increased heat. We were almost prostrate and our eyes burned continually. However, the hardest thing to do was remember everything along our route with no notes: the trucks, how many and what loads; the troops, how many, what units, what physical condition; the tanks, what types; the guns, what quantity, what calibre, what condition; the ammunition dumps and the tank truck and fuel depots, how many, where located; the camps and barracks, how many, where located; the enemy convoy routes, to and from where; the airfields, where located, how many. Fritz and I kept separate accounts in our heads. We would compare them, condense them and recite the figures back to each other. It was rather like trying to carry the inventory of a hardware store mentally. I had already had practice in this kind of mental exercise during my early experiences as Dick's scout in Ferryville, but this was monstrously complicated and made both of us so dizzy we felt sick to our stomachs.

By the end of February 1943 the southern front had been temporarily established at the fortified Mareth Line. I got as close as possible to it within a few kilometres of the English outposts. I felt very tempted to abandon everything and pass through the lines to rejoin my beloved SAS but . . . After changing my travel orders I headed westwards, back through Gabes, Gafsa, and then took the road north to Kasserine and Thala, where Rommel was desperately trying to stave off the Allies' advance.

Rommel had to get as many of his troops as possible out of this area at all costs in order to face the British Eighth Army, which, by this time, had reached the Mareth Line, where he anticipated a decisive battle. The activity behind the front at Thala resembled a disturbed anthill and I had great difficulty avoiding being sequestered into an active German front unit. That was all I needed!

Four days later Fritz and I were back in Ferryville. Not even bothering to change, we rushed over to the apartment. Marc, who was not expecting us back so soon, almost died on the spot when two German soldiers forced their way past him.

'My God! You ought to be hung, scaring me like that. You're worse than the real owners of those outfits, you stupid jerks!'

'Calm down.'

'That's easy to say. I thought my time had come. And the look of you . . . those damned uniforms and those tanned faces. I didn't recognise you. You're damn lucky I didn't blow your heads off.'

After two hours of frantic efforts, passionate arguments and terrifying memory gaps, we put together a comprehensive report on everything we had seen on our expedition. We condensed it, coded it, and gave it to Marc to transmit immediately.

'If you use the full range of frequencies I gave you, alternating with long silences, you should be able to transmit it all in less than eighteen hours without much risk. After you finish and Malta acknowledges reception, put the keys under the mat and get the hell out of here. Go to the other apartment, or go on a vacation if you'd rather, but don't come around here for the next eight days. We'll have a complete radio black-out. I'll see you next week at the same time at the other apartment. In the meantime, I'll try to tie up loose ends. Thanks, Marmot, goodbye and good luck!'

'You're welcome, Herr Oberleutnant, and Heil Hitler!'

I now remembered how I was dressed and had a sudden urgent need to get rid of the uniform immediately. After shaking Fritz's hand firmly I walked back to the hospital, entered through a small side door, stripped and threw the uniform into one of the incinerators in the basement. Then I threw myself on my bed and tried to think.

At around 7.00 p.m. I went around the corner to the local bistro to get a bite to eat. Suddenly I was startled by a strident voice calling me. I turned and ran smack into a very ugly individual called Vincenot. I had met him in the Tunis prison, where he was serving time for an ill-defined crime. He had a high bulging forehead, a chin which jutted out like an Arab's slipper, eyelashes like a seal's and a look that refused to meet one's eyes.

'Alec, old boy, what are you doing here? I figured you'd be in London by now.'

I was disturbed. 'Well, I work here in the hospital.'

'You? Work? In the hospital? You?'

'Yes, I work in one of the wards. I was a medical student, you know, and as I speak German I'm very useful.'

'So that's why I saw you in a uniform.'

'Uniform? What uniform?'

'Why that German officer's uniform, of course.'

'You must have been seeing things. Me, in a German uniform?'

'Well, maybe I made a mistake, but I could have sworn I saw someone who looked just like you wearing a German uniform. Maybe I was wrong. Sorry.'

'That's all right.'

'How about getting together some time to talk about the good old times?'

'You really have a funny sense of humour. The good old times? In prison? The good old times, indeed!'

'I didn't mean anything. It's just a manner of speaking. I'll give you a call.'

'Do that, Vincenot.'

I was irked and felt vaguely uneasy after this encounter but, as I was too tired to worry about it, I had a snack and went to bed. In the middle of the night I was dragged from my sleep by savage knocks on the door.

'Open up! Police!'

My blood congealed. The room was a trap! There was no other opening except the two barred transom windows which gave on to the corridor and these were impossible to squeeze through. I panicked! How could I explain the bundle of money under the bed? How could I defend myself? I flicked on the light and opened the door. Three armed civilians covered me from the moment of my appearance. The largest and fattest of the trio stepped forward and shoved a badge under my nose.

'German police. You're under arrest! Follow us.'

'B-b-b-but,' I stuttered. I was seized by vile terror. 'B-b-b-but . . .'

'No buts; get dressed and get moving. You'll have time enough to talk later.'

The beefy looking one spoke passable French with a heavy Teutonic accent which made me want to strangle him but, for the time being, I had more pressing worries. I dressed clumsily and then asked: 'Can I go to the bathroom?'

One of the three, a Frenchman, took me by the arm and led me there. I was trying to fight off the terror that was making me shake from head to foot, that liquefied my guts, that turned my legs to rubber. I felt I would die from the cold gripping me and making my teeth chatter. When I got to the urinal, I lost all control and pissed my trousers and shoes. I pressed my forehead against the wall, clenched my teeth and repeated to myself: 'Get hold of yourself . . . Get hold of yourself!'

I tried to speak and finally managed a few quavering words: 'What do you want with me?'

'We? Nothing,' said the French cop. 'We're only giving a hand to our colleagues in the Gestapo.'

'Gestapo! Oh my God!' My fear swelled to such unbearable proportions, I reacted. I splashed cold water on my face and began to breathe again. A single thought possessed me: 'I've got to get out of here. I've got to get out of here.'

Out of the corner of my eye I saw a window with frosted

panes across the hall through the open door. Since I was on the second floor, I knew that if I went through it I would land in a flowerbed on top of the laurel bushes. Almost instinctively I lunged and thrust the surprised cop aside. Protecting my face with crossed arms, I crashed through the glass that split into a thousand shards and butted against – iron bars! With a gash on my head I collapsed at the feet of the cop who for good measure whacked me on the head with his revolver butt and handcuffed me. I passed out.

I came to aboard a speeding Citroën. The headlights flooded the road, which allowed me to identify it as the one to Bizerte. I had been squeezed in between two French policemen in the back seat. The fat German, half-turned in the front seat, was watching me.

'Ach! He's joining us again. You try any more foolishness and we'll really take care of you.'

The car came to a halt before the building which had originally held the Public Work Services. In spite of the late hour, lights shone through all the windows and it was bustling with activity. I could hear typewriters clicking, telephones ringing, doors slamming and voices shouting.

They hauled me out of the car, dragged me by the armpits through the corridors to a door that opened off the central hall and shoved me into a brilliantly lit room, where I landed flat on my nose. Four men were sitting around chatting, smoking and laughing. They looked up with a spark of interest at my grand entrance.

'*Ist das der Mann?*' asked one of the men.

'*Ja!*' answered the Gestapo cop who had arrested me.

'He doesn't look so good. What happened to him?'

'Nothing much. He ran into a doorknob.' Everyone found this statement to be excruciatingly funny and roared.

One man approached me as I was lying on the floor and kicked me in the face. Stars and suns burst into fragments. Just as I was recovering the man kicked me again.

'Get up, *schweinhund*.'

A second man, not to be left out, came up and punched me in the stomach; before I even had time to double up I was kicked in the testicles. The air whooshed out of my lungs and I sank to the floor.

When I came to I was very careful to give no sign of life; my mind was clear and for some strange reason I had lost all fear. Instead I was filled with a cold hatred and steeled myself for what was to come: 'They're going to kill me, if not now then later; I'm going to take one of these bastards with me!'

Another man, evidently very important, to judge by the reaction of the henchmen, stepped in. He was fleshy, reddish, baldish and lumpish. 'Is that the man from the hospital?'

'*Jawohl, Herr Oberkommissar*. That's him,' answered one of the lackeys. 'He just got here. We've been softening him up a bit.' Gales of laughter again.

'Good. Get him on his feet. We'll ask him a few little questions.'

I made myself heavy and limp. They heaved me upright. I was standing near a low table with a heavy typewriter on it. In a reflex action, which took the Germans unaware, I lifted the machine by the metal frame with both hands and, spurred on by all the despair, fear and hatred raging inside of me, hurled it into the boss's face, turning that charming countenance into strawberry jam in a fraction of a second. The man screamed and gargled as he staggered blindly. After a moment of petrified silence, bedlam broke loose! A shot rang out; one of the henchmen had reacted tardily and was bawled out by his companions. Two of them carried the Herr Oberkommissar out. I was buried in a heap of men incoherently swearing at me, kicking me, beating me. I could hardly tell what was happening to me, only that I hurt . . . hurt terribly.

A livid German officer stormed in and, as no one took any notice of him, pulled his Luger from its holster and fired twice in the air. Everyone stood still!

'What's going on here? Have you all gone crazy? Where do you think you are – on the firing range? Gestapo idiots! Sons of bitches! Don't you realise that shot came through the wall and almost killed me!' The man, who appeared to be a Wehrmacht colonel, saw my mangled body lying on the floor. 'What's that?'

'A spy. A traitor, sir.'

I eked out enough strength to interrupt. 'I'm not a spy, much less a traitor. I am an officer, the personal translator for the Admiral commanding the Health Service . . .'

One of the cops interrupted, called me a filthy bastard, said I had thrown a typewriter at his boss and smashed his head in so badly that he would probably die.

The Colonel was amazed. 'That's extraordinary. I must admit that we officers of the Wehrmacht disapprove highly of the Gestapo's revolting methods. Well, if I leave you here, they'll cart you out in little pieces; however, as an inquiry is mandatory, I'll have you sent to the Military Court of Inquiry in Tunis.'

Two hours later I was locked up in the Citadel, the military prison in the old Casbah of Tunis. I found myself alone in a dark silent cell. I had been beaten to a pulp; I was bleeding, spitting up blood, hurting. I hurt when I breathed, when I moved, even when I didn't move; I had turned into a knot of pain, but I was alive and, for the time being, out of the clutches of the Gestapo. I moaned and suffered all night as I fitfully slept, starting awake drenched in cold sweat.

My fate had been decided while I slept; the Court of Inquiry had decided I did not fall under their jurisdiction and remanded me to the Tunis Gestapo. I didn't know it yet, but I had just gone from the frying pan into the fire; also, my file was now embellished by the incident with the Gestapo chief. I was in deep trouble. I was still vomiting blood and incapable of standing or walking alone, when a car came to fetch me the following day: new office, new cops, new and old questions about myself over and over again.

There was a bony man, ugly as sin, with a murky look in his eyes which was strangely augmented by his tortoise-shell glasses, which spread his ears further apart than they already were; this one proceeded to give me a preliminary lecture.

'After the unspeakable act you performed against one of our Secret Police chiefs, you deserve to be eliminated immediately in such a way as would be an example to all traitors.'

'What about what they did to me? Just look at me,' I said.

'Shut up!' thundered Ugly. 'Our esteemed colleague is hovering between life and death; your fate will depend on his. Right now we want a complete rundown on your activities during the past few weeks. What were you doing dressed in a German uniform in Ferryville? We have precise information on that from an impeccable source who saw you the day before yesterday.'

'I've never worn a German uniform. I don't know what you are talking about.' Inwardly, I cursed Vincenot, who I was sure had denounced me.

'Are you a Gaullist? We know you were illegally released from the Tunis prison, where you were serving time for just such traitorous offences. Where have you been since then?'

Where? What? Who? Why? When? The questions fell thick and fast, each one more prickly than the last. The Gestapo was well informed and bluffed on the items they were not sure of. One thing impressed me in the barrage of questions that closed around me like a net – it was the one question that was never asked and which undoubtedly would have incriminated me more than any other: not once was the bag of money stashed under my bed mentioned. That was something I would have been hard put to explain away. I then remembered that one of the French cops had stayed behind to search my room while I had put on my little acrobatic stunt in the corridor; like any good bourgeois he had probably set it aside for a rainy day.

During the entire interrogation I gritted my teeth and denied . . . denied again . . . denied everything.

'Well, we don't seem to be getting anywhere. You're too stupid to see that the only way to save your neck is to collaborate, so we'll try other methods of loosening your tongue.'

I found myself naked as a worm, with my hands and feet lashed to a chair which had been screwed down to the floor in the centre of an almost empty room in the basement. There were only two basins of water on the floor, a stool, and shelves with various bizarre instruments.

Already badly battered, I was beaten like an old carpet for two days. They peeled my nails off slowly and delicately; they would wedge a thin steel file under the nail and roll it back with miniature pliers which they used like a sardine-can key. First they removed my fingernails one by one and then my toenails. They attached electrodes to my wrists and ankles, put my feet into the basins of water, and gave me electric shocks in the mouth, nose, testicles and anus, which convulsed me in horrible spasms. After each operation, they repeated the same questions again and again . . . Where? What? Who? Why? When? How? They hung me for hours from the ceiling by my wrists or ankles like a ham in a smokehouse. I was lashed with the whip and the crop and treated to the thumbscrews.

I was wracked by indescribable, insupportable pain. I found that it was useless to try to maintain a heroic front; on the contrary, any noble gesture made them redouble their efforts, so I let myself go. I cried; I convulsed; I contorted myself; I implored; I screamed like the damned; I shitted myself. The brutes were stupid sadists who enjoyed inflicting horror and completely lost sight of their purpose. Several times I reached the limits of endurance, of strength, of pain, of will, of honour; I had been ready to confess, betray or invent anything, but these maniacs took no notice and each time pushed me over the edge into oblivion, from which I would revive to go through Calvary again. But I didn't say anything . . . or rather I did say anything.

Finally, they took my remains not to the military prison, but to the hospital, where a young army doctor slowly nursed me back to life. By the middle of March I was still in a lamentable condition but I was healing and alive.

While I had been in a coma papers had been delivered to the infirmary informing me that I had been sentenced to death and would be executed at the convenience of the military authorities. I received the news with a resigned indifference; at this point it was a sweet alternative. It was only later, when life and hope sprang in me anew, that I was seized by a rampaging fear; however, the slow monotony of prison life anaesthetised me into a numbness which allowed me to live each day as it came.

When I was better I was transferred to a cell on the second floor of the south wing of the Citadel, where I was overjoyed to find many Gaullists and friends from the Resistance in the cells around me. Some had been members of the Tunis network; others I had met during my stay in Tiboursouk and at the Tunis Central penitentiary. A lot of them had known Dick Jones and Coggia. I kept my fears of my imminent execution to myself but woke every morning at five to sit on the edge of my bed and listen tensely, asking myself if today would be the day.

But nothing happened; my lucky star still looked over me.

During the last days of March, a young Tunis radio operator had been arrested and had talked under torture. He said that the night before he was captured he had received a message ordering me to stand by to be picked up either by a British submarine or a PT boat; I had been assigned to a new unit which was to be parachuted into Italy to prepare the ground for future Allied landings. Whether this information was true or not, I never found out, but the Germans assumed I was in the know and could tell them where the Allies planned to land.

The battle for Tunis was now in its final phase; the Americans, the French and the English were converging upon it. At night the prisoners could hear the distant thundering of the cannon. The Germans and the Italians had started packing up and under the present conditions the Germans, considering me to be too valuable to be executed, decided to evacuate me along with the Gestapo and some other army personnel, in order to investigate me later at their leisure. Paradoxically, I had been saved from the firing squad by being unmasked!

10

Die Herren Offizieren

Surrounded by high walls and shaded by old dusty trees, the tranquil prison courtyard buzzed with unusual activity that morning. German soldiers ran hither and thither piling up boxes in one of the corners and throwing documents on a bonfire which had been built against one of the walls; there was a feeling of urgency in the air. A small group of prisoners sitting in the middle talked agitatedly. As I drew near I recognised my friends from the Resistance: Méry, Tiné, Bonjour, Treiber, Mandereau, Boutelleau, and many others. Our number grew until there were approximately forty of us, all happy to find each other again under the open sky, but still afraid openly to acknowledge our friendship having defiantly denied it to the Gestapo.

'Is it over? Are they going to set us free?'

The wildest conjectures were brandished about but everyone kept quiet about their chief concern: Had we been assembled to be shot?

I thought how the day, 1 April 1943, had begun. I had been awakened at 4.30 a.m. by the pounding on my door.

'Get ready,' a voice shouted.

I had been paralysed by fear; this was the dreaded hour, the hour when men were taken out never to be seen again. At 6.00 a.m., as day broke, I heard the same voice behind the door: 'Are you ready?'

In a strangled voice, I said, 'Ready for what?'

The peephole opened and I could see a mouth surmounted by a thick moustache framed in the grille. 'Get your things. You're leaving in a convoy.'

'I don't need anything to appear before a firing squad.'

'What are you talking about? I just told you, you're leaving in a convoy.'

'If this is your idea of an April Fool's joke, it's not funny!'

I heard the familiar noise of rattling keys and sliding bolts; the heavy door opened and I could see a blue rectangle of sky. I looked back at my miserable hole, which now appeared safe and homey; I was sure I was stepping into a trap and was frozen with fear!

The small group in the courtyard finally seemed to be complete. Suddenly there was a commotion; a stretcher carried by two guards and followed by a chubby moustached man came towards us.

'Arthur!' I cried out in spite of myself. It was Arthur Wilding, smiling and relaxed. What a surprise! And on the stretcher, even more relaxed and smiling, lay Dick Jones! 'You were arrested then?' I asked stupidly.

'How did you guess?'

It was good to hear that high sweet voice again. I pointed to the plaster cast covering Dick's left leg and to the rubber-tipped cane he was brandishing. 'What are those?'

'Those are the consequences of my escape.'

'You got away?'

'Then he fell on his head and broke his leg,' said Arthur with a deadpan expression. 'I'll tell you all about it, old boy.'

We were cut short by another interruption. The prison cook began distributing coffee, bread and liverwurst. 'Keep your rations for the trip,' recommended one of the guards. The entrance gates swung open and a convoy of platform trailers parked in a line in the centre of the yard. The prisoners were then lined up for roll-call, chained in pairs and loaded on the trailers.

'Stay flat on the platform. The first one to stick his head up will get it shot off,' threatened a young German soldier standing with his back against the truck cabin, legs apart, a rifle pressed against his ribs. His French left much to be desired but his meaning was very clear. 'Understand?'

I was lying on my back with my arms spread wide, chained to my mate, Gerard. I relaxed; I was weary of guessing games, of building up fragile theories and inconsistent scenarios. The blissfully warm sun was already high in the intensely blue sky. The convoy began to roll and the prisoners could see the pedestrians, streets and buildings pass by. The city was surprisingly calm but we could see people, mainly women, hurrying out on to their balconies to view the strange procession each time it slowed down.

'Bastards! Murderers! *Deutschland kaput!*' The insults rained down. The young soldier who had probably heard it all before, bowed his head and ignored the invective.

One of the prisoners, perhaps from Tunis, called out the names of the streets as we came to them: rue de France, Avenue de Paris, Avenue de Bordeaux. The litany which evoked my lost country depressed me.

The 'tour guide' continued incredulously, 'My friends, we're going into the Hippodrome. The Boche must be out of their minds.'

We crossed a guarded enclosure, drove by several low buildings and came to a halt. The Hippodrome had been turned into an airfield: the runway had been built down the middle, a tall pole with a radio antenna and windsock had been planted at one end; tents had been raised on the sides; aeroplanes were noisily landing and taking off, stirring up clouds of thick reddish dust.

I remarked, 'They are all Junkers-52s. Where are the fighters?'

'A fighter can't land here. The runway's too short and rough,' someone said.

About one hundred planes were scattered around the field. They were being unloaded and quickly reloaded with the most heterogeneous collection of things. The field was busy as a beehive: men were running; trucks were circulating; motorbikes were snaking in and out of the traffic; tankers were refuelling the planes; gangs of bare-chested Tunisians were doing the heavy work, bossed by German Army regulars. An open maintenance area had been set up and mechanics, black with grease, were efficiently servicing the planes; loudspeakers attached to poles blared out orders and warnings and the din was intensified by shrieking sirens or the motorcades which cleared the way for the ambulances; teams of nurses in white coats took the wounded in charge and deposited the stretchers inside the planes with great care. At first glance all this activity seemed chaotic but it was really ruled by strict order.

After a long wait the prisoners, who had been enjoying the sun, were taken, still chained in pairs, to one end of the runway, where seventy planes were waiting to take off. We were split into groups of ten, pushed up a rickety metal ladder into a plane and ordered to sit on the floor of the cabin. Our chains were passed around the metal girders reinforcing the inner panels of the cabin. Our fate was chained to the fate of the plane!

'I don't like this one bit,' I thought and, to judge by their expressions, neither did my buddies. In the semi-darkness of the cabin, the mixed smell of burned oil, gasoline and exhaust fumes turned our stomachs. There were suitcases, parcels, canteens, cases and cartons piled up in every nook and cranny of the cabin; they had been crammed in so hurriedly that they had not even been secured. It was a graphic illustration of headlong flight.

The German passengers boarded, stepped over the prisoners as if we didn't exist, and took their seats. They were mostly high-ranking officers, with a few men who stank of 'cop' and half a dozen 'grey mice', the women soldiers of the German Army. They were rouged, curled, combed; they wore impeccable uniforms, silk stockings, forage caps slanted down to their noses, and bandoleer bags slung over their shoulders.

'Look at the gentlemen's whores,' commented a voice in the dark.

The German voices rang loudly with forced gaiety. They talked about going home, furloughs and new assignments; their suntans gave them a robust look, but we sensed they were only putting up a front – inside, they must be feeling let down and demoralised . . . defeated! One of them brought out a bottle of champagne and they began to toast Victory, return to the Fatherland and farewell to Africa.

Having warmed up their engines, the planes rolled to the end of the runway one by one and took off at the signal flare. They rolled bumpily down the runway gaining speed, left the ground reluctantly and skimmed the hedges of the Hippodrome. They gained height slowly and took their places in the formation which was circling the field in a waiting pattern to allow all the planes to join it. Then the formation divided up into groups, established their flight altitude and flew east. I got to my knees and saw the tops of the hills around Tunis, Cape Bon and then the sea. Soon fighter planes from another airfield joined us as an escort.

The tune of the droning motors lulled me to sleep; I was

brusquely awakened by the staccato grunt of the alarm horn: '*Achtung!* We're under attack by the RAF.'

'That's all we need . . . to be shot down by friends,' I thought.

The plane dived down to sea level and flew almost grazing the waves. We could no longer see the leading plane. I listened anxiously to the comments of the German passengers. They were talking about a dog fight between their fighters and the RAF raging above them, about several Junkers in the rear which had been shot down, about how they couldn't see the rest of the scattered formation. Everything seemed so unreal that I wasn't even afraid; my only worry was being chained to the damn plane. Someone asked to be unchained but his only answer was a kick in the teeth, so we resigned ourselves and retreated into silence. We had left Tunis around 11.00 a.m. and the RAF had surprised us forty minutes later. The pilot managed to lose the attackers and the rest of the flight was uneventful.

Around 1.00 p.m. the Italian coast was sighted. One of the Germans shouted, '*Der Vesuvius! Der Vesuvius!*' so I presumed we were approaching Naples. The plane landed to the loud cheers of the Germans, which contrasted with the worried constrained silence of the prisoners. Four hours later, ten of us were placed aboard an express train heading north. We were shaved, washed, brushed, fed, interrogated, but had not been unshackled. The two German soldiers who guarded the compartment where we sat were overjoyed at the windfall which allowed them to go home.

After landing at Naples Airport we had heard that seven planes in the convoy had been shot down and the others had been rerouted towards northern Italy and had landed in Verona. A miracle had occurred for me: aboard one of the planes brought down had been all the Gestapo and military security personnel who were *au courant* with my case, along with all the dossiers concerning me personally. I had left Tunis facing a bleak future in front of a firing squad, but had arrived in Naples whitewashed of all sin and innocent as a newborn babe; the ways of the Lord are mysterious indeed!

However, the German officials decided that, had the prisoners been completely innocent, we would not have been sent to Naples in chains like beaten starving dogs, so we were shipped off to Germany just in case. At the moment no one was worrying; everyone for his own private reasons was enchanted with the trip. I spent hours wallowing in the opulence of the red plush seats in the first-class compartment of this luxury train.

I saw Italy roll by: Rome, Florence, Bologna, Breschia, Bolzano, the names rang like a melody. At each stop ladies from the Red Cross or Fascist Welfare Organisations would hurriedly approach the train and offer hot coffee, chocolate or consommé, along with deliciously garnished sandwiches, meat pies or fruit tarts. The prisoners, drunk with the excitement of being relatively free, blessed the ladies, especially the young pretty ones, with compliments or outlandish cracks, which were more in tune with their youth and boisterousness than with their proper upbringing. When the sweet charitable young things realised that we were chained and under guard they fled screeching, except for a few who stood staring at us in fascination.

Rocked by the swaying and clacking of the wheels, the prisoners dozed throughout the uneventful trip.

Uneventful?

One guard, thrilled at the unexpected opportunity of going home, began to count his money while the other guard, stretching his legs in the corridor, gazed at the landscape. The first one had taken a crumpled roll of bills from his well-stuffed wallet and proceeded to unwrinkle them by rubbing them over his thigh with the palm of his hand and then arranging them in small stacks by denominations on the seat in front of him. I was watching him absentmindedly out of the corner of my eye when something clicked. 'I must try to escape the first chance I have. Then I'll need German money ... need money ... need money!' Suddenly I was all attention. I poked my neighbour in the ribs with my elbow. 'Gerard, listen.'

'What's the matter?'

'I'm going to ask for permission to pee. You ask for permission to open the window. As soon as I stand up and at the exact moment I pass by the Fritz, you open it ... wide and hard. Do you understand?'

'Sure,' said Gerard smiling in complicity, even though he had not understood what it was all about.

The train rolled on. 'If you please,' I said, raising my hand like a schoolboy.

'*Wass?*' Fritz raised his nose from his money.

'*Abort, bitte?*'

'*Ja,*' the Fritz passed me the key to the padlock of my manacles. I opened them and returned the key.

'*Danke schön.*' I figured one could never be too polite to someone whom one was trying to screw, even if he was German. The guard got a big smile and Gerard got the elbow again. I stood up.

'Sir,' asked Gerard with blue-eyed innocence, 'open the window a little, please?'

'*Ja,*' consented the Fritz who was having a good day.

Exactly as I passed by the German, excusing myself, Gerard slammed down the window; a gust of wind accompanied by the clamour of the train swirled through the compartment scattering the carefully laid out stacks of money. Everyone jumped up; I quickly grabbed a fluttering bill as if I were catching a fly and stuffed it inside my shirt. With an innocent smile I stepped out into the corridor leaving total chaos behind me. Gerard apologised profusely to the guard saying he had not meant to bring the window down so hard, and quickly closed it; the rest of the men busied themselves helpfully trying to gather the strewn bills back into their original orderly piles, exactly as I had foreseen.

Safe in the toilet compartment, I rolled the bill into a cylinder, stuffed it into an empty toothpaste tube which I had been carrying like an amulet from prison to prison. One hundred marks! What luck! Then I conscientiously peed and rejoined the group. The Fritz gave me a funny look but, responding with a candid smile, I took my seat. I put my chains back on again and dozed, reassured by the feeling of security which having money gave me.

It had been dark for a long time when the train went over the Brenner Pass. My nose glued to the window, I nostalgically watched the beautiful snow-covered mountains which were silhouetted against the sky. Innsbruck, Munich, Nuremberg, Leipzig; the whole day passed as we bored into Germany with mixed feelings. The day was rainy and cloudy and a strong wind blew into the train; the more chilled and blue I became the more blooming and rosy were the guards.

'*Schön*! Hey, *schön!*' They had discovered that I spoke German and wanted me to share their joy.

'Humph! *Ja. Sehr Schön!*' I responded morosely, telling myself that the one hundred marks were well worth the concession.

At about 4.30 p.m. we realised we were nearing a large city: the houses were closer together, the traffic was heavier; the click of the shunting switches was more frequent. The Fritzes, bursting with happiness, danced in the corridor. 'Berlin! Berlin!' Since there was no reaction from the prisoners, they shouted authoritatively, '*Berlin!*'

Day was over as the train entered the eerily lit station. A small group of men dressed in broad-belted shiny oilskin raincoats and broad-brimmed black felt hats pulled down to their eyebrows waited for us on the platform, hands in pockets.

The guards, after handing over a thick sealed envelope to them with the requisite 'Heil Hitler', waved farewell to their charges and capered off like kids at a school recess.

'Follow me,' ordered a black hat. We were escorted to a minibus, put aboard and seated. Then one of the black hats next to the driver stood up and said, 'Do any of you speak German?'

'He does. He does.' The pointing fingers forced me to my feet.

'Good. Tell your people we are taking you to the military camp at Oranienburg for the time being where you will await further instructions. It'll take about an hour and a half to get there. I've given orders to the driver to take a route that will allow you to admire some of the landmarks of our beautiful capital.'

I was uneasy at having been singled out as translator but I did the job. It was a truly funny situation: a group of ten chained prisoners *en route* to an alarming, unknown destination on a sight-seeing tour of the capital of the hated enemy country, shepherded by henchmen of the secret police. We didn't miss a thing: Unter den Linden lined by huge buildings housing the Ministries and foreign embassies, the Chancellery, the Opera House, the Tiergarten . . . Street lights, dimmed for the black-out, reflected on the wet pavement. Everything exuded power and wealth. Except for the many uniforms, military convoys and sand-bagged monuments, it would have been hard to believe that this teeming heart of Nazi Germany was engaged in a battle to the death against half the world.

The minibus passed through the dark outskirts of the city.

'*Finita la commedia,*' said Gerard quietly.

The drive continued for more than an hour in silence. The bus stopped at a brightly lit checkpoint in the middle of a dark wet forest. We were checked, started up again and reached our destination a few minutes later.

'Gentlemen, we are here. You shall be treated with all courtesy.' The man turned to his aides. 'Unchain them. Good-bye, gentlemen.'

The minibus swallowed the black hats and glossy raincoats. We could see the red brakelights receding into the dark. Like Hansels lost in the forest, our forlorn little group looked around us. We were in a five-star deluxe camp: cute brown wooden houses framed in white and roofed with imitation tiles were aligned along green lanes; light spilled from the windows, which had been hung with frilly gay curtains; everything was orderly, peaceful and spotless.

'If the *Herren Offizieren* would be kind enough to enter.'

I dutifully translated but no one moved.

'He can't be talking to us,' said one of the prisoners.

'He must be kidding,' said another.

The young soldier standing at attention and impeccably uniformed repeated with a patient smile, 'If the *Herren Offizieren* would please step inside.'

I again translated. Dumbfounded, the ex-convicts filed up the three wooden steps flanked by flower pots, stepped into a large room, brightly lit by rustic ceiling lamps with opaline shades and by matching wall sconces. The parquet floor was waxed to a high polish. There was a row of beds decorated with blue- and white-checked eiderdowns and feather pillows along one wall; they really looked like beds for dolls. There was a massive table surrounded by heavy chairs, softened by little pillows, in the centre of the room. All eyes were drawn to the portrait that hung on the end wall: square-cut waxed moustache, lock of hair licked down diagonally across the forehead, inspired eyes, open mouth, flung-up arm, brown-shirted, Sam-Browne-belted, life-sized, awesomely natural. At first the *Herren Offizieren* were taken aback by the presence of Adolf, but we soon learned to ignore him and finally didn't notice him at all.

We had entered into an equivocal world of folly which we

accepted without question, since we were benefiting: in two short days we had been transmuted from gallows meat to *Herren Offizieren* and were now daintily partaking of boiled potatoes, succulent tiny green peas and carrots, man-sized steaks *à la teutonne*, coffee and crusty rolls with 'butter', honey and jam – all we could eat and served by neatly dressed, attentive German orderlies.

'They're giving us the royal treatment,' commented a cheerful character. 'It's really a shame to have to fight with such charming people, don't you agree, Fritz?'

'*Ja, ja,*' answered the radiant orderly.

Nine-thirty; lights out. 'Aren't they going to tuck us in?' asked the comedian.

The same orderly as the night before awakened us at 7.30 a.m. like a well-trained butler. 'The *Herren Offizieren's* breakfast will be served presently.'

The day began well: shower, breakfast, relaxation. A soldier acting as clerk sat down at the table and began the regulatory interrogation to fill out his forms: 'First name? Surname? Rank?' He got his full quota of tall stories but, as neither he nor the prisoners gave a damn, we all enjoyed ourselves.

An hour later, the 'Dog Master' made his appearance; we knew who he was by the armband which stated '*Hundeführer*'. He courteously asked the *Herren Offizieren* if we would care to inspect the kennels; of course, everyone agreed enthusiastically. We found something entirely unexpected: there were hundreds of big splendid dogs, mostly German Shepherds, in an enormous compound of low buildings with dog runs, individual feeding troughs, showers. Nothing was missing, up to and including a dog hospital, a harness room and a tailor shop. There was a huge obedience-training field outside the kennels where we saw ditches filled with water, brick walls, wooden barricades and rolls of barbed wire scattered all over the place. The *Hundeführers* were teaching their pupils to obey hand and eye signals as well as ultrasonic whistles. Jump, roll over, sit, stay, down, heel, attack, play dead – orders whipped out from every direction. The dogs, defying gravity, even scaled trees to retrieve leashes thrown up there by their trainers.

At one end of the field, there was a row of blue-and-white striped uniformed dummies arranged in varying positions. At their masters' signals the dogs attacked, snarling and slavering ferociously.

'Do you notice that they attack selectively, according to the command given; the calves to bring the enemy down, the throat to kill?' asked the guide proudly.

Further up the field there was a group of soldiers dressed in quilted, heavily padded leather and canvas coveralls. They were warding off the attacking beasts, thus teaching them how to parry the blows and get through the guard of the victim. The *Herren Offizieren* turned green around the gills while observing the training.

'Do you have a dog, sergeant?' I asked politely.

'Who, me? Well, I'm in charge here, but I do have my own dog,' answered Herr *Hundeführer*. Just then a soldier brought the pet. He stood half a metre at the chest, weighed at least sixty kilos of sheer muscle, had a mouth lined with shiny white crocodile teeth and a thick black pelt with tawny markings on the chest and belly. He stood poised like a taut bow, awaiting his master's orders. 'Heel,' and the dog flattened himself into the ground next to his master's boots. 'If you only knew how lovable he is,' the *Hundeführer* said, overcome with tenderness.

'The next thing you know, we'll all be in tears,' I thought, vowing to stay as far away from Fido and his brothers as possible.

We sat around talking for the rest of the day.

'Do you see those prisoners?' asked one of the 'Tunisians', this name being applied to us all by the Germans. We were looking at a group of skeletal men wearing the same striped uniform as the dummies at the kennels, who were pushing wheelbarrows around as they worked in the garden a block away. 'Poor things! Do you notice how they're really nothing but skin and bone?'

'And the guards are beating them, to boot! What bastards!'

'They must be hardened criminals.'

'I think they are Russians.'

'Russians? Why Russians specifically?'

Our guesswork was nothing but shots in the dark. Before we could come to any conclusion the skeletons shuffled off.

We let ourselves sink into the luxury surrounding us: supper, sleep, sweet dreams. At about 4.00 a.m. next morning the room lit up and we could see that it had been invaded by a horde of screaming unleashed demons. They knocked the chairs aside and rained blows on the sleeping men with anything handy: whips, stools, brooms, bayonet sheaths.

'Bastards! Rotten garbage! Terrorists! Bandits! Sons of bitches!' The compliments punctuated the blows. 'Get up! Line up outside! Quick! *Schnell! Raus! Los!*'

Recoiling from the blows and trying to pick up my things, I was stupefied to see that these enraged devils were yesterday's guardian angels acting under the orders of the young, well-mannered blond Aryan soldier who had welcomed us so politely at our arrival. I was still trying to comprehend when a masterly kick in the rear catapulted me out of the barracks. I quickly got up, dressed catch as catch can, put on my shoes, and watched as my buddies were ejected from Eden one by one. Everyone was covered in bumps and bruises; some had been kicked out so fast they hadn't been able to grab their things; some were barefooted; everyone was stunned.

While putting on his only shoe, the group comedian could not help stating, 'We should complain to the management and – '

A rifle butt in the back shut him up and sent him flying; he got to his feet, doubled up and moaning softly.

We were beginning to come to and felt indignant and rebellious, but six soldiers, guns at the ready and accompanied by their snarling pets straining at their leashes, quickly formed a rectangle to surround us. We were lined up for roll-call. A non-commissioned officer gave an order and we were marched towards the camp exit.

In silence we marched past the guard post, crossed a road and approached a massive building which was flanked by a wall reaching as far as the eye could see. The alley and wall were brilliantly illuminated by a series of street lights placed twenty metres apart. We came to a halt in front of the façade of a building which resembled a smalltown railway station: a squat central tower adorned by a square clock, two wings with low sloped black slate roofs and a rectangular portal under the central tower which gaped like a black hole into the unknown. All this was surmounted by an inscription in black Gothic letters: *Schutzhäftlager*.

It was exactly 4.20 a.m., 4 April 1943. None of us realised it but a page in the book of our lives had just turned. Still under the shock of our rude awakening, we stood like well-behaved children where we had been placed. After an hour we heard a bell ring . . . once, then twice, on the other side of the wall. The spotlights were turned on. We heard a dull rumbling, like the noise of breakers on the beach. It was all very incomprehensible and mysterious. I felt I was on the edge of a strange world but I was more curious than afraid. The word *Schutzhäftlager* over the portal intrigued me: *Schutz* meant 'protection'; *Häft* meant 'detention'; *Lager* meant 'camp'; but welded together, the unit made no sense. Did they mean they wanted to protect someone by detaining him or to detain him to protect him? I was still trying to figure it out when the meaning was made very clear.

Strange noises, shouts, indistinct rustles . . . the central gate opened wide and an astounding rhythmic sound was heard; it grew as it reverberated and echoed under the arch, hitting us in the face. It was caused by a column of prisoners in wooden clogs clacking in step on the pavement. They were wearing ragged striped uniforms; they were all emaciated sick-looking skeletons; they carried a brick red enamel bowl tied to their belts which thumped against their buttocks in rhythm with their steps. They were flanked by a line of SS soldiers with rifles in their right hands like hunters, accompanied by ferocious dogs drooling with excitement and straining at the leash. The column was girdled by other prisoners wearing the same outfits and armed with bludgeons, whips and cut-off sections of thick electric cable. They hopped around like kangaroos beating their fellow prisoners under the approving and amused eyes of the dog-men.

'The Russians!' murmured Gerard fascinated.

The column advanced in ranks of five and split up to the left and right as it reached the road according to a mysterious order. Ten, twenty, thirty ranks passed slowly by us and still more poured out; it seemed that the human flood would never be stemmed. Several thousand marched by silently, as if drugged, their backs bowed under the blows, more dead than alive.

'These guys must be crazy!' said someone. We had just begun to realise we were descending into the realm of madness.

Time passed at a snail's pace. Finally, we were allowed to

enter the camp around 7.00 a.m. At the top of the iron grille barring the portal there was another inscription, this time in gold Gothic script: *Arbeit Macht Frei*, which means 'Work sets you free'.

I found the words to be slightly reassuring and tried to tell myself that the poor wretches I had just seen were hardened criminals, not military prisoners like myself.

'Halt!' said the SS escort.

11

The Other Side Of The Wall

The 'Tunisians', as we were known, were marched in to the Oranienburg-Sachsenhausen camp, lined up next to the gate, braced to attention, told to maintain the stance and await further orders. We could not believe our eyes. Next to the other side of the portal five bloodied bodies dressed in striped uniforms lay on the ground. Another prisoner knelt with his arms stretched out as if crucified; he looked more dead than the dead beside him; his head was bare and from a string around his neck hung a placard on which were inscribed words which we could not decipher. Suddenly, he fell forward on his face with a moan. An SS soldier appeared from nowhere with devilish speed and began to flail the poor wretch until, with a super-human effort, he got back to his former position. The scene was repeated a few minutes later but this time, luckily for the prisoner, nothing could force him to get up again – he was dead! The SS guards commandeered two passing prisoners and ordered them to lay the body next to the other five.

A while later a strange vehicle appeared. It was a huge platform on wheels drawn by six prisoners who were harnessed to it by wide straps passed around their chests. There were approximately forty corpses stacked like firewood and through the slotted sides we could see naked bodies – here a foot, there a hand, there a horribly contorted face, here a wide eye that seemed to stare at us. I was so shocked I wanted to scream, to run away, to throw up, but could only repeat over and over again softly, 'Oh God! Oh, my God!'

The human carthorses became efficient maintenance men. They took off their harnesses and working in pairs picked up each corpse by the head and arms, swinging it in perfect synchronisation, low, high and up on to the mountain of bodies. Two others had climbed up and methodically placed the newcomers in their proper places. When they were satisfied that all was in order, they slipped into their harnesses and pulled the cart away out of sight behind a building. The spectacle had been so appalling that we were paralysed; anyhow, what could we have done? Still braced to attention with eyes overflowing, each of us tried to erase the terrible vision that lingered in his mind and to comprehend the incomprehensible.

I moved my head slightly to try to see what was around me. I was facing a semicircular yard with a radius of approximately 120 metres, around the perimeter of which brown barracks were situated in concentric semicircles, looking like the spokes of a wheel. I counted the buildings in the first row; there were eighteen in total and under each gable something was written in white Gothic script. I finally managed to understand that each inscription was a fragment of an inspired slogan – '*Es gibt einen Wag zur Freiheit seine Meilensteine heissen Gehorsam, Fleiss, Ehrlichkeit, Ordnung, Sauberkeit, Neuchternheit, Wahrhäftigkeit, Opfersinn, und Liebe zum Vaterland,*' which translated meant: 'There is one way to freedom: the stepping stones are Obedience, Diligence, Honesty, Orderliness, Cleanliness, Sobriety, Straight-forwardness, Self-sacrifice, and Love of the Fatherland.'

'Maybe we have landed in a Boy Scout camp,' I joked, trying to lift my own spirits.

Ever since we had entered the camp our nostrils had been assaulted by a sweetish stench which seemed to arise from the big smoking chimneys we could see looming to the left behind the barracks.

'Those must be the kitchens. They seem to be cooking steaks for dinner, but they sure stink, don't they?' said one of the Tunisians. We were all too innocent to know yet what was really broiling there.

It was all so strange. Everyone in the camp, except for the SS, moved from one place to another always on the double. Maybe they needed the exercise to keep fit or maybe all those guys were crazy. One jogger crossing the yard towards us stopped, stepped into the guard post and came out a minute later with a paper on a clipboard and faced us who had been observing him indifferently.

'Are you the Tunisians?'

'Yes,' we nodded cautiously.

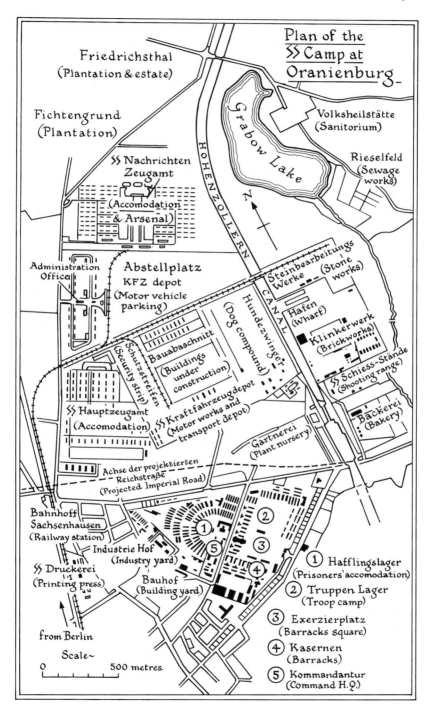

Plan of the
SS Camp at
Oranienburg

Friedrichsthal
(Plantation & estate)

Fichtengrund
(Plantation)

Grabow Lake

Volksheilstätte
(Sanitorium)

Rieselfeld
(Sewage
works)

SS Nachrichten
Zeugamt

(Accomodation
& Arsenal)

HOHENZOLLERN

N

Administration
Office

Abstellplatz
KFZ depot
(Motor vehicle
parking)

Steinbearbeitungs
Werke (Stone
works)

CANAL

Hafen
(Wharf)

Klinkerwerk
(Brickworks)

Bauabaschnitt
(Buildings
under
construction)

Hundezwinger
(Dog compound)

Schutzstreifen
(Security strip)

Schiess-Stände
(Shooting range)

SS Hauptzeugamt
(Accomodation)

Kraftfahrzeugdepot
(Motor works and
transport depot)

Bäckerei
(Bakery)

Gärtnerei
(Plant nursery)

Achse der projektierten
Reichstraße
(Projected Imperial Road)

Bahnhoff
Sachsenhausen
(Railway station)

Industrie Hof
(Industry yard)

SS Druckerei
(Printing press)

Bauhof
(Building yard)

from Berlin

Scale~

0   500 metres

① Hafflingslager
(Prisoners' accomodation)

② Truppen Lager
(Troop camp)

③ Exerzierplatz
(Barracks square)

④ Kasernen
(Barracks)

⑤ Kommandantur
(Command H.Q.)

'OK, let's go to the Schreibstube, that's the Secretariat, then to the shower and then to the Quartermaster.' The man was clean, his striped outfit was clean and his hair unclipped; he looked like a big wheel from the camp. 'On the double!'

'Here we go. These guys must be completely crazy,' I thought. Nevertheless, I was glad to be able to limber up and move away.

On the way we encountered a large column of ragged prisoners, in ranks of five, carrying sacks on their backs marching to the rhythm of a German marching song while being profusely beaten by other prisoners only slightly less shabby and emaciated than they. 'Hali-halo. Hali-halo,' chanted the poor wretches pitifully as the blows descended on them.

Some very important looking prisoners, the working staff of the Secretariat, sat at desks lined up on both sides of a big fluorescent-lit room. Neat stacks of dossiers and printed forms lay on the desktops. 'Last name, first name, middle name, date of birth, profession . . .' Once more the unending refrain. After this little ceremony I was handed a slip of paper with a number on it – F–63205.

The bureaucrat explained, 'That's your identification number: 'F' means you are French. You will wear a red triangle indicating you are a political inmate, which will set you apart from those wearing green ones, who are criminals; the pink are homosexuals, the blue are the stateless, the purple the conscientious objectors, the black the gypsies and those wearing the yellow Star of David are Jews, of course. Understand?'

'Humph.'

'It really doesn't matter. You'll find out about the system by yourself. Hand over your watch, money, papers, all your personal things. Come on!'

I obliged and watched all my belongings disappear into a brown paper bag along with a detailed list. However, I managed to hang on to the toothpaste tube containing my 100-Mark fortune. Glancing at this surreptitiously I saw that the brand was 'Vademecum' and smiled to myself at how apt the name was. The tube had become a small symbol of hope for the future.

We were stripped of all clothing and watched while our

pants, shirts, underwear, socks and shoes were meticulously inventoried, packed into sacks, labelled and taken away to an unknown destination. We were put outside stark naked and startled.

'Brrr! It sure is cold!' grumbled Gerard, clutching his penis as if afraid it would drop off.

Skipping and jumping awkwardly over the broken ground, we were herded to the sanitation block for delousing. Once inside we felt like chickens on a conveyor belt when they are beheaded, plucked, disembowelled and packed. First phase, haircut . . . billiard-ball style. Second phase, shave . . . armpits, pubis, eyebrows, legs. Third phase, disinfection . . . we squatted in a tub of turgid brown liquid and our heads were dunked by a hefty bare-chested fellow for ten seconds; we came up sputtering and coughing out the foul creosote. Fourth phase, showers . . . ice cold, boiling hot, ice cold. 'You'd think these bastards had never heard of ordinary warm water,' complained one of the chickens. Fifth phase, treatment by a specialist who held a 'flit gun' and squirted us generously around the anus and surrounding area; it itched, it stung, it burned!

Under a rain of blows from a new escort and his two helpers, we entered the Quartermaster's quarters. The room was lined with shelves stuffed with old rags. The counters were formed by lines of tables behind which stood clerks. As the line of naked, dripping prisoners filed by, the clerks would run a knowing eye over us and fling a piece of clothing at us. I collected a shirt, a pair of long underpants, a striped jacket, pants and round cap, two puzzling pieces of cloth which I later learned were called 'Russian socks' and a pair of brown canvas clogs with 'Made in Holland' stamped on their wooden soles. At the end of the line we were treated to a shove in the shoulder blades and a kick at the base of the spine which catapulted us outside into a mud puddle which seemed to have been expressly created for that purpose. We scrambled to our feet and did our best to get dressed which wasn't easy as the stinking itching rags woven from wood shavings were either too small, too big, too long or too short. We tried on and traded as best we could but even so some ended up the proud possessors of two left or two right clogs. When the process was finished we looked at each other. One of us burst into wild laughter: he guffawed; he hiccuped;

he cried; he tried to explain but was unable to speak; he pointed his finger at us and gasped for air. At first we felt mocked but we soon became infected with the hysteria: the tears ran down our cheeks; we shook from the spasms; we hit our thighs; we sobbed.

A man dressed in a striped uniform accompanied by two others shouted 'Silence! You're not here to have a good time. One more laugh and you get your heads bashed in! Get moving to the quarantine block where you will be kept for fifteen days until you get your final work assignment. Understand?' Except for me no one had understood but it didn't make much difference. 'On the double!'

Hobbling and limping in our ill-fitting clogs we crossed several alleys and came to a stop at a barrack surrounded by a wire fence. A reception committee was waiting for us as we lined up at attention in front of a wooden box. A fat, greasy-faced individual dressed in impeccably starched striped pyjamas came out of the block and climbed on the box. He had the symbol of his authority hanging from a leather strap around his wrist – a cudgel; he had a band on his left arm with the German inscription *Blockälteste*, which meant Block Boss. His mean closely set prying eyes made him look like a killer boar and when he grinned evilly he revealed a set of rotten pointed teeth. His appearance as well as that of his two aides, who were just a little less attractive than him, set the tone of what we could expect from the rest of the camp hierarchy.

The hog addressed us in German: 'My name is Kurt. I'm the boss of the quarantine block. These are my aides. So you're the famous Tunisians – you sons of mongrel Arab bitches – you vermin who just crawled out of a whore's belly. I advise you to watch your step. If you don't . . .' and he pointed his cudgel toward the smoking chimneys which could be seen over the roofs, 'if you don't, you go straight to heaven in a pretty cloud of smoke.'

We had listened carefully but most hadn't managed to understand a thing. Kurt switched to very basic German. 'Can't anyone in this shitty lot speak God's language?'

'He can. He can!' and I was pushed to the front.

'You speak German? Then tell them what I just said.'

I turned, faced my companions and tried to summarise the

edifying speech of the big boss: 'His name is Kurt. He's the king. We're nothing but shit. If we put our foot in it we'll go up the chimneys somehow or other.' A long silence followed. 'Is that all you want me to say?'

'*Nein*. Tell them that you'll be here more or less fifteen days. It depends on the death rate and how badly workers are needed. Clear? Translate.' It was very clear so I translated.

The hog continued with his welcoming speech. 'Here you'll be taught discipline. You'll be practising sports a lot to keep in condition. We'll also teach you how to march, how to keep clean, how to answer when a superior calls your number and how to introduce yourselves properly. You'll get used to the daily routine, to the roll-calls and to the work. You'll learn to do your duties.'

'What about our rights?' I questioned and managed to block the blow from the cudgel just in time.

'Your rights, you dirty bastard, are to obey, to shut your dirty traps, to submit and to work! work! work! The shirkers will float up via the crematory chimneys. Clear?' The Tunisians were sullenly silent. 'Clear?' insisted the hog.

'Only too clear.'

'Then get into the block. Do as you're told. If not . . .'

'I know . . . up the chimney,' I finished in a low voice.

It was the standard camp barrack: a tar-paper roofed wooden structure painted brown set on a cement slab, with white-framed windows in the back and front and a central entrance door at the sides of which were two signs reading '*Flügel A*' and '*Flügel B*', identifying the two wings. Immediately in front of the entrance door on the narrow corridor were the lavatories; these were equipped with two circular fountains and narrow sunken tiled troughs along a wall. The toilets were eight brick-red ceramic bowls without seats. After passing through the corridor one entered the dining-room, a large room furnished with long tables and benches set parallel to each other; there was a serving board near the entrance and a long tubular cast-iron stove on the back wall. The side walls were lined with iron lockers, like those found in a sports stadium dressing-room. The dining-room opened into a vast dormitory where rows of three-storey bunks ascended almost to the roof beams; the bunks were made up hospital style and covered with blue-

and white-checked spreads, imitating the eiderdowns in the SS
Palace across the street. Everything was spick and span and
smelt sweetly of disinfectant. Each block had originally been
planned for one hundred and fifty inmates but now had four
hundred packed in like sardines.

I was pressed into service as the distinguished bilingual
secretary to fill out my friends' dossiers in multicoloured
quadruplicate. A mixed batch of fifty-odd prisoners, young, old,
were sitting at the other tables around the room occupied in
essential tasks: picking at small lengths of electric wiring to
recuperate copper, sorting out bolts and nuts, cutting up
newspaper into squares in browbeaten silence. We were briefly
interrupted in these activities at midday for rutabaga soup with
a slice of bread on the side.

The time had come for us to attend our gym class. 'Fall in –
on the double. Run in Indian file, lie down. Stand up. Down.
Up. Down. Up . . .' We ran, ran and ran . . . ran out of breath,
our hearts throbbing, our throats choking, gasping, panting,
stumbling. 'At ease.' The ease consisted of squatting with the
arms raised for excruciatingly long periods. 'Run. Hop. Leap
frog. Do push-ups.' We did this over and over again, all the time
being kicked and beaten with sticks, cudgels and rubber hoses.
The gym class was directed by a prisoner comfortably lounging
in a garden chair while he carried the rhythm with a gurgling
police whistle.

After two hours of exercise those few still able to stand were
on the verge of collapse, while the others who had already
succumbed were submitted to various ingenious punishments
for having sabotaged the exercise. The gym class had been
intertwined with highly educational courses: we were taught
the intricacies and subtleties of the German army drill as well
as the etiquette of addressing any authority, especially an SS
man. We were to bare our heads at the command of 'Mützen
ab'; the arm was required to fly up and whip the ridiculous
striped caps off with a military snap and beat them smartly
against the right thigh, as if beating the dust out of our pants.
These lessons in correct concentration camp manners were
considered as important as lessons in deportment at a girls'
finishing school.

*   *   *

The order rang out, 'Fall in in ranks of five.' After standing in reverent silence for a long time we saw a man approach, dressed in the greenish SS uniform. A halo of impressive authority glowed around him. This was the God of the Quarantine Service called Helmuth, but known to the inmates as 'Asshole'. Although the odour of pigpens still clung to him he was now a corporal in the SS, which augmented the dignity of being the block's supreme boss. His beardless dullwitted face had earned him the nickname. He was tubby, had a closely sheared head, wore his forage cap at an angle over his right eye, and had ears which branched out like cabbage leaves. In addition, he had a drooping mouth, bulging eyes and a pug nose. In a word, the perfect example of flaming German youth. His fame as a killer had preceded him; he was credited with hundreds of victims who had been beaten to death, hung, shot or strangled; it was said that if he took a dislike to someone, he took exquisite pleasure in strangling the poor devil with his own hands. A strange relationship like two hands washing each other had formed a perfect linkage between Kurt and Helmuth; they were partners in numerous crimes, sadistic practices, prosperous business diddling, besides Kurt's skill at producing young, defenceless virgin boys for the demi-god.

The prisoners were carefully counted. The roll-call bell rang and blocks of prisoners in ranks of five simultaneously began to march. The ranks advanced rhythmically, their clogs clacking, in a swelling tide toward the assembly square, where we took our assigned positions. Again we were counted and recounted by the block *Älteste*, who wrote down the numbers on a ledger covered with plexiglass to protect it from the rain. Then a crushing silence as we stood in the glare of the spotlights placed around the square, which shielded us from the encompassing darkness. Asshole appeared from nowhere, again counted us and, finally satisfied, signed the form. Only then was a new spotlight over the central tower turned on, lighting up a martial figure advancing through the central alley. Stuffed into an SS uniform, booted, hatted with a much too small flat-top cap centred on his fat head, SS Sturmbannführer Kaindl, the Camp Commander, appeared carrying a little switch pressed under his elbow. Head held high and looking neither to right nor left, he marched rigidly along the human walls formed by the tens of thousands of his slaves, over whom he held the divine power of life or death.

'*Still gestanden. Mützen ab.*' Simultaneously 40,000 prisoners came to attention and whipped off their hats to honour the Golden Calf. The Sturmbannführer received individual reckoning from each SS responsible for his block; again it was checked by an underling, who kept account on a framed blackboard and, after verifying it, proclaimed the liberating word, '*Stimmut*' which meant 'It tallies.' *lte missa est*. At this magic phrase the Sturmbannführer disappeared like a setting sun, and the prisoners were finally allowed to put their hats back on, break ranks and return to their blocks.

As the square emptied, I saw bodies lying on the ground. I sidled up to another prisoner whose number indicated he was an old hand, who explained, 'Everyone who has died or become too weak during the day must be carried to roll-call to be counted, just like the living. In the old days they were held upright by their companions during roll-call. This, however, made the rows look disorderly and the count deficient, so now they are left lined up neatly on the ground next to their block companions. Anyone who cannot summon the strength necessary to stand up is quickly finished off and left with the rest of the dead. The tally of each block must check out – so many living, so many dead. That's what happens.' He pointed at the corpses lying around. A vehicle came to pick up the bodies.

Avid for information, I said, 'This roll-call lasted forever, at least an hour and a half.'

'That's nothing. First of all, the evening checks last longer than those in the morning because then the SS is eager to get everyone off to work, but I've seen checks that last for five, ten and even twenty hours. I remember once when a guy went crazy and hid out in a corner of one of the barrack's attics. That time we stood for twenty hours in the middle of a snowstorm with the temperature at minus twenty-five degrees Centigrade. When they finally found him there were at least five hundred dead from the cold and God knows how many sick who never recovered. As for the fool responsible for this mess, he was hung on the spot.'

I remained pensive. A straightforward control procedure had been turned into a grandiose Wagnerian opera by the camp authorities. Like an alien viewing from the moon, I could visualise that small square populated by thousands of subhuman slaves in a pool of light, participating in the preposterous ritual of a system whose only purpose was to torment and destroy them.

Later, after I had become familiar with the camp I came to the conclusion that there were two purposes served by the concentration camps: first, permanently to eliminate all those opposed to Germany and the Nazi regime; second, to exploit to the fullest the unlimited, gratuitous, sometimes highly specialised labour source which contributed to the war effort, as well as to the pockets of its devoted servants. Therefore, it was imperative for the camp administration never to lose sight of the economical scale of priorities: the dead do not work and the living are expensive to maintain before they die. It was necessary to strike the happy medium where those scheduled to be eliminated should produce a maximum before perishing, in order to make the books balance and maximise the bottom line. Once the prisoners were squeezed to the break-even point, they had to be quickly eliminated so as not to produce a loss.

Then came the classic mathematical problem posed to generations of schoolboys: how long does it take for a bathtub to drain while the tap is turned on? In order to be economically sound, the mortality rate should not exceed the flow of new arrivals. When that happened, entire Polish, Ukrainian or other villages were deported *in toto* for no justifiable reason by the victorious German armies. Bewildered men, women and children found themselves in Ravensbrück, Oranienburg, Auschwitz, Dachau and similar camps, not knowing they were paying for an occasional blunder made by a camp manager. Luckily for those incompetents, their little error of judgement did not have far reaching consequences for them, as the available supply of slave labour was practically boundless. If the reverse situation presented itself the solution was even simpler: just send the surplus workers to their maker via the belching chimneys, always keeping in mind that the weak, sick and unskilled be vapourised first. It was all a question of addition, subtraction and commonsense.

The twice daily roll-calls were really the ledger that served to obtain an inventory of labour supply and provide statistics for short term planning. Thanks to these statistics the camp managers could reach their goal of optimum profits – *Ad majorem Nazi gloriam*, of course.

When we went back to our blocks seats were assigned to us and locker space was given to those still fortunate enough to have something to store. We had to stencil our numbers on strips of tape and sew them on the left front of our jackets and over the pocket of our pants. We were fed the ever present rutabaga soup and sawdust bread with a spot of margarine. Dinner was gulped down in a trance-like state of tiredness. The night wash-up was brief after the morning's thorough ablutions.

Lights out was sounded. Just as I was climbing into the second bunk, which I shared, by chance, with another Tunisian, I was hailed by a voice out of the dark.

'Alec? Where are you?'

'Here, next to the first corner window.'

'Wait for me a minute.' It was a French voice. Curious but wary, I waited. Like a Chinese lantern figure, a silhouette appeared against the window. 'Is your name Alec? Have you just arrived from Tunis?'

'That's right.'

'My name is Paul Mueller. I'm the Private Secretary to the Chief of the camp's Medical Service. That's how I got to see the list of the newly arrived prisoners from Tunis. I saw your name and came looking for you.'

'Oh?' I was polite but noncommittal and on guard more than ever. 'You chose the wrong time. In this black-out you can't even see your hands in front of your face.'

'I know, but I wanted to talk to you. I'm from Luxembourg but all my family is from Metz in Lorraine, so I feel more French than anything else. I try to help the French guys whenever I can.'

My eyes were getting accustomed to the darkness and I peered more closely at the stranger, whose face I could now make out dimly by the light shed through the window. He was of average stature – about five foot ten – and was wearing a fashionable navy blue blazer over his neatly pressed striped pyjamas. Paul continued the conversation by talking about the camp and the quarantine in a voice which had the typical slow

cadence heard in the north-east of France. His way of expressing himself was imaginative and amusing and he often burst out
laughing at his own jokes. I let him talk.

'What about Tunis? How're things going there for us? You
must know, since you were there only a few days ago.'

'Well, you know how it is. If you are locked up in a military
prison, it's kind of hard to get news about what is happening in
a war. How about you? How are things here?'

'You must think I'm an idiot!' Paul's voice had got hard, but I
didn't care. 'All right. I get it. You don't trust me, but you
should. Look, do you know Luxembourg?'

'I've been through it but you are the first person from there
I've ever met.'

'Look, Alec, it's useless to continue in the dark like this. Let's
meet each other and talk again in the daylight. I just want to tell
you that I am where I am because I fought against the Germans
when they occupied my country. They just took us over like a
territory that belonged by right to the German Reich. I can't help
it if everyone now thinks of us as Germans; it's just one more
reason for me to hate them, and I'm not about to take lessons in
patriotism from you or anyone else. Do you understand?'

'Yes,' I conceded, pleased by the spontaneous outburst. 'Well,
here's how it was in Tunis. The Germans and their little Italian
friends were taking the beating of their lives. The Allies had
been on the outskirts of Tunis for four days. We could hear the
noise of battle from down-town when we left. Rommel's men
have been resisting like lions, but they know it's all over. The
Eighth Army has already taken more than a hundred thousand
of them prisoners.'

'Thanks for trusting me. I've got to get back to my place. It's
unhealthy to get caught walking around this place after lights-
out. Can you tell me how I can help you?'

'Thanks a lot, but I don't think there's anything you can do. It
was nice of you to offer.'

'Wouldn't you like a little bread?' asked Paul, reaching into
his jacket.

'No, thanks. There must be a lot of guys who need it more
than I.'

Paul was incredulous. 'No bread? Really?'

'No, thanks.'

'All right. I'll be seeing you then. Oh, by the way, it says in your dossier – of course I've seen it – that you are a medical student and speak German. Maybe I'll be able to get you a good work assignment. Good night. Keep your courage up.' A firm handshake sealed the conversation. I climbed into my half of the bunk and sank into sleep, too tired to worry about anything at this point.

Feeling as if I had slept for centuries, I was brought back to the hard present by light glaring in my eyes and the guards shouting barbarously, 'Bastards! Scum! Filthy rotten sons-of-whores!'

'We've heard that before,' I thought resignedly, but I listened carefully to the rantings just in case.

'To the washroom. Get ready for foot inspection.' I couldn't believe my ears so I waited a few minutes for further orders, but I had heard right. I transmitted the message to my companions in a shout and, seeing that the way was clear of Kurt and his henchmen for a moment, jumped down from my bunk and made a dash for the lavatory. I was among the first to get in so, just to make sure, I quickly washed all over and sprinted out just as the mob began to enter. It was a gross scene: two hundred sleep-stupid, panicky men trying to push through one door, urged on at the same time by the blows of the henchmen descending on their backs. Once inside they found it impossible to move, since they were packed in so tight. Those who had got to the fountains had to climb on top to avoid being trampled and were dragged down by others desperately trying to wash themselves; everyone was screaming in frustration.

I saw Kurt near the door, doubled up in laughter at the practical joke he had pulled on his charges; when he saw me he bellowed, 'What are you doing here? Didn't you understand my orders?'

'Yes, sir. I've already washed and as I wasn't sure exactly what you wanted, I washed from head to toe.'

'From head to toe?' Kurt's eyes bulged. He was ready to strike me when he saw that I was completely wet. 'My God, it's true! How did you manage to do it?'

I disarmed him by giving him a look of complete stupidity. '*Comme ci . . . comme ça.*'

Kurt thought this to be hilariously funny and exploded into

laughter again. I had been expecting a good smack, but found myself being patted so hard on the back that my shoulder blade almost got dislocated.

'*Gut! Gut!* Stand over there and wait a while. *Comme ci . . . comme ça?* Humph!' Kurt was really impressed.

Then the mockery started. The prisoners who had managed to wash their feet had to pass through the dining area to have their feet judged by Kurt's court. Unfortunately, by the time they arrived, their feet had been thoroughly dirtied again by the mud and creosote plastered on the dining area floor, earning them a blow and a sneer from the inspection committee, which sent them back for another wash. The dance went on for a good hour and was kept at the correct tempo by the blows and hysteria which possessed them all. From my little corner behind Kurt I watched quietly; as I had made myself small I was forgotten and had no trouble. Everyone finally returned to his bunk and silence ruled where bedlam had reigned. Before I fell asleep I mentally reviewed the outlandish events of the day; it had ended as it had begun, with a blare.

At 4.00 a.m. bells sounded. 'Everyone up!'

Dazed and worn out from lack of sleep, I got myself out of bed. We had been told to make our beds properly. I had noticed that the beds had been made up in a particular fashion, but had no idea of the work involved. First, the beds must be absolutely square, a process which I had already practised in the French Army, but this was square in the Prussian manner. My block-mates and I not only had no inkling of how to begin but were not especially gifted in chessboard art. We tried to employ a *trompe-l'oeil* technique but were stopped in the act. One of Kurt's aides ripped the sheet off the bunk. Finally, through trial and error, we achieved the correct individual centering, but this was not good enough! A co-ordinated, homogenous effect was desired. All the little checks of all the bed covers of all the bunk levels in the dormitory had to be aligned: on the vertical, on the horizontal and on the diagonal. The prisoners, having finally realised what their tormentors wanted and urged on by blows, finally finished the job. The pristine dormitory was then abandoned for the day.

We were treated to another wash and a breakfast of dish-water coffee and stale bread. It was dark, rainy and glacially cold outside. The north wind which blew in off the Baltic Sea froze our bones to the marrow and caused the huge pines on the other side of the wall to sway. A nostalgic image of Tunis flashed briefly through my mind but I quickly snapped to, conscious of the presence of constant danger. This time roll-call took only an hour and once the assembly was dismissed the prisoners were regrouped in work gangs. My mates in quarantine had been assigned to mysterious chores: 'Rollwagen, Schuläunfer, KWA, etc.'.

I struck it lucky. A new contingent of French prisoners had just arrived and I was appointed to the high position of Bilingual Secretary for the day. As a day-old hand I observed the newcomers, who were even more stunned than I had been, having been shipped under abominable conditions for many days and nights, where a lot had died along the way. While the newcomers were taking their gym lesson I was left to my paperwork in the almost empty block. There were a couple of guys too sick to attend the gym class doing manual work at the tables, the Stubendienst (Kurt and company) and a young twelve- to thirteen-year-old Ukrainian boy named Cyril.

One of Kurt's aides had taken a liking to me. 'Be careful of that one. Avoid him like the plague. He's the Chief's lap dog,' he warned me.

'What do you mean, lap dog?'

'Just what I said. There's a block of about three hundred children under fourteen in the camp and there's a guy who has set himself up as a pimp. If there's one whose skin is sufficiently soft and he shows a leaning toward pederasty, this guy trains him for a brilliant career in buggery. He fattens him up and then looks for a place for him with one of the camp's bigwigs. For the boys it means a full belly and that's very important; believe me, there's a big market for them. Cyril is one of them.'

'What's so special about Cyril?' I asked. Then I took a second look at him. He was a charming creature: crewcut blond hair gave him an equivocal air; he had a cream and peaches complexion, limpid eyes, gleaming teeth and tantalising dimples; his build was slender and swanlike; his gestures were grace itself. 'Yes, he is lovely,' I conceded with a grimace, 'but why tell me all this?'

'I'm just trying to warn you. This kid is rotten to the core. He is a sneak and a stoolpigeon. Don't be fooled by his angelic looks. He'd sell his own parents to consolidate his position. He's a sadistic devil. When he can't find a real reason to squeal on someone he invents one, just to be on the safe side. A week ago he told Kurt that one of the guys had patted him on the rear – as if anyone in here still had any such ideas! The guy is still alive, but he'd be a lot better off dead. So, when the little angel passes by you make like you are looking out the window and don't go near Kurt's room at night when they are at it. You're dead if anyone sees you and informs.'

'Why do you say that Cyril has to consolidate his position? Why should he feel insecure?'

'Well, you see, any day nature will take her course and his voice will break, hair will grow on his legs and a shadow will be cast over his mouth. Overnight the delicious little angel will be transformed into a sordid, nasty pansy. So he has reason to be worried.'

I had been shocked and outraged at the way we had been treated by the camp supervisors, who, after all, were prisoners like ourselves. It took me some time to figure out that the camp was ruled by a double hierarchy. At the very top, in charge of management and security, were the SS, fanatical, often inept, sometimes illiterate rank and file soldiers who, out of lazyness or affinity had delegated their authority to hard-core criminals. These were 'the Greens', the ones who really ran the huge Oranienburg-Sachsenhausen Camp, who acted as police and stoolpigeons and who doled out punishment, giving free rein to their sadistic natures. They were so possessed by their roles that they became more royalist than kings, more vile than their masters. The camp bosses basked in the bootlicking and terror they inspired and enjoyed special privileges which allowed them to indulge in their secret vices and machinations. Living in a perfect symbiosis, the SS henchmen and their parasites thrived.

That same afternoon I had occasion to be enlightened on the mundane aspects of high society in the camp. Kurt had invited a group of friends over and around 3.30 p.m. the camp's high dignitaries began to arrive – a few block bosses, the Quartermaster, some secretaries, even the hangman ambled in. All wore green triangles marking them as common criminals. They exuded well-being, had not had their heads shaved and wore

clean uniforms adorned by a white armband on the left sleeve
denoting their function. Cyril was the hostess and received them
at the door. Kurt's room, like all the other block *Ältestes'*, was
situated at one corner of the dining area. It was strange to see
this oasis of privacy and cosiness in the midst of a world of
hunger, misery and death.

It was small, but was well lit and ventilated by an outside
window hung with frilly blue- and white-checked curtains. He
had decorated it in the manner favoured by smalltime German
civil servants. The bed, set in a corner of the room, was covered
by a potbellied dark red eiderdown draped by a Spanish shawl
on which folkloric dolls sat in state. A train-compartment-style
lamp rested upon an imitation lace doily. His treasures were
displayed on a shelf above the bed – a ball of hollow glass
which, when shaken, caused the snow to swirl around St Peter's
in Rome, a large rock, a green porcelain statuette of a rearing
horse and the carved out base of a World War I mortar shell
which held a bunch of wilted dusty flowers. The worktable
placed under the window held some neatly stacked forms, the
roll-call ledger, some crayons and a glass jar full of trinkets. A
low stool with its feet sawn off held an electric hot plate, where
the water for tea was already boiling. A small electric heater
with a fan was placed in one corner. A pedestal table swagged
with a tasselled runner held the place of honour in the centre of
the room and a cloth-shaded lamp hung over it.

While Cyril fluttered around and served little cakes, tea and
Russian 'Majorca' cigarettes the guests made themselves comfortable. The noise of chatting, throaty laughter and slaps on
thighs escaped through the door but every once in a while the
conversation became serious and voices were lowered to a
confidential murmur. The gentlemen were trafficking, tricking
and thieving, conniving with the SS to form lucrative joint
enterprises, all at the prisoners' expense. The opulence of the tea
party sickened me, who could see images of the starving,
croaking wretches who were spitting out their lungs and
voiding their guts, rotten with TB and dysentery, who were
nevertheless doing their utmost every day to ward off death.

At day's end my companions returned, soaked to the bone
and downtrodden. In broken sentences they tried to describe
what their day had been like – some had tested shoes, some had

pulled a road roller, others had loaded and unloaded bricks, iron bars and excrement. They had been tried to the limit of their endurance; they had been morally subjugated; they had been tamed.

I joined the lot next morning as a shoe tester. At least I had some idea of what awaited me from my Tunisian friends who had done this work the day before, but the more they tried to explain the crazier it sounded to me. In a dimly lit barrack someone flung a pair of boots, an olive-green military raincoat and a bag filled with twenty kilos of sand at me. I tried to put on the boots but not only did they not fit but they were also of different sizes. I was tempted to complain but was stopped by a companion who told me to be thankful they were not both for the same foot, which was what happened to some of the others the day before.

At exactly 6.00 a.m. we began our quality control testing for the benefit of the German Army. The test track was laid out around the assembly square and consisted of adjoining sections of different kinds of road materials – tarmac, packed earth, concrete, cobblestones, sand, cinders, soft earth, gravel and even a huge puddle, to make things more authentic. The track was 700 metres long and had to be circled sixty times in ten hours, with an hour's break for lunch. I calculated that this would amount to a rate of 4.2 kilometres per hour. In spite of unmatched boots I thought I should be up to it.

The *Schuhlauefer Kommando* was really an offshoot of the *Straf Kompanie Klinker*, the disciplinary company of the camp. Here the petty thieves, the queue-jumpers, the fight-pickers, the sassy and the Jews, simply because they were Jews, were disciplined. They had to load bricks into barges at a nearby canal. At least a dozen died daily from brutality, sickness or over-exertion. By comparison, shoe testing was a cushy job. Just the same, shoe testers also died from wear and tear, more slowly perhaps but they died just the same. Since the shoe testing was important, quarantine prisoners were pressed into service to fill the gaps when the mortality rate in the Kommando was too high.

On the first round, I found I still had a lot to learn. I had never been taught to goosestep, which we were required to do when passing in front of the guard post at the central gate. I got a heavy blow on the head for my negligent manners before I even had time to duck. The column boss stepped out and shouted, '*Zwei, drei, vier*'.

'Shit,' complained my Tunisian friend. 'Now we've got to sing.' The whole column began to sing the song that was loathed by all those subject to the German occupation, the song that made the window shutters close when the conquerors marched singing down the street: 'Hali, halo . . . halo. Hali, halo . . . halo.' During the course of the day we had to learn, or at least pretend to learn, a whole repertoire of German songs – marching songs, war songs, folk songs, seafaring sentimental songs. What a spectacle: staggering skeletons singing joyous ballads and martial airs.

'On the double! Pick up your feet. March. Walk. Run.' Through the water, over the stones, into the mud . . . serious research into the lasting qualities of boots and laces but less and less to my liking; I was sweating under the raincoat, my feet were aching and the straps of the heavy bag cut into my shoulders.

It had been raining since early morning and a nasty cold wind had been blowing steadily. At 10.00 a.m. we were given a snack to be consumed while walking; at noon we feasted on cabbage and potato soup, vaguely spiced with caraway seeds, which we swallowed skins and all.

'On the double. March. *Zwei, drei, vier*.' Simple things became very complicated. It was strictly *verboten* to step out of rank, so we had to urinate while moving, being very careful not to wet ourselves or the guy in front.

Each time we passed in front of the infirmary the column boss took a token out of a small sack hung round his neck by a string and dropped it into the slot of a letter box. One . . . two . . . three. When the count reached sixty this ordeal would be over; in the meantime it was march, march, march. Fortunately we were allowed to talk. I chatted with my Tunisian buddy. We talked about the warm sun, the fine sand on Hammamet beach, the lovely suntanned girls, food, Chez Max's shaded terrace facing the avenue; we talked about everything except the war. But even the sunny evocations did not ease the monotony and strain. We were greatly relieved when token number sixty was finally dropped through the slot.

The results of the day's testing had to be carefully recorded:

number of boots, weight carried, wearer's weight, number of kilometres covered, exact time period, weather conditions, everything but the captain's age had to be reported.

When I got back to my block it looked like Home Sweet Home, Kurt looked like a fat mama and my hard clogs felt like soft slippers. In spite of my exhaustion I was pleased with myself because I felt I had come through with flying colours.

Paul came over immediately after the roll-call. I had forgotten all about him and was pleased to see him again. I found that the impression I had formed of him in the dark was correct. Dressed with refined elegance, his hands moving nervously to accompany the words he spoke, he stood out from the rest. Because of his self-assured bearing, unshorn chestnut hair and healthy colouring he looked like a free man. His chiselled features, aquiline nose, piercing blue eyes and bushy eyebrows gave him a resolute look marred only by his flaccid chin. When still, his thin-lipped mouth tended to droop but when he smiled his face was transformed. Only one side of his mouth smiled and his eyes glistened with malice, which gave him a Mephistophelian air, which he apparently cultivated. I could sense an ironic amusement behind all his comments and read him as being highly intelligent, charming, generous, sensitive and direct, but at the same time calculating, wavering and an innate gambler who would risk anything for a laugh. Paul asked, tongue in cheek, 'Did you have a good day?'

'Wonderful! These guys really are crazy, aren't they?'

'Just what did you do?'

'I was a *Schuläufer*, to be exact, a boot specialist.'

'How did it go?'

'Slightly humid, thank you.'

'Have you seen your other buddies?'

'What other buddies?'

'A second group from Tunisia arrived this morning.'

'Really? Where are they?'

'Here in quarantine but probably in the other wing.'

I was so excited that I cut the conversation short to go and see, but I was more and more convinced that we would become friends.

The new batch of Tunisians was there: old Beranger, de Buffon, big-hearted Bernard Méry, Noguerol. When the first

flush of reunion was over they told me about their odyssey: after
the RAF attack on their Mediterranean flight they had landed in
Verona. From there they had travelled north by train, had been
treated to the Berlin-by-Night tour but had been deprived of the
Herren Offizieren treatment; instead they had been entitled to a
three-day all-expenses-paid stay at the Alexanderplatz, the five-
star central prison in Berlin.

Next day I became a horse – a hearse horse – during the
morning and a carthorse during the afternoon. I was hitched to a
six-man wagon and told to look for and pick up corpses and take
them to their final destination: to a clearing station if their new
condition as dead had not been registered; to the pathology lab if
they were of interest for dissection; directly to the crematorium if
of no further use. The corpses were everywhere – in the blocks,
outside the doors of the blocks, in the alleys, but mostly in the
infirmary. I recalled my horror upon seeing the cadaver-loaded
cart picking up the dead on the day of my arrival – only three
days ago, but three days which had branded my soul. Now I was
the horse pulling the chariots of the dead.

Most of my clients were located in Blocks III and V. Block III
was the Septical Surgery Department and I gasped on entering.
Here, patients with anthrax, suppurating abscesses, urinary
infections and gangrene were lying helter-skelter; it stank of pus,
old urine and carrion. It was bustling with activity – patients in
terrible condition were being taken in and out of the operating
room; the dead were being pulled out of their bunks and piled up
in the toilets or the aisles. I later learned that the dead sometimes
managed to stay undiscovered in their bunks for two or three
days, abetted by their bunkmates who thus appropriated their
bread and soup rations. The sick moaned for help but there
wasn't much of anything that could be done for them – only
aspirin and toilet paper for bandages. My fellow team of horses
and I held our breath and closed our hearts to the misery, picked
up the dead by their arms and feet and slung them into the cart
parked at the door. Each corpse was marked by an asterisk with
purple ink on the thigh, followed by date of birth, a cross
followed by date of death and his camp number. The latter was
repeated on the sole of his right foot. The deceased were important to the camp's accounting since the SS seemed to be more
concerned about the prisoners dead than alive.

We plunged into the next circle of hell – Block V. It was even worse than Block III. Here was the Realm of Dysentery, the Antechamber of Death. Understandably, dysentery was rampant throughout the camp and, except for dramatically acute cases, went unacknowledged, the afflicted receiving no exemptions from hard labour and no care. In spite of this, the number of patients admitted to Block V was such that the attendants had no time even to separate the dying from the dead. For lack of space, they lay naked and stinking in rows of six, placed head to foot on two beds tied together. The toilets were spilling over and inaccessible to the sick, who relieved themselves anywhere, even on each other. The whole ward was flooded with excrement. My companions and I skidded in it as we stepped over the bodies in our way. We even found days-old corpses abandoned and forgotten under the beds. We did the best we could but we were completely overwhelmed.

The afternoon job was child's play when contrasted with the morning's inferno. We pulled the wagon loaded with heavy boxes, trash cans, building material and other *bric-à-brac*. Even the blows and curses doled out to spur us on when we slowed down seemed insignificant.

I continued to be a horse for three more days. For ten consecutive hours we pulled a huge road roller back and forth over the camp alleys under low clouds and dismal rain.

I was bored. Next to me in the front row a tall emaciated Russian leaned into his harness with a desperate mulish air. Using my few Russian words and the camp jargon, I struck up a conversation with him. His name was Igor. He was twenty-eight years old and came from Leningrad. He held a degree in engineering but had been authorised to follow his real vocation – music. He played the piano and wanted to become a conductor; he had already stood in for the conductor in several small orchestras. In September 1941 he had been taken prisoner in battle and couldn't understand why he had not been sent to a prisoner-of-war camp instead of a concentration camp. He was one of the lucky 2,000 who had survived the massacre of the 18,000 Russians which had taken place in Sachsenhausen that month. He had been pulling the roller for eighteen months but he only listened to the marvellous music resounding in his head which he would one day interpret. All this information had to be patched together by me through grimaces and isolated words over a two-hour period. I resolved to learn Russian.

At the moment I had other problems to think of. I could not comprehend the incongruous world around me. It was all very well to keep repeating 'These guys are crazy!' but this led to nothing. Since I didn't understand and so did not know how to behave correctly, I was courting death. Anything could happen to anybody at any time. Logic could not guide me out of the monstrous labyrinth. I felt lost, I needed help, so I retreated into myself and began to pray in rhythm with my horse-like gait, repeating endlessly, 'Christ, have mercy on us. Christ, have mercy on us!'

Block, roll-call, work – block, roll-call, work – the camp routine swallowed me up. As day followed day I became sleepier and hungrier and yearned more and more for other places.

I was metamorphosed from a horse to a bricklayer. The bricklayers were employed in raising a structure at the edge of the camp, the purpose of which I had not bothered to ask about. I wheeled bricks from a pile in the centre of a mud hole to the top of a hillock where the structure was rising. I skinned my hands on the rough edges of the bricks. Double time was mandatory at all times but here it was necessary to get a running start to have enough momentum to reach the top of the hill. Just to be sure that the proper pace was kept, a group of overseers lined the path to rain strategic blows on the backs of the runners panting by with their heavy wheelbarrows and woe to him who slid off the rickety slippery boardwalk!

The *Vorarbeiter*, the Supervisor, who was an old 'Red' and had been in the camp since 1933 warned the newcomers, 'I'm not a murderer nor a criminal but the SS are on my back. The day's goal has to be reached. I'll do what I can to protect you but get this straight – the only way to help yourselves is to shut up and do as you're told.'

I was totally immersed in the mechanics of the job for the first two days; I had to keep running at the correct speed, evade the blows and keep the bricks in the wheelbarrow; keep the wheelbarrow on the planks. I was too busy to look around me or even wonder which cog I was in the assembly line. On the third day I got promotion as helper to an old mason who built his walls with professional pride. Thus I was upgraded to the position of receiver of bricks at the top of the hill instead of pusher – a decided step up in the camp's social ladder.

During my first spare moment I looked around and found I was in the midst of the infamous Station Z – the Mass Extermination Station – and what I was helping to construct was the shelter for the ultra-modern conveyor belts which would transport the bodies to the ovens more quickly and more efficiently. The smoking chimneys of the four crematoria loomed over me and further down I could see two mobile ovens parked side by side waiting to be put into service whenever necessary. At an order from the SS Supervisor the prisoners were made to stand aside, but we could still see what our jailers were trying to conceal from us.

At the top of the sloping road which led to the 'showers' – in reality the gas chambers – we could see a long column of about 350 men, women and children being herded in slow procession to their final destination by the SS guards and their dogs. Many of the men were dressed in old-fashioned black frock coats, with their heads covered by broad-brimmed black hats. Most of the women were muffled up in big shawls. They all swayed from the weight of the heavy suitcases they were carrying and appeared to have no idea of what was to happen to them at the end of the road. The children holding on to their parents' hands walked solemnly, as if aware that they were actors in an important performance. A cloud of deathly silence hung over the column as it advanced.

'More Jews!' mumbled the *Vorarbeiter*.

The column halted on a small flat square in front of the 'showers'. An order was shouted and an immense clamour arose from the group. The men, women and children were being separated and they suddenly realised what was going to happen.

I couldn't see much from where I was standing but I could hear clearly the lamentations, the terrified screams, the crack of whiplashes, the barking of the unleashed dogs, as they forced the poor crazed creatures into the gas chambers. The construction crew was ordered back to work which was resumed as if nothing had happened. But in a little while the smoke from the chimneys became thicker, blacker and even more rank. A little later the 'horses' arrived with their cart, loaded the Jews' abandoned baggage on to it and pulled it slowly up the hill. As the days passed I had occasion to see several more similar processions appear and disappear forever.

Work was often interrupted by other grisly episodes. Small groups were shot in a trench dug in front of a bullet-riddled wall. Others were garroted slowly by a new method invented by the SS. The victims' feet were clamped in an iron yoke and the noose around their necks was pulled slowly upwards by a system of pulleys. In the evenings, when I returned to my block beaten and exhausted, I was filled with revulsion and despair at having again been a helpless witness to such horrors.

I felt old. I felt that I had seen it all but I was still an innocent. I had not yet discovered the true meaning of the motto over the entrance gate: '*Arbeit Macht Frei*'.

12

Arbeit Macht Frei

I counted on my fingers that sixteen days had gone by since the *Herren Offizieren* had gone into quarantine; our initiation was coming to an end. That evening, after roll-call, Kurt passed out each man's allocation and work assignment. I had been posted to live in Block 16 and work as a nurse in Hospital Block II. Block 16 had the reputation of being a quiet place; it held a lot of French prisoners and the Block Boss was a fairly just man. However, to be made a nurse in Block II was nothing short of miraculous! From that moment, even Kurt regarded me with respect in deference to my new status.

Next morning, Paul introduced me to the camp's Chief Doctor, SS Heinz Baumkötter, a blond, clear-eyed, clear-thinking man who radiated ease and distinction and spoke in clear-cut sentences. Holding myself tautly at attention while waiting to be interviewed, I asked myself why such a man should be wearing the SS uniform.

'Well, Mueller, is this your new discovery?'

Very much at ease, Paul replied, 'Yes, sir.'

Baumkötter looked me over curiously. 'I'm told you speak German.'

'A little, sir.'

'Where did you learn it?'

'A little in school, a lot with a pretty girl in Switzerland, and some in Germany.'

'In Germany?'

'Yes, sir. Before the war I made several bicycle tours through your country.'

'May I ask why you think you are qualified to work as a nurse?'

'I was a medical student and I think medicine is the only career for me.'

'I haven't seen your dossier yet but I assume it wasn't your love of medicine which brought you here. And from Tunis, at that, by special transport!'

'No, sir.'

'Then?'

'Well, I've landed here because I felt duty bound to fight in this war.'

'And did you?'

'Yes, sir.'

'Do you hate us that much?'

'That's not the issue. It's a matter of principle. I think everyone should fight his country's invaders and –'

'That will be all! Are you an officer?'

'Yes, sir, in the parachute commando.'

I had laid my life on the line.

Baumkötter kept looking at me thoughtfully out of the corner of his eye and then turned to Paul. 'What a horrible specimen you've dragged in this time.'

'Yes, sir.' Paul looked delighted while I felt like the ground was giving way under me.

'I've fallen into the clutches of another crazy guy,' I thought.

'Well, Mueller, what do you suggest we do with him?'

'Put him in Block II, sir. That is, of course, if you approve, sir.'

Baumkötter turned to me. 'All right, but just remember that you are not in Block II to fight a war.'

'Yes, sir.' I could hardly believe my good fortune.

'And . . .'

I froze.

'*Bonne chance*,' he spoke in French.

Then I was introduced to the head of the prison doctors, a former SS doctor called Herman Pistor. He had been convicted of homosexuality and of practising illegal abortions and other wheelings and dealings. He was smooth and unctuous, pink as a suckling pig with thinning flaxen hair. He seemed to be constantly doling out blessings with his carefully manicured hands. Primped, powdered, pomaded and perfumed, he was a walking advertisement for baby soap in spite of his striped uniform. He was an apparition from a forgotten world. He clasped me to his bosom with just a little too much warmth and his handshake was lukewarm, limp and lingering.

Having received the blessings of my two supervisors, I took charge of my new domain. Block II had a festive air about it; the windows were dressed in frilly curtains; the front door was adorned by a flower pot and a double wooden balustrade. Block I, which housed the doctors' offices and surgery, stood across the wide gravelled area and also looked trim and fresh. These two buildings were part of the showcase blocks where official visitors such as government delegations, the press and representatives of the International Red Cross were given red carpet treatment. After their inspection tours, they would leave convinced that they had seen a model vacation resort.

I entered the infirmary, spoke briefly to some of my fellow workers, and then found myself alone with some forty patients, all suffering from acute pulmonary illnesses. While making my rounds I was suddenly struck with the realisation that I was alone! All the responsibility rested on my shoulders.

The wards, which opened on to a long corridor, were well lit, heated and smelled freshly of disinfectant. The two-storey bunks were dressed in the ever present blue- and white-checked quilts. The Pharmacy, opened only at specified hours, was at the end of the corridor and the Laboratory was located in the basement. The latter was well organised and equipped and, when necessary, the technicians there faked the reports, trying to save those suffering from terminal diseases from the crematoria, or to give some poor wretch a longer convalescence before he was sent back to work. All morning I kept pinching myself to make sure it was really true. How could this well-run peaceful hospital be placed next to the death traps I had seen in Blocks III and V?

The doctor in charge of Block II made his rounds about noon. He was a Norwegian called Olaf and had been a prominent lung specialist in his country. Afterwards, while I was supervising the distribution of the patients' soup ration, Paul arrived.

'How many patients have you killed off so far?'

I couldn't find words to express how happy I was to see him.

'Never mind. Look.' He showed me what he had been hiding behind his back. It was a superb navy-blue cap, the most coveted symbol of authority among the prisoners.

I was terribly embarrassed and could only stammer, 'But . . . but . . . why?' I felt awkward at being promoted so quickly to a prominent position without having earned it. I felt I was letting my fellow prisoners down, even though I could be of some help to them by working in a hospital ward – but, was it wrong to try to survive?

'Don't ask any questions. Put it on. You are entitled to it. It's always better to inspire envy than pity. Even the SS might accord you a little respect and, God knows, they're little inclined to give it! Don't think one can get on in the world without selling one's soul to the devil.'

When I returned to Block 16 for roll-call everybody was suitably impressed by my new status; even the Block Boss was proud to have such a dignitary among his flock. My companions congratulated me but I could feel a certain aloofness towards me, as if they were wondering what trickery I had practised to climb up the ladder of the camp hierarchy so rapidly. I felt almost guilty as I watched the work groups return exhausted, haggard, often bloodied and burdened with those whose spirits and bodies had finally given up the struggle.

So I made new friends. I met Dr Gallouen, a newly arrived surgeon from Caen, a smiling man in his sixties who peered at the world ironically over his glasses. Somehow he had managed to hold on to his pipe, in which he burnt sundry things, which he proudly referred to as 'my tobacco', puffing out pestilent smoke continuously. He was in charge of septic surgery and spent his days and nights cutting into mucky wounds, abscesses and gangrenous infections. He never let up, anyone in need could call him and he would come running. The men called him 'Papa Maurice'.

'You want to know what's wrong with you, Alec? You're still a silly Boy Scout. You're killing yourself. If you don't slow down we'll soon be taking care of you. Look at you – thin as a rail . . .' And while still scolding me he would dash off to attend another call. It was Maurice who soon died of total exhaustion – who never regained his freedom – who never saw France again.

Partly because of my new status I had become isolated from my block mates so Paul's friendship became all important to me. In the evenings the two of us would wander through the alleyways talking about everything and sharing our dreams. Frequently, Paul received huge fat packages from his family in

Luxembourg; no one dared to pilfer them or ration him, as was the case with many other prisoners. Thus Paul was the owner of hams, Ardennes sausages, lard and butter; he even had bottles of Rhine and Mosel wine, which was strictly forbidden but which he was allowed to keep. The gold reserve at Fort Knox, the Crown Jewels in the Tower of London, the Topkapi treasures were baubles compared to Paul's hoard. Paul, however, was not only generous but also smart and shared his treasures around him.

At first, I was irresistibly drawn to the wall that isolated the camp from the ordinary world. It was a three-metre-high cement block wall surmounted by four rows of electrified wire. At regular intervals along its two-kilometre perimeter, fifteen flat-roofed platforms equipped with floodlights were used as watch-towers; they were manned night and day by an SS team of three or four men armed with machine-guns. Approximately three metres inside this first obstacle there was an electrified fence and the carefully raked sand passageway between the wall and the fence was constantly patrolled by SS guards and their dogs. There was a broad gravel road posted by skull-and-crossbones warning signs along the inner circle of the electrified fence, followed by rolls of barbed wire.

In spite of this formidable barrier calculated to dissuade anyone from trying to escape, every once in a while some desperate soul would dash across the gravel road and fling himself on the electrified fence, preferring a quick death to a slow rotting away in the camp. For days I stared at the walls but finally came to an ineluctable conclusion — if one wanted to get out there were only two possibilities: up the chimney stacks or through the front door. Since the second solution was much more attractive than the first, I decided to mull that one over.

One day Nicolai came into my life. Exactly when or where I was never able to recall but like a bird that suddenly begins to peep on your balcony, Nicolai was simply there. Later, when I tried to question Nicolai, he would smile impishly and reply, 'Don't you know, Alec, that I simply fell out of a cloud?'

Nicolai was Russian, completely Russian. He could not have been anything else. Not quite sixteen, he was very tall for his age, had clipped blond hair and high cheekbones which accentuated his Slavic look. His long-lashed eyes changed from blue to deep violet, reflecting his constantly changing moods; thick golden eyebrows gave character to his childish face and his smile could charm the birds down from the trees. He was a beautiful boy but what made him most endearing were the whimsical facets of his passage into manhood: the melodic voice which suddenly became a crow; the way he got tangled up in his own feet; his big unfinished frame; his frolicking, contagious laughter; the way he expressed himself in a bizarrely accented speech; his hilarious mimicry. From the time the Germans had taken him from his family up to the moment, eight months later, when he came to the camp, he had seen and lived through horrors about which he never even hinted, but when he mentioned the Germans naked hatred shone on his face.

I never found out anything about his parents, where or how he had lived, what schooling he had received, but Nicolai both read and wrote Russian and spoke like an educated person. Was he a country child? He certainly was a child of nature; he knew all about the stars, the sky, the wind and clouds and could forecast the weather and the coming of the seasons; he was always on the look-out for signs – a falling leaf, a passing bird, a budding flower, a sprouting blade of grass, a crawling ant.

One day, I was strolling through the camp with Nicolai chattering like a magpie behind me. Nicolai had a strange way of walking – he either walked a few paces behind me gesticulating wildly or took my arm and walked silently in step with me. We ran into Paul, who took an immediate liking to the boy. From then on, the strange trio often ambled around the camp after roll-call.

As time went by, I became more familiar with the layout of the camp. There was, naturally, a kitchen, a bakery, an administration building, a Telex room, a radio station, a garage, a kennel, a vegetable garden, a chicken coop, a luxurious pigsty and the SS quarters, but there were also other very special installations. I had already seen Section Z, the extermination centre, which worked day and night spreading the foul odour of death and causing the cinders of the dead to fall like snowflakes on the camp. There was also 'Pathology', a place where cadavers of special interest were dissected and which housed a unique collection of monstrosities, deformities and abominations. There were the Disciplinary Block, the Jewish Block, the Russian Block, the Children's Block, the Watchmakers' Block and the Blocks for the Living Dead, 'The Musulmen'. There were warehouses packed to the ceiling with SS treasures: mountains of gold teeth, gold bridges, gold coins, gold wedding bands, jewels and paper money from all countries, all lifted from the dead or their belongings.

At the edge of the camp, there was a charming Swiss-style village which housed important hostages, such as famous scientists, professionals, prominent politicians, high-ranking German or foreign officers who had dared to criticise the Nazi regime. On the edge of the camp there was also the famous 'Bunker', a cell block where criminals suffered special punishments, great cruelty and tortures with two goals in sight – insanity or death.

Outside the camp, but forming part of the network, were the Factories, where the *Kommandos* manufactured bricks, aeroplanes, trucks, tanks and recycled scrap material into essential gadgets for the Reich. The satellites of the camp reached into the industrial outskirts of Berlin. It was a world unto itself!

As I learned more about my surroundings, I became more than ever convinced that there was no chance of survival in a system which focused on the utter destruction of the individual. The only way to survive was to escape. I also became fully aware that the longer I took to initiate the escape the less likely I would be physically and psychologically 'fit' to carry it out. I must not allow myself to be lulled into acquiescence by the monotony of my surroundings. If I was going to try it, it had to be done quickly before it was too late!

The Oranienburg-Sachsenhausen camp had been founded twelve years before. Since then, hundreds of thousands had died there or been exterminated, but still it kept growing. Although many were willing to gamble their lives trying to escape, there had never been a successful attempt. Tight security measures as well as an elaborate stool-pigeon network inside the camp had managed to thwart any attempt. Even the mention of trying to escape invariably led to torture and hanging and curbed even the most intrepid. The concentration camp itself quickly smothered any fighting spirit or yearning for freedom by killing the man within the man and reducing him to the level of an animal, concerned only with his basic needs: food, shelter and how to evade fatal blows and overwork. Even if someone managed to get out, how and where was he to go? In his striped outfit, shaved head and starved appearance, the fugitive would surely be spotted by one of the civilians living in the vicinity who, well aware of the existence of the camp, would conscientiously report him to the authorities. Rare was the man who could face up to these challenges.

During the first years of the camp's existence two or three men had escaped, but they had been Germans who had worked in an outside *Kommando* in central Berlin where the supervision had not been so strict and they had been helped by German anti-Nazi organisations. Others had tried but these had been attempts inspired by desperation rather than the outcome of serious planning and every time these epic heroes had been brought back like dismantled puppets, torn apart by torture and usually dead. The survivors were dragged through the camp and then hanged immediately; the dead were exhibited near the central tower sporting a placard reading, 'I tried to escape!' as a shining example to those remaining.

I came to the conclusion that it was vital to consider all possibilities before making a final decision. To go by myself was dangerous but to have a partner one had to confide in someone, which was even more dangerous. But I had to get out and I began to think and plan seriously.

Time crawled by and the days lengthened. Suddenly spring arrived. There was a sweetness in the air and my heart lightened when I caught glimpses of patches of blue sky, but life in the camp remained as grey and grim as ever.

The camp managers continued to dream up cruel new games for the prisoners to play. One night an entire block was ordered to dismantle their bunks and take them together with their bedding to the assembly square; there, half-naked and under a torrential rain, they were forced to make and remake their beds in the prescribed Prussian manner. They were allowed to go back to quarters just before roll-call – all this because some poor soul had not managed to make his bed before dropping dead.

One man dared to complain about the soup so the block boss had the soup caldrons pulled to the end of the table and the grumbler and all others at his table were forced to jump into the boiling soup, then drink the dregs while enthusiastically praising the excellent consommé.

They dreamed up sessions of preventive delousing, of naked and barefooted promenades through the snow for health, of long leisure hours of perching on top of the gabled roofs – they really let their imaginations soar. Not a day went by that there was not a 'delightfully amusing' story circulating through the camp. All the prisoners could do was to keep as low a profile as possible and their mouths shut.

I, of course, also suffered the practical jokes and indignities inflicted on my block mates. They no longer distrusted me but, as I did not share their lot completely, they made me feel like an outsider, so I turned increasingly to my other friends in the world of the hospital.

One day, a young SS doctor sent for me. 'You're to go immediately to the *Schlag* Service. They're waiting for you at the *Bockzimmer*.' It was Chinese to me but I got a translation. *Schlag* was a punishment which consisted of flogging a prisoner according to an established ritual. *Bock* was a sawhorse over which the prisoner was laid while the *Schlag* was administered. As in other places there are rooms specially designed for certain functions such as the Ballroom, the Billiard Room and the Throne Room, here in the camp they had the *Bockzimmer*.

Grave misdemeanours, such as forgetting to salute an SS, having your collar standing up, walking with your hands in your pockets, losing your cap, or stealing potato peelings, were punished by *Schlag*. The tariff varied in accordance with the seriousness of the offence . . . Five . . . ten . . . or twenty-five lashes, but it could go as high as a hundred and this meant death! The camp management, always eager to do things according to the book, had made it mandatory for a doctor and a medical assistant to be present at the floggings.

I was given a list of the culprits which I was to have checked and signed. There were five in all, looking greenish and trembling with fear at the *Bockzimmer* door. First they were ordered to lower their pants and present their buttocks to be approved as medically fit. The SS doctor did not actually stoop to examine them, he merely said, 'Fit for the *Schlag*'. 'Fit for the *Schlag*', I wrote next to the man's name on my list.

The first culprit was brought into the room where two other attendants stood beside the *Bock*. There was another prisoner wearing a white armband marked with the letter Z. Since Z was the last letter in the alphabet it was quite appropriate to designate this man's calling – he was the specialist in the 'final solution', which he solved using several techniques, hanging, gassing and strangling. Flogging was only a menial job for him. Z held his professional tool which was also called a *Schlag*, a metre-long steel rod enclosed in thick supple leather. An expert had doubled the prisoner over the *Bock*, blocked his feet in stirrups, lowered his pants and raised his shirt. His body was bent forward so that his buttocks lay high, his back horizontal, his arms strapped to each side spread-eagled and his head left hanging. Once the prisoner was correctly positioned, the specialist stepped forward to administer the full quota of lashes. This time it was twenty-five, for arguing with his Block Boss who bawled him out for losing his spoon.

'Hah!'

'*Eins*,' said the victim who was obliged to count the strokes in German.

'Hah!'

'*Zwei*.' This time the prisoner groaned.

'Hah!'

When they reached eleven the poor guy, who had been yelling like a stuck pig, passed out. This had been expected. There was a bucket of water handy and they doused his face to bring him to. The session continued.

'*Zwoelf*' . . . 'Twelve.' The unlucky victim had called the number in his native tongue, Polish.

'That doesn't count,' said the specialist. However, since he was in a good mood today he kindly said, 'Start at ten.' Normally, they would have started at zero.

Finally the flogging was finished. When they unstrapped the prisoner he was unable to stand, so they dragged him to the doctor who, not deigning to look at him, said, '*Alles in Ordnung*.' 'Everything in order,' I wrote next to the man's name.

The second man was old and all skin and bones. He did not let out a sound other than counting for the first eight lashes. At the ninth blow he did not count. He was ordered to count again but once more he failed to respond.

'The bastard is dead,' complained the frustrated specialist.

'*Alles in Ordnung*', said the doctor.

The session continued.

After the flogging the victims were in such a terrible condition that I asked the doctor if we weren't going to dress their wounds.

The doctor laughed. 'You must be crazy,' he said and signed the control sheet without blinking an eye.

I had to concede that my question had been a stupid one. I knew how difficult it was to be admitted to the infirmary. To be dying or wounded was irrelevant, as the SS, who were devotedly working to exterminate them all, were not very interested in saving them. Only a few prisoners ever received any kind of medical attention; the rest died unattended all over the camp. I had been crazy to imagine that the SS could have the slightest interest in healing those it had just destroyed.

I was sick to my soul when I came out of the *Schlag* Block, but what could I do? What could anyone do? At the least sign of protest the prisoners were kicked and beaten, starved, dunked in barrels of freezing water, sent to the *Schlag*, the Bunker or the gallows. The Germans had an extensive repertoire to keep the prisoners in line! The only way a prisoner could defend himself was to pass unnoticed.

One evening during roll-call, the prisoners could see the stage set for the spectacle their rulers were getting ready to produce. Way down the central alley opposite the entrance gate, a wooden platform had been erected; two wooden poles on each side held a crossbeam from which hung a noose; it looked like a cowboy movie set. After roll-call a current of foreboding rippled through the assembled prisoners whose eyes were rivetted on the gallows. Then we saw a terribly battered figure shuffling up the alleyway, escorted by two SS guards and the hangman. He could barely hold his head up and a placard stating his offence hung from his neck over his chest. He was wearing a red triangle and I heard it whispered that he was a Russian army man. I couldn't read what was written on the placard, but that was really immaterial.

The prisoner stepped on the stand and was hoisted on to a

plank which spanned two wooden crates. The hangman lowered the noose around his neck and made sure the slip-knot was working properly. An SS officer faced the camp commandant and his staff and read out the sentence, which was translated by prisoners into several languages that no one could hear well enough to understand. When the hangman approached the condemned man he straightened up, faced his companions, waved goodbye and shouted some words which were snatched away by the wind. Then he indifferently raised his head and looked at the sky.

At a signal from the SS officer in charge the hangman kicked the plank out from under the prisoner, who only fell about twenty centimetres because of the short rope so that, instead of his neck breaking cleanly, he went through terrible agony. His feet fluttered frantically to find the floor, his hands groped to loosen the noose that was slowly strangling him. After an interminable interval his movements slowed, the jerking of his body became less violent and his hands dropped limply to his sides. One final jerk and it was over; he hung still.

During the execution, the SS men at the gallows had joked and smoked unconcernedly. Suddenly music burst forth; the camp orchestra, formed by forty prisoners, broke into a gay mazurka, followed by several perky polkas, and the whole camp marched to the strains of violins. As each column passed in front of the gallows an order rang out: '*Augen links*' – eyes left. The showmen wanted to be sure that the lesson just presented was not lost on anyone and God help the one who turned his eyes away!

I saw the young man dangling, his head tilted like a sleeping child's, blue faced, snot running out of his nose, tongue hanging out, eyes bulging towards the sky. I had become hardened to most of the horrors I witnessed daily but this image was graven in my mind forever. I screamed silently to God, 'Why?' as I continued to march like a robot.

I had occasion to see this scene repeated, sometimes double garrottings, sometimes triple. Some of those executed behaved like heroes; others lost their nerve and went to their deaths sobbing, screaming, imploring. I never forgot! Each execution was abhorrent, all the victims deserved to be remembered; above all, their executioners deserved never to be forgotten.

I go by the road,
I go by the street,
Tira, la, la,
Oh, white high roads,
Ye knew my feet.

Day was ending and the prisoners were taking advantage of the few moments to relax before lights-out. Nicolai, Paul and I were walking, our hearts and feet in unison, down Gallows Alley admiring the extraordinary Brandenburg sunset, typical of the region. The sky was ablaze with a blood red glow which cast purple shadows around the watch-towers and the tall pines swaying beyond the wall. We let ourselves be carried along by the feeling of friendship and momentary pure happiness. Paul had got it into his head that we should teach Nicolai French and, as there was insufficient time to begin with basic grammar, he had decided that Nicolai should learn French romantic poetry. I had humbly suggested that it might be better to teach him the names of the Paris Metro stations or the recipe for Quiche Lorraine, or even the rules of the game of Bellotte, but Paul had been adamant; after all, it had been his idea initially so now good-natured Nicolai proclaimed to the winds:

I go by the road,
I go by the street . . .

He rolled his r's most amusingly and gave an unexpected rhythm to the language. His cheeks were flushed with bashfulness, his eyes shone with pleasure. Now and then he would explode into youthful laughter which rang out so joyously that Paul and I would join in.

Paul stretched. 'How well off we are. Isn't life beautiful?'

I stopped dead in my tracks, looked at Paul, looked at Nicolai who was smiling with the angels, and then looked around me. 'Do you realise what you said, Paul? Do you realise where we are?'

'Of course, I know exactly where we are! To hell with it! There's nothing we can do about it! Why spoil this moment?'

'I was sure that's what you were going to say and I have been waiting for just such a moment to talk to you.'

'About what?'

'I wanted to tell you that you are an ass and so am I and if we aren't careful both of us are going to wind up being contented asses.'

Paul was furious. 'Have you gone out of your mind?'

'No, I just mean that our relative comfort – and I'm not belittling it, I'll never be able to thank you enough – our snugness makes us forget that we are at the mercy of madmen and anything could happen to us at any time. We are becoming prisoners of our own contentment. We are fools!'

Paul was now livid. 'Come on, Nicolai, I've had enough of this idiot.'

Nicolai stopped and looked at his friends. He hadn't understood a word but could sense the discord between us. He was frightened and walked dejectedly away.

I took a deep breath. 'Paul, listen to me. Don't interrupt, just listen. All right? Tell me, do you have any idea of why you're really here?'

'Not really. A lie, a false accusation perhaps, but I don't really see what that has to do –'

'I know you were in prison and were dragged through the *Volksgerichtshof* (the People's Court). The first miracle is that your head didn't get chopped off. True? You were then acquitted, miracle number two . . .'

'True, but –'

'But, instead of being set free as you should have been, you were sent here. And not only have you survived but you can still afford the luxury of feeling that life is beautiful.'

'But –'

'But nothing. I think you've got this far due more to your wits than to luck, but you can't count on this forever. Stop and think. The Allied armies are getting nearer every day. They'll be here in a year – maybe even in a few months. Then what will happen to you?'

'To me? Why me? I'll be liberated like everyone else.'

'How naive can you get? Liberated? Ha! Do you think these bastards, including Baumkötter, whom I sort of like and respect, are really going to let you tell the world exactly what you've seen here? And just suppose, God forbid, the Germans win. Do you think they will liberate you? Or suppose they transfer Baumkötter? You might find your whole little world could come crashing down around your head and all those fair weather friends of yours could turn into ravenous wolves, snapping at your heels.'

Paul had become very silent; his anger had vanished.

I continued, 'Now I'll tell you a secret. No one here knows, because my dossier was lost on the way here from Tunis in a plane which was shot down, but I've been condemned to death. And since the Germans are a thorough lot, I'm sure they'll find out some day who I really am and then it'll be all over.'

Paul turned pale. 'Oh my God, Alec!'

'Forget about that. Don't you think it would be worth it to try to join the Allies and be in on the kill?'

Looking wistful, Paul agreed, 'Of course. More than worthwhile.'

'Then?'

'Then what?'

'Well, I've made up my mind I'm going to try to get out of here and I believe that, if you're the man I think you are, you'll come with me.'

Night had come without us realising it and lights-out sounded. I hurriedly finished what I had to say. 'Think it over, Paul. If you weren't my friend I'd have never spoken to you as I have.' Both returned, running, to our respective blocks but neither of us slept that night.

Next day we kept running into each other in the corridors; while not speaking we waved hello to each other; each of us was as pale and distraught as the other. I was scared; I had laid myself wide open and as long as Paul was not committed I felt endangered. When we finally met in the evening I remained silent, not knowing what to expect.

'I've thought it over, Alec. You're right. I'll go with you. But don't think I'm doing it to save my skin. It would be short-sighted to risk dying trying to escape just because I might die here later. I also want to fight. All high sounding considerations aside, I have a score to settle with these bastards too.'

I breathed again. I had won my friend over and I could now see a chance of success with the two of us united.

Nicolai interrupted us; he beamed as he saw that his two friends had made up. Certain that it had only been a squabble, he asked, 'Ça va?'

'*Oui, ça va,*' we answered in unison. Our eyes met and we repeated, 'Oh yes, everything is really fine!'

We began to lay the groundwork for our escape. From the start we knew that our only possibility of getting away was from an outside *Kommando*, preferably one working on a small construction job where vigilance would be less tight. We divided the problems to be solved: Paul, who was familiar with the workings of the camp, would decide on the ways and means of escape; I would procure the necessary supplies and would be in charge of the operation from the time we managed to get free until we arrived in Luxembourg, Paris or London. I had to scavenge for civilian clothes, leather shoes, a compass, money and maps, as well as prepare a detailed plan of what we were to do from the moment we left the camp; any hesitation would be fatal. Getting supplies was a brain-wracking problem. I had to obtain these incriminating items from men who did not know each other and convince them to hold them until H-hour without arousing their suspicions.

Morning roll-call was moved from 4.30 to 3.30, a sure sign that the summer of 1943 was almost here. From a few clandestine radios and SS gossip heard rumours that the Allied Armies continued advancing on all fronts. Rommel and the Italians had been pushed into the sea. In Russia, the Germans and Italians were retreating. The American war effort, backed by the enormous productivity of their industry, was beginning to make itself evident. The Resistance movements in all the occupied countries were gaining momentum.

In Sachsenhausen, except for a few innovations such as compulsory soccer games and music blaring from the loud speakers every Sunday afternoon, discipline was tightened, punishments fell thick and fast, hangings multiplied, mass extermination accelerated, and more than ever the prisoners' strength was sapped by the two endemic plagues – hunger and lack of sleep. The diet was the same for everyone, which disguised the fact that the nourishment derived from ever thinner soup and smaller bread rations eventually reached below starvation level. The symptoms of starvation were evident: stomach cramps, bloated bellies, fainting spells, cottony legs, foggy heads, apathy. Since everyone looked the same no one noticed that they had inadvertently turned into walking skeletons, whose only sign of life was the fire burning in their eyes, sunk deep in their sockets. The heavy work requirements demanded from these human wrecks never lightened. In addition to these miseries, insomnia undermined all possible resistance.

The prisoners were forever trying to catch up on their sleep, but how could we rest in the overcrowded stuffy dormitories, awakened at all hours of the night and having to get up at the crack of dawn to work without respite until ten at night, always wary of harassment. When we finally got to bed we were usually too exhausted and tense to fall asleep, so all day long we tried to snatch a few winks. We slept while marching, eating, working and sitting on the toilet. Some became 'Musulmen', emaciated skeletons already three-quarters dead who were put into a special block and given lighter work, but when even this became excessive they died like snuffed-out candles. For those who lingered long in the twilight between life and death and were considered irrecoverable, orders arrived periodically sending them to the *Himmelsfahrt Kommando* (the Heavenbound Commando). I saw many of my companions depart by this route during the next few months.

One morning in June, after roll-call, the SS Chief called me and with a smirk told me, 'You're excused from work. Get all your things together and report to the *Schreibstube*. You are to be liberated.'

I felt like the earth had opened up under me. I was only too well aware of the various connotations the word 'liberate' could have. My mind reeled: had my file been found revealing my death sentence? Had an old buddy talked carelessly? All I could do for the moment was to go to the *Schreibstube*. The clerk there smilingly informed me that I was being sent to Berlin for an interrogation and that then I might be liberated.

'Who else is going?'

'No one else. Just you.'

All of my personal possessions were returned to me to my great surprise. Even more surprising, I was sent to take a tepid shower and given a shave and trim. They ordered me to sign a document in which I swore under dire threat that I had never been mistreated nor would I ever divulge anything about what I had witnessed while in the camp. I signed willingly enough and, under the envious eyes of the clerk, was put aboard a small bus with an SS guard.

I only had time to send a message to Paul but had been unable to see him.

'Where are we going?' I asked.

'To Berlin.'

'Why? Where in Berlin?'

'To Prinze Albrechtstrasse.'

'What's there?'

'Gestapo Headquarters.'

The trip was endless for me. My feelings wavered between unreasonable hope of liberation and the numb fear evoked by the Gestapo.

13

Comings And Goings

Handcuffed, I arrived at the gate of an enormous building two hours later. This was the headquarters of the famous *Reichssicherheitshauptamt*, headquarters of the National Security Service of the German Reich. The place was hectic with comings and goings, crowded corridors and staircases, checkpoints, telephones ringing behind closed doors, and uniforms, uniforms, uniforms everywhere. The SS guard stopped in front of a door labelled *Abteilung IV E-4*. I shivered when I saw the number; I remembered it was the number belonging to the sinister counter-espionage section. The guard pressed a bell button and announced himself through a speaker set in the wall. A green light flashed, the lock snapped open and we stepped into a small vestibule. A clerk came out of an adjoining room and took delivery of the prisoner. 'Last name? First name? Date of birth?' He signed the receipt. My guard took it, clicked his heels, saluted with the mandatory 'Heil Hitler' and left.

The clerk ignored me. He was busily perusing some papers which seemed to pertain to me since every once in a while he would grumble, look at me disgustedly and return to his reading, while scratching his crotch through his trouser pocket. Finally he called a secretary.

'The judge will see him tomorrow at 8.00 a.m. Meanwhile put him in the basement.'

He rang a bell to summon another guard who amiably stuck a big calibre gun in the small of my back. 'Hands on your head. Let's go.'

More corridors, stairways and uniformed crowds. Fifteen minutes later, I found myself sitting on one of the chairs placed around a large wooden table in a vast, brilliantly neon-lit hall. There were six metal beds hinged upright against one wall with the mattresses visible through the springs, six night tables, two sinks, a mirror, a toilet, a roll of toilet paper and two coat-hangers hung on each side of the heavy door which was equipped with the traditional Judas window. Strains of sweet German folk music flowed from a speaker concealed in the ceiling. I was astounded; such luxury and tranquillity I had not seen for a long time. Best of all, not once had I been mistreated or cursed on the journey; I spent a most agreeable day and a peaceful night.

I was awakened by a ringing bell and the lights going on. I washed, had my 'coffee' and bread and waited, my heart throbbing with misgivings. Two SS guards opened the door and escorted me back the way I had come the day before. As we passed a cell block I heard dismaying moans and groans from behind a closed door.

'*Ruhe!*' One of the guards gave the offending door a well-directed kick. I realised that not all was as idyllic as it appeared in the *Reichssicherheitshauptamt* and a growing fear gnawed at my guts as we mounted the stairs.

Judge Lorenz's office was spacious but dark as the light barely filtered through the heavy drapes covering the window. A long work table facing three easy chairs was placed diago-nally in the corner; on it rested a cast-bronze lamp, casting a yellow light on a leather writing pad. The secretary whom I had seen the day before was seated in front of a typewriter at another table. Bookcases stacked with leather bound volumes gave the room a stately air and an enormous photograph of the Führer adorned one of the walls.

I was shoved into one of the easy chairs. The SS guards were replaced by yesterday's plump clerk and a bony mean-faced private. A clock behind the desk chimed and Judge Lorenz entered. Everyone rose.

'Heil Hitler.' Lorenz put an end to the courtesies with a regal gesture and everyone sat down.

SS Colonel Lorenz looked like an intellectual member of the Catholic Action Party. He was tall, very slim and fine featured. He was greying at the temples and sported the small brushy moustache favoured by the Führer. His intent grey eyes bored through rimless glasses which sparkled when he moved his head. He spoke softly in clean-cut sentences. Occasionally a slight tick made his nose twitch as if he had a bad cold and had forgotten his handkerchief. He looked me over for a long while. 'Last name? First name? Date of birth?' The conversation had been conducted in German and the translator sat down.

'I see you speak German.'

'Yes.'

'Are you Jewish?'

'No.'

'Are you a Gaullist?'

'No, I'm a medical student. What's a Gaullist?'

The judge, who was not accustomed to impertinence, made an almost imperceptible signal. The clerk slapped me twice across the face so hard that I felt my head was going to come loose.

'I repeat, are you a Gaullist?'

'My ears are ringing so I cannot hear you.'

This time Lorenz didn't have to signal. I was again slapped back and forth. I felt sure that the Germans had no precise information about me or they would have executed me a long time ago. In any case, I thought my best defence was to divert Lorenz's attention from the crucial questions.

Lorenz, however, continued unperturbed. 'Do you know why you are here? Do you know the charges against you?'

'Really, Colonel, I think it's your business to know that. After what your people did to me in Tunis and at Sachsenhausen, why ask me?'

'Don't behave like an idiot! If you don't answer my questions things will go very badly for you.' Lorenz had addressed me in practically flawless French.

To hide my surprise I turned slightly aside. I continued my strategy. 'Let's be realistic, Colonel. There is nothing that I could have said or done before my arrest in Tunis five months ago that could possibly be of interest to you now. You know much better than I when and where the Allies landed and where the front now lies in Italy or Russia or any other place. You know so many things of which I haven't the slightest inkling. Any information you could get from me would be completely obsolete. You are probably as aware as I am that Germany is finished.'

Lorenz turned livid. An expression of naked hatred flickered in his eyes, his mouth twisted, his hands balled into tight fists as he rose and approached me with jerky steps. He struck me as hard as he could, yelled an order which I didn't understand and the two soldiers descended upon me. They trounced and thrashed me and dragged me out to an adjacent room by the ear, twisting and tearing it. Exit Alec! It was 8.05; the inquiry was over!

From then on I had only distorted images of what followed. Anything and everything went; heels crushed my hands; I was kicked, knocked, pelted and pummelled, banged and boxed black and blue, beaten to unconsciousness. When I slowly started coming to I heard a long moan, just like the one I had heard in the morning. It was pitch black and I hurt – I hurt unbearably whether I moved or not. A sticky substance was running out and clogging my nostrils and my mouth tasted of lead. I stuck out my tongue slightly to moisten my cracked lips and felt my bleeding broken teeth. I tried to move my arm which was compressing my chest and was frightened by a gurgling wail. I forced myself to swallow the blood which was choking me. I stopped breathing for a moment and the sobbing rattle also stopped. Then I realised I had been hearing myself! Slowly I changed my position but at the slightest movement the piercing pain produced flashing stars and trailing comets behind my eyelids. I opened them a slit and realised I was not in the dark but that my eyes were swollen and caked with dried blood. I willed myself to awareness. The Gestapo had certainly not lost their knack since they had worked me over in Tunis. I inventoried the damages; only some teeth, my nose and a few ribs seemed to have been broken; nothing vital. The smaller injuries were the most painful: my ear seemed to have been torn off my head, my Adam's apple and testicles had been smashed.

I lay on the floor like a wet mop until the lights really went out and I fell back into the oblivion of sleep in which terrible nightmares of Lorenz, beatings and whippings pursued me. I felt slightly better the next morning and managed to bring myself to a sitting position and sipped something from a bowl which had been passed through a small trap door. I desperately wanted to wash myself because I was wallowing in my own faeces but I was unable to stand. I sank into despair: I thought I would die but apparently my time had not yet come. Next morning they made me get up, wash, shave and dress, then they handcuffed me and led me away.

The Alexander Platz! From the armoured prison van I got my first glimpse of the enormous building that occupied the whole length of the beautiful square from which it took its name. The guards half dragged, half carried me through the vaulted entrance. I had thought that because of my battered appearance I might have inspired pity in the passers-by but all I got were glowering looks and churlish remarks.

'They'll never know how right they are,' I thought to myself as we crossed a large hall where people were lined up before counter windows; it was the police station. At the end of this hall we passed through a door and entered the prison. Here I was put through the traditional formalities. In twenty minutes I was fingerprinted and stripped of my belt, shoe laces, tie, money, watch, etc. Once again I had ceased to be a man and had joined the ranks of the dispossessed.

The guards took me through empty corridors and up stair-cases and halted in front of door 306. They pushed me in gently and closed the door on my heels. The ward was about ten metres by twenty-five metres and the entire centre was occupied by scaffolding which formed four decks of bunks. About two hundred prisoners were either perched there or standing around. Many bare-chested were busily delousing themselves. A dozen men sat around a table in front of the first of the four barred windows, which opened on an interior courtyard, cosily chatting and smoking; they probably constituted the local aristocracy. A slightly stooped man stepped towards me; his hair was white and his round face friendly. He looked at me with compassion and held out his hand.

'I'm Hans Friedman. I'm the boss here, chosen by popular vote of the inmates. You poor fellow! They really worked you over! Come!' He took me by the arm and led me to the table where the others made room for me. They said hello briefly and returned to their former activities.

I found out that most of the men in the ward were common criminals, besides a small sprinkling of German political prisoners and a handful in transit, like me. Hans, my new friend, leaned against the wall and held forth at the head of the table. He had been a famous Berlin lawyer who was here while his affairs were being investigated. He told everyone who would listen that he had been imprisoned for resistance to the Nazi

regime but his detractors claimed that the reason was embez-
zlement and corruption of minors. He was kind and charming
to me and soon had the opportunity to prove his good will.

Dinner was announced at 5.30 p.m. A group of prisoners
counted off by Hans were allowed to go out into the corridor by
twenties and line up in front of the trollies which held four
100-litre thermoses containing boiling soup. Each prisoner
picked up a bowl and received a ladleful of an evil smelling
steaming concoction. They were allowed exactly two minutes to
gulp it down, put the bowl on the floor and take a piece of bread
and spongy sausage back into the ward. Of course they burned
their mouths but they submitted to the needless ragging without
complaint. I had not been informed of the procedure and
suffered excruciating pain when the boiling liquid touched my
split lips and broken teeth.

'*Los! Schnell! Schnell!*' screamed the runt who supervised the
serving.

'I'm sorry, but it's too hot.'

'It's not hot. *Los! Schnell! Schnell!*'

I couldn't drink it.

'Put it down!'

But I was hungry. Soup was sacred so I stubbornly tried to sip
a little and didn't notice that everyone else had finished and
gone back in and that I was creating a bottleneck. One of the
guards raised his fist menacingly and started towards me. But I
had already received too many blows and flung the still
steaming soup at the guard's face.

'It's not hot! Not hot!' I mocked while the runt howled in
pain. Another guard pulled out his gun and the comedy
threatened to turn into a tragedy until Hans intervened. A towel
was brought, the mess tidied up and Hans took the runt aside to
talk to him discreetly; he finally nodded and calmed down. The
guard whom I had shared my soup with kicked me along to a
rat-infested dark dungeon where I spent my first night at the
Alexander Platz. I had ample time to recall the incident with the
Fort Ain-Roumi guards. 'This is getting to be a habit,' I
admonished myself. After two days on bread and water I was
taken back to Room 306 where Hans greeted me like a prodigal
son.

'I'll grant you, you were right, but that wasn't the thing to do,' said Hans and I agreed. 'I told them you were out of your mind from the beatings and that if they would forget the whole thing they could pass by my office for a hundred marks each.' Hans had even procured a medical certificate for me which allowed me to drink my soup inside the ward.

After this stormy introduction I settled down into the prison routine but that didn't prevent me from dwelling on the possibility of escape. The sole bright spot of the day was a half-hour's promenade around a small cobblestone courtyard but here there was no chance; the guards were ever vigilant and the walls too high but I noticed another door, small and barred, which opened on to the courtyard. I asked where it led and was told 'to the Admissions Office', which I remembered from the first day. This aroused my interest and I kept watching the door.

I made a new friend, Jan Alexandrovicz, a young fervent Catholic patriot, son of a Polish general, who had fled to England to fight the Germans. Because of this the Germans had arrested and deported the entire family – his mother to Ravensbrück, his sister to a military brothel, his little brother to his death on the journey and he himself to the Alexander Platz. He had lost a leg during the bombing of Warsaw but stoically he dragged along his wooden leg and his grief. He had been rotting away for a whole year when he had caught tuberculosis. Although he coughed and coughed no one paid any attention. He had never lost his faith, courage or hope for even a minute. From time to time, his almost translucent pallid face would light up with a sad smile. He usually spoke in a soft voice but when he mentioned the Germans his look would become implacable and his voice hoarse and cutting – frighteningly so.

Occasionally something amusing interrupted the drab slow days and made me laugh. Hans was a Francophile and spoke French fluently. He often asked me to recite a poem or sing a French folk song and then the whole ward would follow along, picking up the tune. I sometimes had to pinch myself to remember where I was when I heard 'A la Claire Fontaine' or 'Montagnes Pyrénnées' ring through the hall.

One day, a young Frenchman from Lorraine, who had been drafted into the STO (Service du Travail Obligatoire – Forced Labour Service), arrived in 306. His name was Albert Labuche and he had been arrested for setting snares for rabbits in the Tiergarten, Berlin's Central Park. He accepted his eight-day sentence with utter indifference. What he had to say was of great interest to me. Albert had been living in an STO camp installed in a former restaurant in Charlottenburg in an area of Berlin. Originally there had been sixty living there but now, due to the bombings and regrouping of the work forces, there were only ten. The home guard in charge of them had also gone, a precinct policeman was supposed to come by to check up on them but as yet he had never appeared, so the few Frenchmen still there were taking advantage of their relative independence and taking it easy.

'You'll always be welcome to come and stay with us, Alec, if you ever get out. We're all friends and do as we please. There's plenty of room. We live in style so don't hesitate to come and stay if you want to.' Little did Labuche know what he was offering and to whom. I carefully memorised the address – just in case.

Several days later I was summoned to the Secretariat.

'Orders have arrived sending you back to Sachsenhausen by the next convoy which leaves the day after tomorrow.'

Time was running out; I had to do something before the trap door snapped shut on me again! The following morning, during the early exercise period, I saw a guard coming through the small side door. I shoved him aside and flew like an arrow up the corridor and through the Admissions Office. I cleared three steps in one leap and bolted towards the door leading to the Police Station. Miraculously it was unlocked! I was puffing like a steam engine, my stomach was heaving in my throat, choking me as I stormed through the door flinging aside a policeman who had been peacefully leaning against it. The Police Station was crowded and I charged like a rugby player pushing and skirting the people obstructing my way to the exit. I could smell freedom fifteen metres, ten metres, five metres away. Just as I was ready to make my final leap, a policeman who had been watching my dash slammed the door shut on my nose. I crashed against it and shattered on to the floor. All the police had to do was pick me up.

It had been an impromptu desperate attempt but it had almost worked. Once again, they handcuffed me and, vanquished, I let myself be taken to the Admissions Office where I was met by the same prison warden who had told me I was to go back to the concentration camp. He took me into his private office. He looked tired and old.

'So it didn't work, did it? Too bad for you. Theoretically I should put you in solitary confinement, but where you are going is a lot worse!' He made a gesture of helplessness. 'For us, *alles ist kaput.*'

Less than a month had elapsed. While all sort of things had happened to me, the camp had remained unchanged. I brought back news – above all, the news of the German retreat on all fronts. The beast was dying, it was just a question of time and patience but patience was not my strong point and my Berlin excursion had opened new horizons for me. Once again, I had been bounced back to where I started from, but now I was desperate to be free as I had heard that a group of Tunisians had been taken to Berlin for interrogation. I feared that my death sentence could surface like a body which had lain on the bottom of a river for a long time.

Paul was the first to welcome me back. I had not expected to see him again since a small number of the Tunisians had been liberated in the interim. I felt nothing had been lost and that I was lucky to be alive, so I picked up my uniform, my duties and my secret plans.

In August 1943 a Frenchman from Tunis who was to be the doctor for all of the camp's ill and defeated, regardless of race or creed, arrived. Emile-Louis Coudert had been arrested in Tunis in April, had been sent to the camp by a roundabout route and had arrived long after the other Tunisians. He quickly joined the small group of friends. Great surgeon and patriot, big hearted, big mouthed and bawdy, he came to hold the post of Chief Surgeon within a few weeks, a position he was to maintain until the liberation of the camp. He looked like a strong, hairy, unlicked bear covered with red fuzz. He seemed to have been carved with an axe out of roughly hewn wood; bald, square-jawed, sensual-mouthed, rugged-faced, he wore thick glasses on the tip of his potato-shaped nose. He boisterously bellowed out his opinions, his joys, his frustrations, and swore like the heathen he was, but he also had the rare talent of listening. He sat silently at his patients' bedsides listening and observing them carefully, comforting them with a warm voice and handling them lovingly.

In the operating room he was the undisputed authority; his speech and movements were deft and spare. He began operating from the moment he arrived and saved thousands of lives. He even stood up to SS doctors who had never encountered such a man before. He managed to control the camp gangs and the surreptitious petty plots without once demeaning himself. His reputation as a famous Parisian surgeon and as a notorious rogue and womaniser had preceded him.

The scorching summer days and the blue sky made our imaginations soar. Discouraged by my absence, Paul had allowed our escape project to lapse but now, bit by bit, the details began to fall into place. Thanks to Labuche's invitation, one of the main problems – where to find shelter when we reached Berlin – had been solved.

My hospital routine was interrupted one August morning. I received orders to prepare one of the small wards for very special patients. The whole thing was very mysterious; special security measures were to be taken and special equipment was to be installed; the patients would not be allowed to leave their quarters under any circumstances. Several days later, seven patients who had been showered, shaved and disinfected arrived. Their hospital gowns hung to their heels, dragging on the floor. These patients were Polish-Jewish children, aged seven to eleven; they had been brought to the hospital to serve as guinea pigs. As a 'medical experiment' they were to be injected with drugs to test their effect.

I could not find out anything else except that an SS doctor would be in charge of the 'treatment'. I was horrified; I had already seen these incompetent doctors operating, removing healthy organs only to keep their hands agile and improve their surgical techniques. I had also witnessed 'experimental' grafts and organ transplants, tests to measure resistance to extreme cold, and other grisly experiments which had killed or maimed adult guinea pigs. I told Paul about my predicament since he categorically refused to abet such abominations. We talked it over and came to the conclusion that the only solution was to have me transferred. In the meantime, I would have to pretend to co-operate. The children were given an acclimatisation period in order to have them in optimum condition for the 'experiment'. Knowing they would die and not knowing what else to do, I played with them and spoiled them for a few days.

Then my good star came to the rescue – I fell ill! I had been ignoring my aches, pains and general malaise until I fainted as I was returning from roll-call one day. I was taken to the hospital delirious from a high temperature. I had caught double pneumonia and my friends fought to pull me through. I hovered between life and death for days. When I regained consciousness, the first face I saw was Paul's regarding me anxiously. Olaf came and announced that the fever was abating and the crisis was over. Nicolai had somehow gained entrance to the hospital and smiled radiantly at the doctor's words. Like a magician, Paul produced a fragrant yellow object – a lemon! No one could believe their eyes; we had never seen a lemon in camp. Paul cut it into sections while giving us a lecture on the curative powers of Vitamin C. Nicolai also had a surprise up his sleeve; he had been looking very solemn but suddenly could not contain himself any longer and, beaming, he offered me something wrapped up in a dirty rag – his bread ration.

I was up and about eight days later. Another nurse had taken my place. The Polish children were kept in strict quarantine and I never found out what was done to them. I had been transferred to fill a position in Block IV – the TB Block. Here patients came not to be healed but in transit to the crematoria. The block was dark, stuffy, overheated and overcrowded. The bunks rose to the ceiling and all the windows were inaccessible and hermetically closed but what shocked me most was the smothering silence. The sick lay listlessly in the last stages of tuberculosis. They knew they were dying. In a world where people fought over a handful of potato peelings these didn't lift a finger to take their bowl of soup. They didn't even have the strength to cough. Their burning, staring eyes followed me but when I leaned over them I couldn't understand their incoherent rasping gargles. No fight, no hope, only despair. When they died, the bodies were piled up in a corner of the toilets. The only available medicine was a limited quantity of aspirin which did about as much good as a plaster cast on a wooden leg.

Dr Pistor was in charge. By nature a conscientious man, he arrived promptly at 8.00 a.m. looking prim and proper, the perfect epitome of Christian charity. He would go straight to the table which held the charts, pick them up squeamishly by the edges with his manicured fingernails, count how many had been received, discharged or had died, regard me benevolently and say: 'Alles in Ordnung? No problems? Good. Good.' Before I could reply he was out of the door expelling the miasma and other germs from his lungs.

Priests and ministers were lodged in Block 15, in front of where I was quartered. I tried to persuade them to bring the solace of religion to the totally abandoned patients, but received a categoric 'no' from all. Although it was perhaps true that these men had tried to do as much good as possible within the limitations imposed on them by the authorities and this type of visit was strictly forbidden by the rules of the camp, I was bitterly disappointed that no one was sufficiently convinced of his belief to risk the rare honour of martyrdom and bear witness to the faith.

Autumn came, bringing in its wake cold winds and rain; the prisoners were perpetually soaked and shivering. The roll-calls became most unbearable and when the snows started many began to die. I blessed my experiences in mountain climbing where I had become hardened to rude weather.

One day, an SS guard bearing precise orders presented himself at the hospital with a gravely ill Polish prisoner. The patient was interned in a small, rarely used isolation room and the guard stationed himself beside the bed with a sub-machine-gun between his legs. I asked Paul, who generally knew everything, who he was. Paul told me that he came either from Block XVIII or Block XIX. Almost everyone was curious about these buildings. It was forbidden even to go near them. They were surrounded by a barbed-wire barrier and they and the adjoining alley were literally encased in wire netting. They were called the Printers' Blocks. Approximately 150 men worked there and they were isolated even from the birds. The inmates were skilled specialists: copymen, painters, printers, miniaturists, designers, engravers, photographers, counterfeiters. They were equipped with the latest machinery, special inks, papers, varnishes and paints. There were two groups working twelve-hour shifts who produced such good bogus Bank of England notes that the Swiss banks and even the Bank of England were fooled. The 'printers' also produced false dollars as well as documentation for the German Services which were so top secret that the Reich preferred to have them printed in the camp.

These prisoners ordinarily never left their blocks, never attended roll-calls; they had no contact with anyone; their SS guards lodged with them, which explained the presence of the guard in the small isolation room.

Anxious to hear what went on exactly in these blocks, I started to chat with the guard, warning him to be careful of the endemic microbes which teemed in the air of the room.

'Look around you. I'll give you some disinfectant to wash your hands but, above all, be careful never to eat anything while inside the block.'

The guard got panicky and kept stepping out frequently; he did take the precaution of locking the door to the isolation room but trustfully left the key with me in case of an emergency. I took advantage of his absence to get acquainted with the prisoner, speaking half in Russian and half in German. I agreed to try to get some important papers printed in the 'Printers Block' out to London. I didn't exactly know how but I was willing to give it a try. The sick prisoner recovered and was returned to his cage.

Two weeks later I admitted another inmate from the 'Printers Block'. This one was a Belgian, which made conversation a lot easier. He confirmed the agreement and told me that, although all of them were risking their necks, the information he would give me was well worth it: communication codes of the armoured divisions, battle plans and secret codes of the Wehrmacht, which were to go into effect on 1 May the following year.

Thus I came into contact with what I had heard about but had not been able to believe existed: a network of resistance within the camp. I began to receive the papers in the first days of December; they were brought by prisoners unknown to me who immediately disappeared. The only characteristic I was able to note was that they were mostly German, all wore red triangles indicating they were political prisoners, and they generally held high positions in the camp hierarchy.

I got a pleasant surprise at the end of December – a package from Paris, the first one. It was badly wrapped, torn, and half of the contents had been lost *en route* but what was left was wonderful: a dark blue woollen sweater and a pair of woollen gloves, which I was allowed to keep after haggling with the block boss, cookies, raisins, a little jar of jam and . . . chocolates! Best of all was the psychological link I felt had been forged between me and the outside world, especially with my mother, who had addressed the package to me in her own handwriting. This also meant that my 'letters', printed forms, which the prisoners were allowed to mail out once a month had been received. Now I was no longer a parasite, always taking; now I could also give. Other pillaged and pummelled packages followed and were most welcome because they provided the means of exchange for the requirements needed for the escape.

As Christmas drew near, the cold became more and more bitter. Fear stalked through the camp. The SS executioners bettered their methods for disposing of useless hungry mouths without gassing or shooting. They openly applied shots of benzene to the sick, who died after fifteen minutes of violent convulsions. Death stalked the camp!

The infamous torment of the prisoners grew directly in proportion to the defeats suffered by the German Army. I was disheartened and asked myself if this thing had no limits and just how long it could go on. Unexpectedly I received another summons to go immediately to the *Schreibstube*. Once more my stomach tied itself in knots. This time, a surprise of a different nature awaited me. I had been transferred to an outside *Kommando* – to Falkensee, a new satellite camp to Sachsenhausen – and was to be in charge of the infirmary there. The clerks at the *Schreibstube* congratulated me warmly on my good fortune because the job was not only easy but also a promotion; from my point of view it was a setback to my escape plans.

Meanwhile, Paul had been pulling strings, hinting that he needed to breathe fresh air for his health. The *Vorarbeiter* of the outside *Kommando Fichtengrund* (Spruce Vale), who was overjoyed to have such an important person among his workers, arranged a light work assignment for him in exchange for a few niceties. Paul had reckoned that once he was a member of the *Fichtengrund Kommando* he would be able to wangle a transfer for me to the same group. Now, for the second time, all our plans were in jeopardy: first, the Gestapo outing, and the Alexander Platz, and now this!

Paul and I conferred during the following two days. I was determined to get back to the camp within a month; the only question was how this could be accomplished. We decided that, during my absence, Paul would prudently proceed with his end of the preparations. A new idea occurred to Paul who asked for my Red Cross parcel. That very morning I had received a package sent via Lisbon by a sweet Swiss girl who had somehow managed to locate me; I handed it over without question. As we said goodbye we were suddenly overcome with awe at our own audacity for even attempting an escape.

The week before Christmas, I was put into a van making the half-hour run to the Sachsenhausen train station. I was accompanied by a filthy Russian and a grimy Pole who seemed to regard the whole thing as an amusing excursion; by coincidence, it was the same van that had taken me to Berlin. Our SS guard, iron cross dangling from his tunic, had the mature look of someone recently returned from the front; with his rifle slung over his shoulder, he did not seem over-enthusiastic about his new post.

'I've nothing to do with your being here. I'm just taking you to the new camp. If you behave properly I'll leave you alone, but if you act up I'll shoot you without blinking an eye. Understood? Forward march!'

We caught the train to Oranienburg where we changed to the S-Bahn, a small underground electric train which took an hour to reach the junction with the Berlin underground. The train was crowded and our striped uniforms caused quite a commotion among the civilian passengers. I thought that our gaunt look would arouse pity but, on the contrary, one fat woman made random nasty remarks and then shook her fists at us as we were pushed into a corner by other angry passengers while the SS guard, irony of ironies, tried to protect us. When we got off at the next station our faces were scratched and covered with spittle; our escort was very upset as he had also received his share. We walked to another platform to change trains and were put in the last carriage which was equipped with barred windows and reserved for the mail or for prisoners. Utterly exhausted, we sat down on the bench while the guard seated himself on the opposite side with his gun resting between his knees. He was still angry but he looked at us in a new light, almost with sympathy. He asked the Russian: 'Who are you?'

The Russian regarded him empty-eyed, not understanding.

'And you,' he turned to the Pole who jumped up like a Jack-in-the-box, whipped off his cap, stood at attention and declared in a parade ground voice, 'Schutzhäftig 58367.' He had certainly been well conditioned. The SS guard's face fell so, not wanting the flickering flame of warmth which seemed to have been kindled in the guard to go out, I quickly stated: 'I'm a French officer from Tunis.'

'Terrorist?'

'War is war.'

The SS guard looked glum.

'Don't you agree? Haven't you been fighting too?' I insisted.

'Yes, it's true,' said the guard thoughtfully.

At the next stop another SS guard got at in with a strange looking prisoner. A hood and kerchief were tied over the head and the pants were very wide, almost like a skirt. It was a skirt! I was so shocked that I cried out, '*Mais, c'est une femme!*' Although I had spoken in French the two guards had interpreted my meaning and broke into good-natured laughter.

The creature, who was now sitting opposite me, pushed back the hood which had hidden her face and the kerchief which had hidden her hair . . . and an angel appeared! We held our breath in wonder as we gazed at a lovely young girl, between sixteen and eighteen years of age. Her short cropped hair was the colour of summer wheat; her eyes, of a deep cornflower blue, didn't look outward but guarded her soul; a triangular shaped face, high cheek bones, a small impertinent nose and a child's swollen lipped mouth. She was short and stocky, like the peasant girl she was, and her dirty uniform bagged on her. She cowered in the seat like a weary scared animal. She carried traces of the beatings she had received; her lips were cracked and a long scar which hadn't quite healed marred her face, but the most touching thing about her was the vacant look in her eyes of someone who had seen and borne too much!

As the train began to roll my heart was thumping loudly, and I could hardly take my eyes off her but I finally managed to look out the window.

The impact of the Allied bombings on Berlin had had quite different results from the first random British raids over Cologne and the Ruhr Valley. Since July, the prisoners in the camp had listened gleefully to the ever more frequent air-raid sirens which upset the camp routine, giving them unexpected rest periods which they welcomed and sleepless nights which they considered well worth-while when they looked upon the worried faces of the guards the next morning. The devastation of Berlin was impressive. One thousand American Flying Fortresses flying in low formation razed the city by day and the RAF Lysanders continued the blasting by night.

As the train passed through the outskirts and the centre of Berlin, I could see the sky through gutted walls, toppled-over cement blocks and twisted iron beams littering the streets. The SS guards who glanced furtively at the wreckage tried to hide their distress and started to talk with a bitter sense of humour about the fall of Stalingrad and the recent German defeats, rejoicing in the fact that they were still alive and unscathed.

Then their conversation turned to women. Suddenly one guard had a brainstorm. 'Tell me,' he said to me, 'how long has it been since you've had a woman?'

Completely taken aback, I didn't know what to say, but decided that the best policy was to play the clown and tell the truth. I held out my hands, shrugged my shoulders helplessly and let out a deep sigh. The guards burst out laughing. I thought the baiting was over, but a guard pointed to the girl.

'Do you want her?'

'What?'

'I mean it. If you want her you can have her.'

'What about her?'

'That doesn't matter a damn. Does that bother you?'

'Well . . .'

I felt desire stirring inside me. 'Yes, I would like her.'

'Then take her into the toilet and be quick about it. But don't try to play any tricks on us!'

I stood up, stunned and deeply embarrassed. The girl had followed the conversation passively. Had she understood? I looked at her questioningly, but her eyes were remote. I held my handcuffed hands out to her but she didn't budge.

'Los! Mädchen, los!' The guard spoke sharply.

She returned from far-off places, looked at me and slowly stood up. The guard prodded her in the back and she followed me submissively. As we walked out of the compartment the guard, not wanting to be taken for an imbecile, cocked his gun and warned us, 'It's forbidden to lock the toilet door.'

It was freezing cold, noisy and cramped in the toilet. I closed the door and asked her in German, 'What's your name?'

She looked at me absently and didn't answer. I insisted, this time in Russian, 'What's your name?'

'Katia.'

'Are you Russian?'

'Ukrainian.'

'How long have you been a prisoner?'

'Six months. They took everyone in my village. Who are you?'

'I'm French. I'm called Alec.'

'Alec, please don't hurt me.'

I looked at her raptly. A surge of need and an immense tenderness invaded me. I passed my handcuffed hands over her head and held her in my arms. She remained still but I drew her close to me until I felt her whole body pressed against me, felt her yield, saw her head drop backwards and her eyes close. I kissed her face, her eyelids, her neck, and then gently kissed her mouth, which opened slightly; and I entered a warm enchanting world. Reluctantly, I lifted my arms and released her. I then began to caress her ever so tenderly. Her breasts were sweet and firm; her flat belly quivered under my trembling hands as they travelled down her. When they touched her thighs she arched her back and moaned softly. The idea of possessing her flashed through my mind but for all kinds of reasons I erased the thought. While she leaned against the wall I husbanded her young girl's body with mine. She had let her thighs part slightly and with every movement and swaying of the train long shivers shook our bodies and waves of pleasure inundated us, carrying us to the border of ecstasy.

Someone knocked on the wall and broke our trance. I sighed deeply. She looked at me with starry eyes and said just one word in a soft, deep voice, 'Alec.' Again someone knocked on the wall.

'Come, Katia.' We left the sordid little washroom, the glow of the happiness we had known so briefly written plainly on our faces for everyone to see.

'Well,' said one guard.

'Well, well, well,' said the other. 'Tell me, Frenchman, does she fuck well?' he asked loudly.

I looked at Katia and said, 'Yes! Oh, yes!' and after a moment softly added, 'Thank you.'

Katia had already retreated into her own private world and her face had lost its knowledge of love but it seemed to me that the shadow of a smile hovered on her lips.

Day was coming to an end and the train slowed down. The Oranienburg guard stood up and said, 'Here we are.' The three prisoners rose reluctantly and, while the guards were saying goodbye and exchanging wishes for a Merry Christmas, I looked at Katia for the last time. Her eyes met mine for a second, burning desperately; I waved at her as I stepped off the train and, very slowly, still holding my eyes, she nodded slightly and then gazed off into the distance.

An hour later, we walked through the gate of a camp lost in a deep dark forest; night had fallen and the raw light from the reflectors gave it the air of a stage setting. Falkensee was a small camp which had only been operational for three months. A central alley gave on to an assembly square, surrounded by administrative buildings and flanked by two parallel alleys lined with a dozen barracks holding about 1,000 prisoners. The whole complex, which lay in the shadows of huge pines, formed a square. At each corner there was a watch-tower and the perimeter was formed by two lines of three-metre-high electrified barbed wire but there was no wall to bar either the view or the prisoners' dreams. Everything was brand new and clean, while the snow that covered all made it look almost pretty.

But things had not always been rosy here. The camp had originally been part of the Starken Camp, the worst of the Sachsenhausen satellites, where workers of the Demag factories, part of Herman Goering's industrial empire, had lived under hellish conditions. Due to the reign of terror of beatings and torture inflicted by the sadistic supervisors, Starken had been known as the Death Camp. From July 1942 to July 1943 more than seventy-five per cent of the inmates had perished. Falkensee had been constructed to meet the demand for new factories and Goering's ever growing greed. It was located more conveniently near the Demag factories than Starken itself which was

six kilometres away. There were a lot of French prisoners in
Falkensee who had organised themselves into a group which
was generally well liked. Most of the camp's bosses were
political prisoners and, as a result, life was a little more
bearable.

I settled in and inspected the infirmary. It was a small wooden
structure set slightly apart from the others. It contained two
twelve-bed wards, a small isolation room, a minor surgery
room, a small pharmacy and a supply station, all very clean,
orderly and well heated.

Before lights out I wandered through the camp. The trees in
the forest rustled in the wind behind the fence, which ran
directly behind the infirmary. I could smell freedom in the scent
of the pines. The electrified wires were barely visible and seemed
trivial to me, only the low humming coming from them
reminded me that death ran through them. I really had the
impression of being in the wilderness and could ignore the
watch-towers, glaring floodlights and menacing machine-guns
pointing at the camp.

I took a closer look at the infirmary which had been set up on
stilts, and it occurred to me how easy it would be to dig a tunnel
there. All sorts of wild ideas hatched in my head but then I
curbed my imagination. What about Paul? I felt contrite for
having forgotten my friend momentarily. I went to bed with
images of Sachsenhausen and the train trip dancing through my
head; I fell asleep in Katia's arms, lulled by a lingering sweetness
and the whirring of the wind.

On the following days I organised myself; I admitted patients,
dressed several nasty wounds and when I got a case beyond my
competence I called in a local doctor, a pale stooped young man
wearing a pince-nez who was terrified of the atmosphere of the
camp and panicked at making any decision.

All of a sudden, I realised it was Christmas Eve. I gathered a
few pine cones and branches to decorate the infirmary. A
certain mellowness swept through the camp and showed on the
prisoners' faces. One of the Frenchmen invited me to share in
their Christmas celebration. Everyone gathered in Block V;
those who had recently received packages from outside shared
generously with those who could only contribute what they had
managed to save out of their meagre reations. The eyes of these

homeless, lonely, depersonalised beings shone as they sang about things they had almost forgotten. Old memories surfaced in my mind: wonder-filled Christmases from my childhood with both my parents; jolly Boy Scout Christmases; sheltered Christmas Eves in snow-covered mountain huts; all the things lost in the past perhaps never to be recaptured. Suddenly I could not hold it in any longer; I rushed out into the freezing cold, leaned against the rough bark of a pungent pine and sobbed my heart out.

14

Sweet Liberty

Twenty days later, I was returned to Sachsenhausen, a very ill man. After Christmas I had done everything I could to make myself sick. I dosed myself with tons of cod liver oil, pills, lifted from the Norwegian Red Cross packages and a cocktail made from anything available: aspirin, turpentine, liquid soap, shoe polish. I had used all the tricks I had learned on my way through prisons and army barracks and had brought myself to the edge of total collapse. My kidneys shut down, my body wasted away from diarrhoea, I refused to eat and I was burning with fever. The village doctor, who had been called in urgently, was baffled and simply could not cope with such a case. After eight days of observations, consultations and hesitations I was declared acutely ill and shipped back to the main camp.

When I arrived, Paul and Emile Coudert came to see me immediately. Coudert could not make head or tail of my confusing symptoms but, sensing something was fishy, finally made a diagnosis sufficiently vague to meet the approval of the mystified SS doctor and I was put under observation. That evening I told Paul and Coudert what I had done; Coudert, who could not imagine why I wanted to return, was outraged.

'You are absolutely crazy, you stupid ass. You could have killed yourself! You're . . . You're . . .' He was so indignant that he began to stammer. Paul took him aside and did his best to calm him down and then returned later to let me know how the preparations for our escape were going. He had really got things moving and everything was falling into place, but I was too sick to take it all in and went to sleep telling myself that I had to get back on my feet as fast as possible.

Paul arrived the next day loaded down like Santa Claus and, as he unpacked, he told me that during my absence he himself had been sent out daily to work with the *Frichtengrund*

Kommando, which was building barracks to house the SS survivors of units from the Russian front who were being regrouped. *Frichtengrund* was located on the edge of the forest beside the road to Oranienburg. Paul had driven a hard bargain before accepting the transfer and had been guaranteed that he would not have to work at all.

As soon as he had arrived at Frichtengrund he had begun an active campaign of charm and demoralisation through his winning personality; of course the generous sharing of his packages of goodies helped considerably. Ham, bacon, sausage and lard usually paved the way to the heart of any normal German but Paul was also able to offer sugar, coffee and jam which were scarce even outside the camp. The SS guard in charge of the *Kommando*, a young Rhinelander called Wolfgang, was captivated by the new prisoner who smilingly offered him wine from grapes grown on the sunny slopes of his homeland. The two became bosom buddies and spent entire afternoons sitting in the office beside a humming stove smoking and sipping wine in cosy warmth while outside the thermometer registered minus twenty degrees Centigrade and workers dropped dead from the cold, overwork and abuse. They talked a lot about the war and Wolfgang confided to Paul that he was worried about the recent turn of events. His house had been hit by a bomb, his father killed, his mother crippled and his fiancée drafted to work in a factory. Paul fanned his fears by harping on the reprisals the Allies were sure to take against the SS, the Gestapo and such as he who were renowned for their ill-treatment of the inmates of the camp. Bowing his head, Wolfgang admitted that he was afraid and didn't know what to do, especially as the SS officials were becoming more and more iron-handed every day and the slightest mistake or any wavering from the true Nazi spirit was immediately punished; one had only to look around to see former soldiers who had been stripped of their uniforms and now wore the stripes of prisoners.

Paul took a shot in the dark and offered Wolfgang a way out. If Wolfgang would help him escape Paul promised him privileged treatment from the Allies after Germany surrendered. At first Wolfgang was stupefied. Paul pretended he had a friend who would go with him who worked for the Allied Secret

Service and could guarantee Wolfgang's safety if they got away. He then showed him my Red Cross package, which Wolfgang carefully inspected. He was impressed, it was authentic down to the seals and stamps and the contents! . . . York ham and bacon, English chocolate, English marmalade, English cigarettes and English vitamins . . .

When they met the following morning, both looked haggard from worry and lack of sleep. Paul, however, felt more sure of himself since he had not been singled out at the evening or morning roll-call. The moment they were alone he uncorked a bottle, poured two glasses, looked the young guard in the eyes and asked:

'What shall we drink to?'

Flushed, Wolfgang raised his glass and toasted: 'To freedom.'

Paul let out a long sigh of relief.

Then Paul told him I had to be transferred to *Fichtengrund* with similar privileges to himself. He also needed two SS uniforms. Wolfgang protested at two. Paul also asked for the location of the front gate, the password for the day, a map and a train time-table. Amazingly, Wolfgang not only agreed but asked if he could go with us. Then I, or what was left of me, had been brought back. I could not find words to express my admiration for Paul's audacity in arranging the escape plan. I asked Paul the date.

'21 January.'

I made a quick calculation: eight days to get back on my feet, three days to get my stuff together. 'What about leaving on 2 February?'

Paul was delighted. 'That's Candlemas.'

I figured out that on 2 February it would be exactly ten months since I had passed through the portals which had informed me that '*Arbeit macht Frei.*'

For ten months, for ten eternities, I had lived in this insane world where sometimes minutes seemed to last for centuries. My sense of time had been subjected completely to feeling. Instead of perceiving time as divided into hours, days and weeks, alternating cycles of terror, joy, pain, dreams, desolation and hope, the real substance of life, were all I could recall of the time I had lived behind the wall.

Bombs fell more and more frequently on Berlin and German

morale fell lower each time. Wolfgang came to regard Paul more and more as a heaven-sent deliverer.

Thanks to my friends' devoted care I was up and about in eight days. Undoubtedly the best medicine of all had been the prospect of freedom. I donned my uniform and made the rounds of the camp to pick up what I had accumulated: two well-cut unmarked jackets, two pairs of trousers, two pairs of leather shoes, two shirts and other useful items such as a compass, a map of Berlin, etc. I stashed it all in an unused cupboard in a corridor in the Pathology Block. I described to Paul what I could remember of the road to the train station which I had travelled twice going to Berlin and to Falkensee; I told him the name of my Berlin friend, the address of the French STO and the password, just in case we should get separated. At last I opened the famous toothpaste tube and got out my 100 marks. To my horror I saw that part of the bill had stuck to the tube, smelled like mint and had turned pink. I soaked it, washed it and laid it out flat to dry; once dry it was perfectly all right except for a faint odour of mint which still clung to it but this was neither illegal nor subversive.

Paul and I had decided to say nothing to anyone until the last minute but it was important that someone else know in case we didn't make it. Thus we decided to give a small dinner party on the eve of 2 February and invited Emile-Louis Coudert and Papa Maurice. We took a long walk with Nicolai before the party, showered him with presents and embraced him affectionately before bidding him goodnight. Nicolai didn't understand what was happening but was enchanted. He had already started towards his block when he hesitated and turned around. An expression of anxiety flickered over his face.

'Until tomorrow, Alec?'

'Of course, Nicolai, until tomorrow.'

'Tomorrow really? Really tomorrow?' insisted Nicolai, not quite believing me.

'No, Nicolai. Not tomorrow.'

Nicolai gaped like a fish out of water and turned grey. 'Not tomorrow!' He made a forlorn gesture and shuffled away, his back bent. Then he stopped, turned around again, tried to smile through his tears and waved goodbye. 'Not tomorrow!'

Paul had decided to squander his hoard. The four of us met in a room in one of the hospital blocks for our farewell dinner. Paul uncorked a bottle of special Rhine wine which he had been saving for the occasion and filled the glasses. Galouen and Coudert watched him eagerly. Paul solemnly lifted his glass: 'A toast to tomorrow because tomorrow Alec and I shall either be free or dead.'

The two friends gaped in shocked silence for a few moments, then the questions flew thick and fast. 'How? When? Where?'

'We can't tell you. It isn't that we don't trust you. If we didn't you wouldn't be here but everyone who knows us will surely be questioned afterwards and the less you know the better for all concerned.'

As we emptied our glasses the air-raid sirens began to shriek; the lights went out; we could hear men running and shouting orders. The dinner party was cut short. We embraced each other, choked with excitement, fear and concern.

It was a bad raid. We could see the bursts of flak way up high flickering like lightning. The searchlights wove a spider's web across the sky, sometimes snaring a plane in their beams. The armada of bombers passed over the camp and a few minutes later we heard the distant thunder of the explosions over Berlin; then the orange-red afterglow of the incendiaries, diffused by the clouds of dust and smoke, kindled the sky. The hearts of thousands of prisoners sang with hope; our silent jubilation could almost be heard.

The raid seemed to last forever. I lay on my bunk, arms under my head, reminiscing about lost friends, endless days and all I had learned. I didn't dare let myself think about tomorrow. Everything had been prepared and rehearsed over and over again. A sack containing my equipment and the envelope with the top-secret documents provided by the 'printers' lay beside me. I got up quietly around 4.00 a.m. in pitch blackness, went into a small room that served as a surgical supply room, put on a suit and leather shoes under my striped uniform and cape, and hung a small bag with the secret documents around my neck. A bell rang at 4.30 for roll-call.

Roll-call was interminable and the waiting was fast becoming unbearable. When assembly broke up and began to disperse into separate work groups I quickly made my way to the *Frichtengrund Kommando* to which I had been assigned the evening before. Paul, looking very pale, was already there and our eyes met briefly from a distance. I reported to the *Kommando's Vorarbeiter* who welcomed me warmly. I saw a few acquaintances from the camp who were surprised at my presence.

I explained evasively that, since I was recuperating from a bout of pneumonia, the doctor had prescribed fresh air and no contact with the TB patients. I didn't really think I had been very convincing but then an order rang out and their attention was turned elsewhere.

'Line up. Ranks of five. Roll-call.' The workers were recounted. The column began to march towards the converging spotlight beams and came to a halt a short distance from the central gate. 'Line up.' Again the count was taken. 'Forward. March. *Links, zwei, drei, vier.*' The SS guards, accompanied by their slobbering pets, had joined and surrounded us, guns at the ready. The prisoners' clogs clacked rhythmically as we marched down Gallow's Alley. We passed the guard post heads high, fingers rigidly stretched downward, jaws jutting forward martially, the bowls suspended from our belts knocking against our buttocks. The passage of the *Frichtengrund Kommando* through the main gate was duly noted on the ledger. Daylight had not broken and the road seemed very dark to our eyes, blinded by the glaring spotlights; actually it was lit faintly by the glimmer of the snow-covered ground.

We walked quickly. I recalled the first time I had seen a workers' column. Today I was a member of a similar ghostly procession; the world had come full circle, but bundled up and sweating in my double layer of clothing, I was walking towards freedom . . . towards life! I refused to consider that anything might go wrong. My heart quieted to a normal rate and my breathing became easier. I started to observe the forest which I had seen so often silhouetted against the sky from behind the high wall. Escape Phase I was over.

We reached the work camp forty-five minutes later. Again line-up, roll-call, recount. I felt as if I was in a dream. The whistle sounded and the prisoners dispersed to their different assignments. Only Paul and I turned and walked towards a door where Wolfgang was waiting for us. He looked so young, so blond, so robust, so red faced, so edgy. He pointed at me with his riding crop.

'Is that him?'

'Yes, that's him.'

'Did he agree to everything?'

'Yes, I did. To everything,' I said.

'Officer's word of honour?'

'Yes. You have my word of honour.'

'Did you get the green light?'

'Of course. Otherwise I wouldn't be here. Are you coming with us?'

'No, I can't. I must stay but here are my particulars.' He handed me a small card on which he had written down his name, address and serial number.

I put it in my pocket and said authoritatively, 'This will do.'

My tone of voice caused a typical reflex reaction; Wolfgang sprang to attention, puffed out his chest, clicked his feet together and saluted.

He led us to an empty half-finished barrack and with a gesture waved Paul in. Paul found a heap of military clothing behind the door. He stripped hastily and donned the uniform which fitted, the belt, the cap, the tunic. The result was nightmarishly impressive. 'What about my friend?' he asked Wolfgang, who had been on look-out at the door.

'I could only get one uniform but there are any number of kits available next to the cots in that barrack over there, which is occupied. We can take him there and he can take his pick.'

Accompanied by the two 'SS officials', I was taken to the barrack, a distance of about one block. The barrack was empty. I stepped in and saw ten blue- and white-checked made-up beds. A small locker stood beside each one. I opened one at random and found a set of military gear. I took off my striped uniform and sat down on the bed. I was just reaching for the uniform on its hanger when someone opened the door and came in. Tousled hair, towel around his neck, knitted vest, pants unbuttoned, suspenders down to his calves – he was obviously just coming from the lavatory.

Dumbfounded he stammered, 'But . . . but . . .' Then he saw the striped outfit.

Before he had time to add two and two, I lunged, grabbed a heavy wooden stool and brought it crashing down on the intruder's head, who thumped to the floor. I looked at the door but no one else was there. My temples throbbing, shaking like a leaf, drenched in sweat, nauseated, I somehow managed to get the trousers on. They were much too short – too bad! I pulled them down over my shoes. The tunic was impossible. I couldn't even button it. Luckily I found another one more or less my size in the next locker. Belt. Cap. A small haversack into which I stuffed all the things I was carrying in my striped cape. I grabbed the limp Fritz by the feet and dragged him forward a few feet and pushed him well out of view under the bed. I put on my cap, checked myself quickly and flew out the door.

Paul and Wolfgang, completely unaware of what had happened, were waiting calmly. I quickly told them what had just occurred and Wolfgang turned ashen.

'I can't be seen with you. Take that wide paved alley over there, go straight for half a block and you'll find the gate to the camp. There's usually a guard at the post. He's the one who lifts the barrier. When you get there stop a few metres from the post and come to attention. He'll let you through without question. What with all the things that have been happening lately, the control has become slipshod. Goodbye. Good luck. If you're caught, I don't know you and you don't know me. If you get away, don't forget me.' He smiled wanly. 'Incredible!'

Paul and I smiled back and walked on shoulder to shoulder. When we got to the main alley we stepped up the pace and assumed a military air. Practically no one was around. We only met a few soldiers who did not even glance at us. Our throats contracted in fear when we were about thirty metres from the gate. What if the man I had knocked out had been found? What if I had killed him? Then we saw the guard run from the guard-house shouting and disappear from our sight. We were terror-stricken but continued to advance so as not to call attention to ourselves.

I whispered, 'If that's because of us, we'll shove him aside and it's each man for himself. If we get out, we'll meet at the STO camp in Charlottenburg.' Paul nodded.

The barrier was up and the road was clear. When we got there we realised why the guard had behaved so strangely. He was greeting a friend and the two were joyfully slapping each other on the back. Remembering what we had been told, Paul and I came to attention but seeing that no one was paying us any attention we continued to walk . . . and walk. We walked past the barrier and down the small road. Instinctively I looked at my watch; it was 6.35 a.m. We turned right and approached the first houses of a small town a few moments later. A man in uniform walked towards us. The skull-and-crossbone insignia on his cap identified him as an SS officer. I froze.

'Salute, you idiot! Salute!' hissed Paul, as he raised his arm in an exuberant Heil Hitler salute.

I pulled a blank. How the hell did one salute? Hand to the cap like the French, the English way, Jesus, how? Then looking at Paul I followed suit and lifted my arm olympically. Fortunately I had imitated Paul closely enough that the SS officer did not take it amiss. He returned the salute and continued on his way. We looked at each other in disbelief; we couldn't imagine we had passed ourselves off as the real thing. Paul cut a fine figure: he wore one stripe, which made him some kind of non-commissioned officer and the armband distinguished him as a *Hundeführer*. An additional black armband adorned with silver letters stated '*Leibstandarte Adolf Hitler*', making him a member of the highest SS aristocracy. My uniform was humbler – I was a private and belonged to the '*Leibstandarte Gross Deutschland*', but I did have an Iron Cross and so I puffed out my chest in spurious pride.

We arrived at the station after a twenty-minute walk just as day broke. I looked up the schedule and verified that there was a train to Berlin due in ten minutes. I walked up to the ticket window, pulled out my 100-mark bill and held my breath hoping that the pink tinge and minty odour would not awaken the ticket inspector's, suspicions. The ticket inspector was impassive.

The workers of the early morning shift were packed into the train like sardines; people looked harassed. The talk concerned last night's big raid. Many were wondering if they would be able to find their work places at all. The train was slowing to a stop when a young girl standing next to Paul suddenly began to abuse him. I was horrified. I didn't know what had happened but I knew we had to avoid attracting attention at all costs. As I listened to the girl's tirade I realised that Paul, who hadn't been near a woman for over four years, had not been able to resist the temptation of the sweet young thing pressing against him and had lovingly patted her on the behind. Luckily, the train stopped at that moment, people were in a hurry to get to work and the incident was closed.

I knew the way; we went down a staircase which gave on to a subterranean passageway. We were so absorbed in reading and following the signs so as not to lose our way that we didn't even realise we were walking straight into a trap. A Feldgendarmerie patrol identified by the metal plaques on their chests was lining up all military personnel against the wall and checking their papers. The air raids and the chaotic military situation had produced a veritable epidemic of deserters and AWOLs and the army was trying to put an end to it. Paul and I consulted rapidly and were just getting ready to lose ourselves in the mob when a brawl broke out in front of us.

A soldier whose papers were not in order was loudly cursing the Military Police. Yes, he had come from the front. Not only that, he had been wounded. His home had disappeared. He had no news of his family. Nothing was going to stop him from trying to find them – leave or no leave! He was striking out and the Military Police were holding on to him. Taking advantage of the providential confusion, Paul and I stepped out of line with an innocent air and walked nonchalantly towards the stairway leading to the Berlin U-Bahn platform. Paul was already halfway up the stairs when he turned back to look for me . . . Then he saw me still at the bottom, holding on to the arm of an old lady climbing the steps with great effort.

I had had to solve a problem which could have proved disastrous: I had pulled down my too short trousers and had done all right as long as I could take short steps, but to climb stairs when the crotch of my trousers was nearly around my knees was another thing. I stood there trying to realise the magnitude of the practical joke being played on me by Destiny when a little old lady took me by the arm.

'My poor boy! You have been wounded! Just take it easy and I'll help you. My son is a soldier too so when I do something for one of our brave boys, I feel I'm doing it for him.'

Calm had been restored in the passageway and if one of the military policemen had happened to look towards the stairway he would have seen the edifying spectacle of a wounded German hero lovingly supported by his proud *Mutti*.

After an uneventful U-Bahn ride we got off at the Charlottenburg Station, where we had no difficulty in locating the restaurant where Labuche's STO camp was installed. The establishment had seen better days. There was a street-side terrace covered with an awning. A sign over the building announced that here was the 'Restaurant-Weinstube'. Casement windows with imitation leaded stained glass ran around the façade but had been boarded up. We knocked on the carved double oak doors situated on the corner which were opened cautiously by a round pot-bellied bald-headed man who peered nervously at us over his round glasses.

'*Merde!*' he exclaimed in frightened French when he caught sight of our SS uniforms. His round vividly black eyes darted from one to the other.

'Herr Labuche?' I asked.

'Labuche? Home. Liberated. To France. Not here.' The answer was stammered out in halting German.

We pushed Butterball to one side and went in. 'Don't be afraid. We're French. We're friends of Labuche. Are you alone?'

'Yes.'

'Then you'll have to help us. We must get rid of our uniforms first and then we'll explain.'

The little man did not waste any time. Very efficiently he helped us to strip and then cut up and throw our telltale clothes into the coal furnace.

There was an inscription engraved on the belt buckle with the inspiring words '*Gott mit uns*' which Paul sentimentally kept as a souvenir. 'What a motto!'

'I hope you feel the same way when they hang you from that thing!'

In a trice, Paul and I had the appearance of two innocuous civilians. I introduced myself as an ex-medical student from Paris and Paul as a businessman from Metz. 'We are prisoners of war who managed to escape from a Stalag. We had tried twice before to get out but were caught. The third time was the charm.'

'I'm Georges Veron. I was a waiter at the pavement café at the Terminus St Lazare Restaurant in Paris for twenty years. You must have been there.'

'Of course,' I answered, 'but let's get down to business. If anyone questions you, you never saw any SS uniforms. You don't know anything about us, but you think we are STO workers whose camp has been bombed. All right?'

'You bet. How about a cup of coffee?'

'Can you tell us who lives here? Are you checked up on? Labuche told me you were sort of isolated and quiet here.'

'Well, there are only ten of us here. We're all French, all good friends, and all fed up to the back teeth with the Huns. As far as the check-up is concerned, it's practically nil. The local police station was blown up recently and we think they must have forgotten about us. The rest of the guys left for work about 5.00 this morning as usual and should be back around 6.00. You're welcome to stay here. There are extra beds and you can fix your own meals on the stove.'

Georges showed us around. The main dining-room of the restaurant had been converted into a dormitory holding thirty double-deck bunks but, since there was more than enough room for all, the residents had been able to convert the room into private cubicles by nailing khaki-coloured bedspreads to the bunk frames. The huge bright kitchen contained all sorts of professional restaurant equipment, several commercial stoves and numerous cupboards.

We sat down at a big table surrounded by a dozen or so chairs, so we presumed that this room was being used as a lounge. Our rumbling stomachs reminded us that we had not eaten anything since last night's celebration dinner. The memory brought to mind the faces of our good friends – Coudert, Nicolai and the others – and it dawned upon us that we had indeed made it and we were filled with intense joy.

We decided to take it easy for a while. We needed to get some food coupons but first we had to get our bearings, so we agreed to get in touch with an old friend, Boris de Brodski, who had been part of the group of Tunisians who had arrived at Sachsenhausen after me. Like me, he had been sent to the *Reichssicherheitshauptamt* but, unlike me, he and a few others had been set free by the unfathomable SS system. Boris had written to a friend at the camp giving his new address. He had been assigned quarters in Spandau, a suburb of Berlin.

'I suppose they won't realise we have escaped until this afternoon so they won't put out a bulletin on us until tomorrow morning. Maybe we should get in touch with Boris right now.'

We telephoned Boris at lunch time and made a date to meet

him at a nearby café. I got there half an hour before to make
sure I was not walking into a trap. I intercepted Boris walking
towards the rendezvous and led him to another restaurant
where Paul was waiting.

Boris, a raw-boned stooped man with wavy grey hair, wore
thick glasses which magnified his mouse-like myopic eyes. His
fumbling fingers finished off the picture of the proverbial spy. I
tried not to laugh.

Boris said, 'I see they let you go too.'

'Well . . . not exactly.'

'What do you mean, not exactly?' Boris burst out. 'You
didn't by any chance . . .?'

'Shh!' I interrupted him. 'Not exactly by chance. Mum's the
word.'

'You must be out of your mind getting in touch with me. Surely
you realise that I'll be the first one to be suspected of helping you.
They'll stick me back in that hell hole . . . or hang me . . . or . . .
What have you done!' He was in a panic.

'Slow down, we aren't putting you in a bind. We've already got
a place to stay, and money. Besides, they don't even know yet we
are missing. All we want from you is information – which places
to avoid, which transportation to take, where to get food coupons. Really, all we want is a practical guide to Berlin.'

De Brodski answered all our questions and even went so far as
to give us a few food coupons, but refused to listen to a word
about our future plans. To cover our tracks Paul spun a tall tale
of trying to get to Switzerland and we parted good friends – Paul
and I full of useful information and de Brodski empty of all
knowledge and wanting to remain in that happy state.

Overcome by fatigue and hunger, we started back. Paul volunteered to do the shopping and arrived an hour later loaded down
with sausage, margarine, vegetables and a large quantity of
bread. His face beamed as he put the things on the table under the
approving gaze of Veron.

'You know, Alec, she is something!'

'So soon? Who?'

'The baker's wife just across the street. She's young, pretty
and, best of all, her husband's away fighting a war, leaving her to
run the bakery. Just look at what she gave me and she refused to
take even one coupon for it.'

I thought about the episode aboard the train that morning and wondered exactly where Paul had put his hands this time, but tactfully I kept quiet. While we were fixing dinner the rest of the crew came back, they welcomed us and I was relieved to see that they showed no undue curiosity about me and Paul. Before going to bed I conscientiously checked all the exits just to be on the safe side.

As we lay on our bunks Paul said, 'Pinch me.'

'What?'

'Pinch me. I can't believe how lucky we have been.'

And it was true! All the improvisations had gone like clockwork; I was disconcerted at how smoothly it had gone.

My mind then went back to the camp and I began to reflect on the consequences our escape would have on our companions. I could envisage the prisoners of the Kommando lined up in ranks of five for the roll-call, being counted and recounted, the ensuing search with Wolfgang aggressively leading it, the return to Sachsenhausen, the report of the frightened guards and *Vorarbeiters*, the rousting out of the entire camp, to be counted and recounted again and again under the bitterly cold snow. How many would survive the night?

'Luck? Do you really think it's luck? I'm not so sure. Don't you think it's time to render unto Caesar what is Caesar's?'

'And to God what is God's!' finished Paul.

From habit we both awoke at the usual middle-of-the-night hour to go to work and it took us a few minutes to remember that it was over! We were free!

15

Berlin

When Paul and I walked through Berlin in early February 1944 more than half the city had been reduced to heaps of bricks and cement slabs, twisted iron and shapeless rubble; whole city blocks had been levelled and we could see endless debris as far as the horizon.

The wind blew through the skeletons of buildings and only wall segments still covered by patterned paper stood as reminders that someone had once lived there. The two of us were appalled at the sight of freakish fragments forgotten by the destruction: a gilt-framed mirror hanging between heaven and earth; a bathtub clinging to the wall by its drainpipe; a chest with a vase of flowers whose colours clashed with the dusty greyness; a set of kitchen pots hanging on their hooks; a coat rack with a jacket dangling from a hanger. The crumbling buildings had spilled their innards into the street stopping most of the traffic. Curiously, some neighbourhoods appeared intact from a distance, but when we approached them only scorched walls stood gaping as through blind eyes. Some sections were still undamaged but the unremitting Allied bombers pounded them day and night.

The ragged, dirty Berliners silently scavenged the ruins like busy ants. The biting north wind blew snow flurries around old men, kerchiefed women and children who were stubbornly digging with their picks and shovels into the rubble and embers, while apprehensively raising their eyes to the skies, dreading the next attack. Here and there we could see parked ambulances, firemen and homeguardsmen doggedly trying to unearth the dead and looking for survivors in caved-in cellars. Thousands had taken refuge in one of the underground stations which had received a direct hit and now, forty-eight hours later, people were still bringing up bits and pieces of the butchery.

Could this be crime and punishment? The mills of God? We had more reason than most to think so, but when we witnessed the carnage, the mangled bodies piled in the ambulance, when our eyes met the panicked look of a child whose silence was more eloquent than any sobs or screams, even we could only ask ourselves the same question everyone else was asking – Why?

Looking at the blasted-out windows in some of the buildings, I had an idea.

'Look, Paul, it's dangerous to wander through the streets like this. We need money, we should get a hammer, nails, a pair of pliers and scissors and offer to board up people's windows with cardboard to keep out the draughts.'

That evening we went to the restaurant around the corner. It was humid, hot and stuffy and smelled of stale tobacco, cabbage and beer. While we ate the *Eintopf* (one-dish meal imposed by the Führer as an austerity measure symbolising solidarity with the regime) we kept our ears open to the conversations buzzing around us. From what we could hear, German morale was sinking. Even hard-core Nazis were pessimistic. We heard the same refrain over and over: 'When will it be over?'

By morning it had stopped snowing but a thick fog had settled over the city making it appear even more ghostly. Carrying our tools Paul and I cheerfully set out upon our new business venture. The evening before Paul had got hold of a small Tyrolean hat adorned with a shaving brush tuft and he looked totally Teutonic. I had opted for a stolid proletarian look and was wearing a worker's cap. For some reason I couldn't understand, the effect had not quite come off and I looked more like a tout at the racetrack but decided it didn't really matter. We went across town to avoid being recognised as residents of the STO camp just in case something went wrong.

When we rang the bell at the first apartment, a small woman wearing her hair in a tight bun on the top of her head opened the door. She was alone in the windswept apartment and suspicious and frightened of strangers, but when she heard of the service we were offering she gave us a warm welcome. We set to work quickly, cut cardboard to size, removed broken panes and old nails, scraped off old putty and began to hammer.

I had had good training in the use of tools during my Boy Scout days but not so Paul, who hit his finger, then the nail, then his finger, then the nail . . . We finished around noon and received a magnificent fee – so much cash per hour, so many food coupons worth their weight in gold and a luscious lunch – real *pot-au-feu* and apple tart!

We got another job in the same building during the afternoon but when we finished Paul declared that he definitely was not adept at carpentry and, anyway, the baker's wife had made him several very interesting propositions so he could foresee a brilliant future at the bakery.

In the middle of the night, the air-raid siren woke us. At first we remained in bed but then became so afraid that we rushed to the cellar next door. There, among the old men, women and children and under the iron rule of the Cellar Chief (there was always a Chief for everything in Germany) we underwent the most hair-raising raid imaginable. 'Bizerte was nothing,' I thought.

Innumerable waves of bombers kept passing over with their fiendish droning, shaking the house to its foundations. The anti-aircraft batteries scattered throughout the city were firing frantically and I could hear the empty shell casings fall like dense hail on the roofs and streets. A long whistle presaging the arrival of a bomb swelled to a screech; everyone tried to burrow into the ground. Then dead silence followed by an ear-splitting detonation which shook the house. Earth trickled down from the ceiling of the badly built shelter, the light dimmed and we thought our last hour had come. No sooner had we straightened up than the next bomb announced its arrival.

The candle-lit stricken faces of the people in the cellar looked like grotesque masks. The women howled and their terror was transmitted to the children who took up the chorus. A gaunt, uncombed woman hastily dressed in a bathrobe, who would have been considered attractive under other circumstances, clung to me. I had no idea what to do with her. When the raid was over we could hear cries for help, moans and the scary crackling of fires through the airvent even though it was partially stopped up with boards and slabs of concrete. More than a dozen bombs had fallen in our vicinity in less than half an hour.

We couldn't believe our eyes when we finally left the shelter. The entire city seemed to be ablaze; it was as bright as day. Thousands of fires had been started by incendiary bombs and were melting the snow. People were slogging around in the slush. No one knew where to begin. Some fire trucks circulated aimlessly; the fire hydrants were either broken or buried and the fires which smouldered were difficult to locate. The house next door had suffered a direct hit and was a mass of rubble, licking flames and a cloud of dust. The house had caved in on the cellar and there was no sign of life. The woman still hung on to me; I gently disengaged myself and slowly walked away with Paul.

We met our housemates at the restaurant and everyone was elated to be still alive. I asked if the big public shelters were not safer than the poorly constructed house cellars.

'It's not even worth considering,' said Georges Veron. 'They're bigger, of course, but not any safer. Besides, foreigners are forbidden to enter and the police check identity cards at the exit.' I made a mental note of this.

Paul crossed the street next morning to earn his daily bread. I walked to the buildings where we had worked the day before. A bomb had struck nearby and broken more windows and opened holes in the façade which gave me some made-to-order opportunities to earn my living. 'I don't think I'll have a hard time getting customers today,' I thought as I mounted the steps and rang the first doorbell.

'What is it? What do you want?' said a woman's worried voice through the closed door. I explained my business and mentioned the two customers of yesterday as references. The door opened a crack but the chain stayed on. I was examined and finally the door opened.

'Come in. Please forgive all my precautions but a woman who lives alone cannot be too careful nowadays.'

I could not see her clearly in the dim vestibule but noticed that she was tall, slender and dressed in what was probably the early morning uniform for the women of the neighbourhood – a flannel bathrobe, woollen socks, her hair in a turban and a towel in her hand.

'Come take a look and see what you can do.'

I followed her through the apartment – five ostentatious,

expensively decorated rooms, carved furniture, crystal chande-
liers, allegorical pictures and a profusion of knick-knacks. It
was ice cold and everything had been turned topsy turvy by the
raid. I suggested I should do the kitchen, bathroom and
bedroom first so they could be heated and made habitable and
that the furniture which was getting soaked from the rain and
snow should be moved immediately. The lady agreed and I went
to buy some nails, thumbtacks and cardboard which were being
sold like hot cakes on every street corner.

When I returned loaded down like a mule I put my things
down, shook the rain off and took off my jacket. 'I'll get
straight to –' I stopped in mid sentence and looked at her.

God, she was beautiful! Her hair was a warm glowing gold
and tumbled in short curls around her fair face. Her eyes were
crystalline and sparkled like aquamarines – or was it amethysts?
She had changed into navy blue slacks and a turquoise sweater
which moulded her shoulders and high taut breasts. She was
amused at my confusion and gently taunted me, 'You were
saying . . .? You were going to do what?'

'Get to work,' I stammered, trying to recover from the shock.

'All right, then, get going.'

While I repaired the windows she tidied up the apartment. I
kept watching her out of the corner of my eye and, of course,
pounded my fingers with the hammer. 'I'm as unhandy as Paul,'
I thought ruefully. But my eyes were drawn irresistibly back to
her. Her every movement was filled with poise and grace but
there was nothing coquettish about her.

Shortly after noon I stopped. 'If you don't mind I'd like to get
a bite to eat. I'll be back in an hour.' But she invited me to
lunch! We sat down to an improvised meal in the kitchen,
which was dim now that only a little light came in through the
boarded up window and from a candle burning on the table. I
kept discovering her. She must be in her thirties . . .

Her glance caught mine and I quickly said, 'What a delightful
lunch!' She laughed. What sparkling teeth . . . and her smile! It
carved a dimple in her cheek making her look so very young . . .
her lovely voice sometimes sank into huskiness . . . and her
hands! They were nimble fingered, strong and sensitive and she
underlined her words with graphic gestures . . . I was spell-
bound.

'Aren't you hungry?' she asked.

'Oh, of course! Of course I am. Excuse me.'

I tried to follow what she was saying. Her name was Hanni. She was married. Her husband was in the Army but she had had no news of him. He was lost somewhere in the Russian snow. She was – an astronomer! But the observatory where she worked had been destroyed, so at the moment she was staying at home as she didn't want to leave Berlin. She had no children and remarked that, looking at the destruction surrounding them, for the first time in her life she felt glad. She was rich but didn't give a damn about money. And now she could only watch her world collapse around her, and all because no one had stopped the madman who was leading Germany to her doom.

I told her of my life, of my dreams, of my love for the mountains, of medicine, of people I had known, of the occupation of France, of my family, of my friends, of everything except the last few years – these I skipped saying I would rather not talk about them. I told her I had lost everything I owned in a raid and was now trying to make ends meet by doing odd jobs, biding my time.

As I listened and looked at her, I felt lured by a strange magnetic current radiating from her. I shook myself to break the spell. 'Let's get to work unless you want to sleep in an icebox tonight.'

We bustled around as before but something had subtly changed between us. She stayed close to me and examined this stranger who had invaded her privacy. The atmosphere between us was charged with a delightful undefinable tension. We became more and more aware of each other and were filled with a sweet foreboding.

'Damn!' said Hanni loudly when she dusted the same knick-knack for the third consecutive time.

When I was finally satisfied that her shelter for the night would be fairly warm darkness had long since fallen. 'Shall I come back tomorrow?'

'If you want to.'

'Good night, Hanni.'

She gave me her hand and I trembled at the touch. I walked home with my head in the clouds. I kept seeing her – her face, her gestures, the expression in her eyes – I kept running into lamp-posts and bumping into people, stepping into puddles, but my heart sang.

Paul was waiting anxiously for me at the camp. 'I was worried about you. It's very late. How did it go?'

'Oh, all right. I worked all day but still have to finish up tomorrow. What did you do all day?'

Paul's face was drawn and his eyes were ringed with dark circles. 'Oh, me? I spent the whole day at the bakery. I haven't had one free moment.' I was discreet enough not to ask what he had been doing. Paul was hungry. 'Did you bring anything for dinner?'

I came down to earth with a thump. 'My God, I completely forgot to charge!' Somewhat embarrassed, Paul admitted that he had done the same. Fortunately there were some noodles left over from the day before.

Next morning I rose at six, shaved closely. Lacking shoe polish, I brushed my shoes to a high gloss and set off to work the moment day broke. Hanni was still half asleep when she opened the door.

'For heaven's sake, Alec, what time is it?'

'I don't really know but it's certainly more than time to see you again. I couldn't wait any longer.'

She gave me a funny look and blushed. 'Come. Let's have a cup of coffee first.' Her hair was entangled from sleep and I could hardly resist the temptation to run my fingers through it. Her sleepy eyes smiled at me; she looked so vulnerable!

I breathed in deeply; I felt alive again. I got busy and she disappeared only to reappear a while later wearing a soft grey dress, white woollen stockings, buckled flat shoes, a band holding back her shining hair, a gay scarf encircling her neck. She looked sporty and sophisticated, her eyes were shining! How lovely she was!

She had climbed on to a chair to hang an ornate antique mirror when I saw her lose her balance. In a split second I had the mirror, put it on the floor, helped her down and held her in my arms. Our cheeks touched. Hers were warm and smelt of hyacinths.

'Oh, Hanni, I love you! I can think only of you!' My voice shook; I was trembling.

Pliant in my arms, her lips opened slightly and slowly I kissed her with infinite gentleness and felt her respond. I was inflamed by the searing fire of her thighs and breasts pressing against me and as our kiss deepened I was transported. Never leaving her mouth, I carried her into the bedroom and laid her carefully on the bed. Her breath quickened and she moaned softly as my hands touched her and I discovered the delights of her body as I slowly undressed her in the dim light. I ripped off my clothes and I cried out with pleasure and urgency as I felt her naked against me. It had been so long . . .

I tore myself away when night came as I didn't want Paul to be worried about me.

On the following days we drew the drapes to hide the ugly patches in the walls and shut out the world, and kept the apartment warm and snug by burning wood scavenged from the ruins.

We came from such different worlds and if it had not been for the winds of war we would never have met. We had known fear and loneliness and were starved for warmth, tenderness and love. We found ourselves now in the eye of the hurricane – idle, available and freed from the restraints imposed by society.

I tried to ignore the small voice which whispered that what war had granted, war could destroy. I knew our passion was ephemeral and that we could be torn apart at any moment, that we would then have to continue on as before, or almost . . . This premonition, however, only added depth and urgency to our feelings.

We laughed, talked and hungered for each other. Together we reached into a world of luminous love.

'Hanni, talk to me about the moon.' And Hanni drew me into her universe. She sat stark naked on the bed clasping her knees and lifted her eyes dreamily to the ceiling as if she could see the sky. She spoke of the stars, the planets, the cosmos, the harmony which ruled the infinity of the space in which they moved. She spoke of her studies, of the research that was being done – of still unexplored radiations that might one day clarify the question of matter, of the established order which ruled all celestial movements in the seemingly chaotic cosmos, which only feebly reflected the immense glory of its Creator. I was enthralled.

'What about your husband? Do you love him?'

Her face hardened and her eyes veiled over. I regretted my question.

'Oh, Erich is an admirable man from any point of view. He is a polished patrician, a lover of music, he is – he was a successful lawyer but everything was over between us before the war began. But when he went off to war I felt it was my duty to stand by him. However, as you can see, it is enough for an apprentice carpenter to come to nail cardboard on the windows for my enormous sense of duty to evaporate. But why this morbid curiosity, Alec? It can only conjure up ghosts between us. In all the centuries I have loved you this is the first false note I can remember. What about you? Who is the woman in your life? What's she like?'

I was silent for a moment, then looked at her very seriously and said, 'Well, she's not much to brag about. Her hair looks like a wheat field after a storm. Her pert nose catches the raindrops. She's freckled like a guinea hen and as narrow hipped as a gnu. She has dirty feet from walking barefoot. She claims she's an astronomer and it must be true because, when I make love to her, I see millions of stars.' She flung a pillow at me. 'Hanni, oh Hanni! I love you!'

'Alec, take me to the mountains.'

And I told her of nights spent in mountain shelters, of the absolute confidence which reigned among climbing companions, of the slow climbs, of the glow of dawn on the glaciers, of the dark blue of the unfathomable crevices, of the grasping on sheer vertical cliffs, of the intoxication of reaching the summit. 'You see, each time I got there I was getting a little nearer to you without knowing it. Where else can you almost touch your stars?' I paused. 'Hanni, how old are you?'

She wrinkled up her nose and sighed, 'Thirty-one. I could almost be your mother. Why?'

'Because you have the ardour and surrender of a young girl and the sensuality and wisdom of a woman.'

Aroused by my words, we again lost ourselves in passion.

When Hanni returned to earth she ran her fingers playfully over my body. 'You're as thin as a rake, Alec. You're covered with scars and welts. Tell me, where do you come from?'

'Let's not talk about Hell when we are in Heaven.'

'You're right . . . You must have been in a raid.'

'Yes, Hanni, in a raid!'

The time came when we were out of firewood and food. I remembered Paul. We parted as if for the last time. As I left the apartment I saw she had again metamorphosed into an elegant woman of the world.

I spoke to Paul, ran his errands and sold my watch, a birthday present from 1939 which had served me well. I bought a bouquet of flowers, a rare commodity in the winter in Berlin, to offer to Hanni on our fifth anniversary – we had known each other for all of five days.

At 3.00 p.m. the sirens shrieked and I had a ringside seat for the spectacle of a daytime air raid. The rumble of the anti-aircraft guns gradually increased until I was enveloped in noise. The slow thumping of the heavy artillery blended with the barking bursts of the machine-guns and I could see hundreds of blimps blithely balancing in a sky punctuated by little black puffs. Then I saw the majestic Flying Fortresses approaching, indifferent to the flak and the Luftwaffe fighters that swarmed around them like hornets. They came on and on in ranks of six, wing-tips almost touching. The cold winter sun reflected off their silver cabins. They seemed to be powered by a irresistible supernatural force.

The first one was hit! It fell from the formation in a tailspin, trailing tendrils of black smoke. Some planes fell on the city, their cargo detonating in a reverberating roar. Others exploded in mid-air, their fragments slowly swirling downward. I saw men shoot through the air like bullets, their trajectory suddenly arrested by the snapping open of the white flowers of their parachutes which floated them down to earth. Soldiers, anti-aircraft crews, old scrawny men of the Home Guard, anyone who had a weapon shot frenziedly at the helpless human targets. Some of the punctured parachutes turned into crackling torches and their burdens fell like stones. Some, only slightly damaged, softly deposited their dead on the ground. The ones who survived miraculously were immediately attacked by civilians – a fear-crazed mob which stoned them, tried to tear them to pieces or threw them dead or alive into the pyres of their own making.

I was warned off the street by an air-raid warden and not

wanting to risk a public shelter I took refuge behind a pile of
rubble. The effects of the raid were devastating. Even though I
was far from the centre of the city I felt I was being blown away
by a hurricane. The sound of the explosions was ear-splitting
and their breath carried away trees, cars and pieces of walls.
Long sky-rending shrieks added their horror to the cacophony.
The earth shook, split open and spewed out plumes of mud and
debris. Everything was ablaze. People were driven out of the
shelters and blinded ran around in circles holding their hands
over their ears. I couldn't stand it much longer.

I was lying flat on my stomach next to a piece of wall, my
nose buried in the golden chrysanthemums I had bought for
Hanni. A deafening silence, even worse than the preceding
pandemonium, marked the end of the raid. But then came the
cries, the moans, the gurgle of the police whistles so utterly
incongruous in this apocalyptic world. People improvised rescue operations and again I saw burnt, mutilated dead. As I ran
across the street I saw a small boy in short pants and white
socks, lying spreadeagled on his stomach. The child had been
decapitated; I screamed, threw up and then ran away.

Suddenly I thought . . . Hanni! Oh, my God, Hanni! I ran and
ran! I didn't dare to say her name out loud, but it rang like an
invocation in my head as I ran and ran through streets filled
with ruins and smouldering fires, as I pushed through the
stunned crowds, as I hurdled obstacles. Hanni! Oh, my God,
Hanni! I saw her face, heard her voice. I ran like a man
possessed clutching her flowers. Finally I got to the wide avenue
that led to her apartment building. Large trees lay splintered
across it and scorched car carcasses littered it. Night was
already falling when I came to a dead stop! In front of me,
where the building should have been, there was only a pile of
smoking rubble. A thick cloud of unsettled dust still floated
above it. A handful of people moved aimlessly around. My
knees buckled and I tried to scream out the question that was
suffocating me, but only managed to open and close my mouth
like a guppy out of water. One of the women who was standing
there looked familiar.

I finally brought out: 'Have you seen Frau von . . .'

She looked at me and sighed, 'Yes, I saw her when they got
her out. The whole house collapsed, there were practically no

survivors but they are still looking. She was . . . She was terribly . . . It was horrible!'

I doubled over as if I had been kicked in the stomach. I choked down a sob and, blinded with tears, turned on my heel, then took a few steps forward and flung the flowers on the rubble.

I sat on a wooden box and wept hopelessly. Oh, my God, Hanni! She had become as necessary to me as the sun! Oh, my God, Hanni! Visions of her flashed like lightning through my grief. Oh, my God, Hanni! I was all alone again, drowning in despair.

Slowly I turned and wandered through the dark streets.

I wandered for hours. It was well past midnight when I knocked on the door of the STO camp. How had I got there? I couldn't remember. The door had been bolted shut because of the hour but Paul opened it immediately.

'Thank God, Alec, I've been worried sick. Where have you been? What happened?'

My face was caked with soot and streaked with tears. Blood had clotted on my forehead from a cut I hadn't even felt. I was covered with mud and cinders. I looked at Paul and walked to my bunk like a sleepwalker and collapsed.

I didn't wake up until three the next afternoon and then just lay there hurting – incapable of sleeping any longer but also incapable of facing the world. At six I forced myself to rise.

'Come on,' said Paul. 'Let's take a walk. It will do you good to get out even if the weather is foul.'

The sight of the ruined city brought back my agony. The wind and sleet scoured our faces as we walked as in the old times.

'Do you remember our evening strolls in Sachsenhausen?' Paul said as he put his arm around my shoulder. 'I don't know what happened to you but try to remember what we've already come through. It might help you to see things differently.'

'You're right, Paul.' I realised I owed some kind of explanation to my friend. I searched my mind carefully for the right words so as not to cheapen my love. Stifling my sobs, I told Paul about Hanni.

Next morning I asked, 'When are we going to leave Berlin?' It was the first indication that I was recovering. We had consulted our friends and had heard the wildest stories about what others had tried or done. Someone had crossed Germany clinging to the under-carriage of a railroad car; someone had walked from village to village leading a cow on a leash; someone had gone dressed as a mourner carrying a funeral wreath. None of these brilliant ideas were of any help.

One idea seemed feasible. A convoy of gazogene trucks which were coupled by twos (one towing the other) left every fortnight for Metz in France. A French mechanic who worked at the parking lot smuggled us in and hid us in the empty cylinders of the second truck. At the last moment, however, the destination of the convoy was changed to Poznan in Poland and we scrambled out and got away just in time.

An hour later, I told Paul about a new inspiration: the mundane idea of taking a train – just like Berliners would do when leaving the city.

'I've checked out the schedules and made a list of the checkpoints. I've really studied it and it isn't that difficult. The local commuter trains are rarely checked. The police really only care about the big express trains. It's the same at the ticket windows. The slow trains are old. They don't have any passageways and the two-door compartments open directly on to the platforms. There aren't any vestibules. There is no connection between cars.'

Paul drank in my words. 'That's not half bad, you know, but what about the risk when we get on?'

'We'll have to look into that. Maybe we can get on at a small suburban station. We should not take any ride that covers more than a hundred kilometres. It's 700 kilometres to Luxembourg and even if we take back routes it should only take us five days at most. Besides, as everyone knows, Luxembourg is just another German province . . .'

I received a hard kick in the shin.

'Hold it! Hold it! Calm down! I didn't mean it like that. All I was trying to say was that we don't have to cross a border for you to get home. Even without any papers we stand a good chance of making it. All we have to do is look tired and worn out like everyone else. What is everyone doing nowadays? Repairing their houses, right? So if we carry a roll of tar paper, a trellis or a bunch of pickets we should be able to melt into the crowd.'

'That's good! It really is! Much better than leading a cow around on a leash. But don't you think our looks will give us away? I'm passably decent, but you – you look half starved.'

'So much the better. At least we don't look like deserters. But, Paul, let's get some rest and sleep on it. We can decide about it tomorrow.'

We spent a restless night. The next morning we decided to give it a try. We split up to get our props; the results were astounding! Paul with his Tyrolean hat, a certain baker's Loden coat, a roll of wire and two boards tied together looked like the classic illustration of yesterday's bombing victim. My costume did not have as much verve. I wore my Sachsenhausen navy blue suit, a heavy brown raincoat and a wool cap and came off as a down-and-out factory hand but with my roll of tar paper I thought I could merge into the background.

I concealed the papers from the Printers' Block as well as a 5mm pistol I had picked up in Hanni's apartment. Paul and I bade a fond farewell to Veron.

We chose to walk to the station rather than take the U-Bahn. At 3.00 p.m. we took a last look at the 'Labuche Palace Hotel' where we had spent twenty-five days. I sent up a short prayer for our companions in Sachsenhausen and said a final passionate goodbye to my love, Hanni.

Twilight had come and big snowflakes fell softly about us as we entered the Friedrichstrasse Station. It was sinister and cold. A drab crowd milled around, splashing through the puddles formed by the melting snow which filtered through the broken panes of the glass roof. Sandbags had been piled up on the landings and in front of the offices, there were piles of firewood strewn about. The wooden barriers, which were now useless, only added to the confusion. Everyone was in a hurry to escape this rat-trap station, to go home, but Paul and I had a longer road ahead of us than most.

16

The Styx

I took my place in line standing in front of the ticket window. 'Two third class tickets to Luckenwalde, please.' I looked at the posted train schedules and found my train: Berlin–Dresden, second and third class, departing 16.57, Platform C. Luckenwalde was the fourth stop on the itinerary. We had decided we would get on separately to minimise the risks, so I tried to look like I knew where I was going while Paul trailed me a few feet back. The station was swarming with soldiers, green-uniformed *Schupos* (policemen), hands deep in their raincoat pockets, slouching felt hats almost to their eyes, looking disinterested – the Gestapo stuck out like sore thumbs.

Once we thought the game was up when a *schupo* walked towards me with obvious intentions of checking me out. My heart skipped a beat; all I could think of doing was to give the policeman a dazzling smile, which took him completely aback.

We scrambled for seats in a compartment dimly lit by an old oil lamp. The compartment stank of sour sweaty bodies and stale tobacco. After a tense interminable moment the train jolted forward, pitching and swaying, but Paul and I felt as if we were gliding on clouds.

Our milk-train was overtaken several times by fast steam-driven expresses which bore slogans painted on the side in big white letters: '*Räder rollen nur für den Sieg*' which, roughly translated, means 'Wheels roll only towards victory.' My eyes met Paul's; we were both thinking the same thing: 'Don't be too sure!'

Every time the train stopped one of us would get off to check if any police got on board, but because of the foul weather even they seemed to have decided to stay home.

Next stop, Luckenwalde, 18.20. Five minutes! We got off in a whirling snowstorm, squinted up and down the platform trying to spot any checkpoint. Suddenly, out of a snow flurry came a loud '*Merde!*' We made out a blurred figure trying to pick up something in the slush. I approached him cautiously, ready to make a break for it if necessary. 'Are you French?'

'How did you figure that out?'

'I'm French too. Do you live around here?'

A third voice answered, 'We work for the STO near Berlin but we sleep here in a barrack. What about you?'

'Our work camp and barrack were bombed out and we are being transferred to Halle, but there aren't any more trains tonight. We're looking for a place to sleep.'

'Come with us. There's plenty of room.'

We walked for twenty minutes through an agglomeration of snow-covered houses and came to a wooden barrack which was an exact replica of the blocks in Sachsenhausen. I shuddered as I came to a dead stop!

'That's home', said the Frenchman.

'Do the police ever come by to check?'

'You've got to be kidding. No one's checked up on us for months!'

They fixed something to eat and sat around talking for a while. The news was good. The Allies were advancing and the Germans were scared and chafing under the ever stricter food rationing. Everyone agreed that soon we would be able to start thinking about going home to France.

Once again I was struck by the passivity of all these young Frenchmen. They had been drafted into the STO and accepted it. Shipped to Germany, they went obediently; put to work in German factories, they drudged away submissively; they lived like slaves — undernourished, underpaid, overworked, bossed around, forbidden to move around freely or to sleep with German women. All this they took with meekly bowed heads, waiting like good little boys to be liberated, to be taken by the hand and led home safely. I was sure there must be exceptions, but it was hard for me to swallow.

We spent a warm, comfortable night, got up at 5.00 a.m. and walked with the rest to the station. When we got there I asked one of the fellows, 'Would you mind getting our tickets for Halle? Our German isn't fluent.'

The man looked at me dubiously but got the tickets for us.

'Here they are. By the way, I didn't know you were so photogenic.'

'What?'

'Yes, you really are. Just take a look at your photo on the poster posted above the ticket window. I suggest you pull your cap lower over your eyes. That way you might look less like yourself.'

Intrigued, I went to take a look and blanched. There among a number of tattered posters was a new blue one on which Paul and I appeared with our prison number underneath. Our names were printed in bold type with the legend: 'Wanted for murder, dead or alive.' There was a description of us and the reward for our capture amounted to a small fortune. I stared at my likeness and wished the ground would open up and swallow me. I went back to Paul and told him to take a look. From a distance I saw the worker who had warned me wink, put his finger to his lips, raise his thumb and wave goodbye. 'He was all right,' I thought. 'Maybe I should change my opinion about the STO workers.'

We soon discovered our posters adorned every train station, post office, police station and air-raid shelter throughout Germany, but we kept on reassuring ourselves that the photos really weren't such good likenesses. Besides, everyone had other things to worry about now. We soon got used to seeing ourselves at every turn and stopped worrying about it.

The trip to Halle was uneventful but it took three and a half hours to cover the hundred kilometres. The train stopped constantly to make way for the military convoys passing it. The ones going to the front were loaded with well-secured new equipment and soldiers in brand new uniforms who waved at the cheering crowds and the pretty girls, but those returning from the front looked shabby, the equipment was rusty, battered, muddy and loaded on helter-skelter, and the soldiers looked unkept, tattered and gaunt. When these trains passed Paul and I would smile at each other ironically. '*Räder rollen nur für den Sieg*'!

Halle was a picturesque town with timbered houses, gabled slate roofs, and painted in sherbert colours: peppermint green, melon pink, raspberry rose, caramel brown. We had already bought our tickets for the next leg of the journey – Halle, with a changeover at Nordhausen for Göttingen – because we had found it safer not to purchase them prior to departure. The weather was sombre and threatening. Low grey clouds hovered over the town and snowflakes swirled about in the thick cottony fog that enveloped everything. People were smothered in thick drab clothes and splashed through the slush. Paul and I were standing next to the cathedral in the principal square of Halle, famous for its medieval architecture but we were too hungry and cold to be impressed by the beautiful buildings.

We were looking around for a place to eat and warm up when the air-raid sirens shrieked. Everyone ran. Like shepherd dogs the air-raid wardens and the police herded the people into a shelter on the corner of the square. The flak was already heavy! We tried to free ourselves from the human stream but were swept inexorably into the tunnel leading down to the shelter. The sky was so overcast and the visibility so poor that I wondered how the Allied planes would know when they were over their target. As it turned out, they didn't seem to care; the entire town was a target for destruction.

The enormous shelter was carved into solid rock and buttressed by reinforced cement columns. There must have been over a thousand people inside, sitting on benches in rows and facing the entrance like an audience at the movies. Wave after wave of planes thundered over at an incredibly low altitude, their bombs shaking the earth. The air-raid warden who had posted himself to one side of the iron entrance door peeked through a Judas window and commented to the crowd, 'They're American.'

A volley of bombs hit the square and shook the shelter like a tidal wave. The lights flickered then went out and the crowd screamed. Everyone was hysterical when the raid ended after twenty minutes and the doors to the shelter opened.

'That really was something,' I said. Inadvertently I had spoken in French. A small group of nuns dressed in navy blue habits covered by white aprons and starched white cornets with lapettes which fluttered like seagulls on wing pressed up behind us. They were in a frenzy as their convent abutted on the cathedral. One of them, a scrawny Sister of Charity, screamed, 'Help! Foreigners! Spies! Arrest them! Kill them!' and the rest of the kind Sisters of St Paul took up the chant!

Paul and I had to get out! We bent over and rammed through the solid wall of behinds in search of the exit. We shoved aside the air-raid wardens and police and ran towards a more charitable environment. The people were too stunned to pursue us. In our flight through town we saw things that even we, hardened as we were to horror, had never seen before. The ravage was shocking.

The station was a heap of rubble but a few trains were still running. The conductors anxiously looked at the sky and were in a hurry to leave. We found our train to Göttingen and climbed aboard. Part of the track had been blown apart but through careful manoeuvering the train got by and we arrived at Göttingen after dark.

Refugees were lying all around the station. Paul and I stood in line before the Red Cross booth and received coffee, a sandwich, a piece of cake and a reassuring smile. We found a reasonably dry corner, curled up on some newspapers and slept until morning. We cleaned ourselves up as best we could in what remained of the station-master's office, breakfasted on more sandwiches and smiles and then stood around, as all train services seemed to have been suspended.

Finally service was resumed and we left at noon. As usual, we chose a car in the centre of the train and on this leg we had a chance to play a little game of cat and mouse which we had carefully thought out. The ever systematic German police boarded the last car of the train at one station. At the next station they would board the next car up and so on. We had only to wait before they boarded the last car before ours, get off nonchalantly and board a car which had already been checked. When the coast was clear we returned to our car. We finally arrived in Giessen at 9.00 p.m.

We felt as if we had landed in an overturned ant hill. People scuttled in all directions calling out to each other. Police and military patrols criss-crossed the narrow, snow-covered streets. There were checkpoints everywhere and houses and cars were being searched. We found out that three planes had been shot down near the town. The parachutes had been found but the pilots had disappeared, so the manhunt was on! Since we had no wish to be a consolation prize for the headhunters we slunk out of town as quickly as we could.

We stopped when we were four kilometres away at the edge of a frozen creek beside a forest. Not daring to sit down, we stayed on our feet. We talked, told each other stories, slapped each other on the back, boxed – anything to keep warm. When the cold became more intense we pranced and danced. The temperature must have dropped to minus twenty-five degrees Centigrade. The full moon dragged a huge halo across the sky, a sure sign of more snow to come. The barren trees stood out like Chinese quill drawings and the crackling of their frozen branches and the thousands of other night noises made us jumpy.

I tried to get a rise out of Paul. 'Considering everything, maybe we were better off in Sachsenhausen,' but Paul was too cold to respond. Day finally broke and the sun began to thaw us out. We refound our fingers and managed to unwrap a sandwich and a piece of sausage to eat. We decided it was safer to wait until mid-morning to return to Giessen. When we arrived we found that calm had been restored, so we went on to Koblenz, arriving in the late afternoon.

Suddenly Paul remembered, 'I have a cousin who lives in Bittburg. If only she were there! To sleep in a real bed!' We went to the post office and looked in the telephone directory. She was listed! What luck! We were so delighted we prankishly saluted our poster on the way out. We returned to the railway station and took the train to Bittburg.

She was home! She opened the door, she opened her arms and Paul disappeared in her bosom – then me. She was more than beautiful; she was super-wonderful. She was roundish, sixty-ish, her face shone with kindness and fun. She looked like someone who would tell marvellous stories and make blackberry jam. She was warm and smelled of sweet rosemary. I thought that everyone should have a cousin like her!

Paul had a long story ready to explain his sudden appearance. He, who usually lied so convincingly, began, 'Well, you see . . . Uh, I want to . . .'

'I don't want to hear anything. Do me a favour. You look exhausted and smell ghastly. Why don't both of you go upstairs, get out of those wet clothes and get cleaned up? I still have some of dear Jos' clothes which should fit you. Take your time and I'll have dinner on the stove. We can talk afterwards.'

It took two strong showers for each of us to scrub the grime off. There was soap, soft bath towels and clean clothes! Then, like two pointers, we followed the tantalising odours wafting up from the kitchen. As we sat around the table we talked about everything: Paul's family, the death of her husband the previous year, food, books, about the war, the camp and our odyssey of escape.

Then Paul asked, 'Which is the easiest way to get to Luxembourg?'

'The best way is to take one of the early workers' trains at Trier. These are never checked. You can stay here quietly until tomorrow evening and then set out for Trier.'

We spent a sumptuous night in a real bed with real sheets and then a lazy luxurious day. The cousin waved goodbye to us with a linen handkerchief from the platform around 8.00 p.m. Since it was a Sunday, we had the compartment to ourselves. Because we had had such a relaxing day we let down our guard and both of us stretched out on the benches and fell fast asleep. We awakened, startled, to hear a voice say *'Kontrol!'* A hand fell on my shoulder shaking me. 'Tickets and papers!' My heart speeded up as if it would burst, but I forced myself to open my eyes slowly as if reluctant to wake, while trying to gain time.

Two men loomed over us. The one with a lantern, probably the train conductor, was fat and florid. The other, although not in uniform, had the unmistakable air of a policeman. He was bigger, darker and thinner.

'Quick,' I thought, 'I must do something quick!' I stretched lazily and then lunged at the one nearest me with a wild scream. I caught him by the belt and threw him against the window with all my strength. Taken by surprise, the man's arm windmilled as his back broke the glass. I crashed my fist into his Adam's apple and somehow managed to shove the upper half of the man's body through the broken window. I released him for a split second, grabbed his calves and heaved the rest of him out. The man disappeared into the dark without a sound. I turned.

Paul was in trouble. He had been watching my struggle through half-open eyes but the stunned policeman had finally reacted and fallen on him and they were in the midst of a life and death struggle. Paul looked panicstricken as he desperately tried to keep the policeman from drawing his revolver, but he was weakening and rapidly losing ground. Punch happy, I grabbed the policeman from behind, locked my arm across his throat and yanked back hard. Paul directed two well placed kicks to the groin and solar plexus and it was all over. The man went limp.

'The window!' I gasped.

We pitched him out feet first and on the way out he left the seat of his pants and part of his buttocks on the shards of the broken window pane. The lantern was still burning on the compartment floor, so I picked it up and threw it out too. We collapsed, soaked in sweat, blamed ourselves for our needless stupidity and tried to clear our minds.

The train slowed down.

'Do we get off?' asked Paul.

I thought for a second. 'No, it will take at least fifteen minutes for them to regain consciousness and decide what to do. Besides, they are too far apart to be of much help to each other. The policeman, who is the more dangerous of the two, is probably in a worse condition than the other, so we had better try to get as far away as we can from the scene of the accident. We don't even know where we are!'

Everything aboard seemed to be peaceful and no one seemed to have heard the brawl. Figuring we had covered a good twenty-five kilometres, we got off at the third stop. It was a dark, deserted place and we walked away at the end of the platform, avoiding the station. We found ourselves on a country lane. Paul had oriented himself by the station signs of the two previous stops.

'I know a little about this area. Treves should be about five kilometres from here. This road seems to follow the railroad tracks. Come on.' It was even closer than he had calculated and soon we walked through the Porta Nigra Gate.

We found shelter from the cold in a handy Public Works shed. This time we both stayed awake!

Around 5.00 a.m. I asked, 'Do you think we ought to take a chance on the train?'

'Well, I trust my cousin.'

'I'm with you.'

The train to Luxembourg was crowded with workers on their way to the coal mines and the Arbed steel foundries. Paul and I, our noses glued to the window, watched the landscape unroll.

Paul stiffened; he had seen a long horizontal line cutting across the distance. The train soon rumbled across an iron bridge spanning a river whose dark turbulent waters carried ice and flotsam. 'The Styx,' murmured Paul, for thus had we named the Rhine when we dreamed of escape in the camp. The Styx, that eerie, unfathomable river of the Ancient Greeks which meandered around the Kingdom of Death. We had crossed it and were once more in the Kingdom of the Living!

We got off the train at Sandweiler, a small town seven miles from the capital city of the Grand Duchy of Luxembourg. Paul was home! '*Moyen – wie has et!*' he cheerfully greeted the station master in the Luxembourg dialect as we set out for the capital. 'We'll be there in an hour and a half.'

The road, straight and icy, ran through a forest of beeches. The hoar-frosted branches of the gigantic trees were outlined against the indigo sky and millions of ice crystals twinkling in the sun gave life to the ancient trees. We were filled with a deep primeval joy at the fairytale spectacle. We kept up a good pace and were soon out of the woods and into fields sloping down towards the peaceful unharmed city of Luxembourg with its tiled roofs, its Gothic spires and its big bridges which spanned the Grund (the gorge on which part of Luxembourg is built).

Paul's lips quivered and his voice broke as he said, 'I can't believe it. We've really made it!' We fell into each other's arms impulsively. Yes, we had made it!

The city was just awakening and there was little traffic. Only a few blue-and-cream trams rattled down the main avenues and a few warmly dressed pedestrians scurried around on their early morning errands. Walking through the streets we glanced into the shop windows which, although scantily supplied, had nevertheless kept an almost Swiss air. Paul, flushed with excitement, was almost running and I had a hard time keeping up.

His smile became even brighter as he hurried on. We rushed through downtown and crossed the bridge over the Grund, finally arriving at a tree-bordered square. The sun was trying to pierce the early morning mist, which lay like a cotton crown on the tree tops.

Paul slowed down. 'This is the Place de la Foire. Let's get a drink at that bistro on the corner but we'll enter and sit separately, just in case someone recognises me. If everything goes all right I'll go alone to my sister's which is close by. I'll find out what to do and come back for you in half an hour.'

'You're crazy! That's the first place where they would look for us. You're going to walk straight into a trap!'

'I don't think so. They might have tapped the telephone but even the Germans can't keep a constant watch on the houses of all deserters, draft dodgers and suspected Resistance fighters in Luxembourg. The police here are on our side, anyway.'

A full-length portrait of a lady wearing a diamond tiara and an evening gown adorned with a ribbon order – none other than the Grand Duchess Charlotte of Luxembourg herself – benevolently greeted me as I entered the stuffy bistro. The room was gloomy and the daylight grudgingly tried to filter through the heavily draped windows which opened on to the square. I saw Paul sitting unruffled in front of a glass of white wine. Paul had told me what a townsman would order so I said, 'One Ebling, please.' A fat jovial lady smiled at me and disappeared behind the bar.

Paul rose, paid his bill with German marks which were circulating freely in Luxembourg, and winked at me as he left. Only the ticking of a clock broke the silence as I sipped the slightly sour bubbling wine. Then I heard murmurs from a room behind the bar. The nice lady, who must have been the owner, spoke to me in a strangely accented French. 'I think you'd be better off with us in the "Stuff".'

'The "Stuff"?'

'In Luxembourg that means a small living-room.'

'Why, Madame?'

'It's just that when we saw you two coming we recognised your friend and since there are a lot of people coming and going at this hour we suppose you'd be more comfortable in our company. Besides, the "Stuff" has a back door to the courtyard.'

Taken aback at having being so easily spotted, I tried to regain my composure as I rose.

It was cosy in the 'Stuff'. The owner, smoking a cigar, was leaning on his elbows at a dining-table and reading a newspaper spread out in front of him. He looked up at me. 'Tell me how things are in France.'

I hemmed and hawed.

'Come on. Leave him alone,' said Madame with authority and her husband retreated into his newspaper.

Time crawled. I squirmed in my chair. What had happened to Paul? What if he didn't come back? What should I do? A small blue-eyed, pink-cheeked, thirteen-year-old girl came in and whispered a few words to the owner. Then she came straight up to me and asked, 'Is your name Alec?'

I was wary of answering.

'Paul's my uncle. He sent me to fetch you because he says it's too cold to be walking outdoors.'

I tried to pay for my drink but the couple refused to accept. Madame pushed me gently out the back door. 'Go on. Good luck whoever you are. *Vive la France*!' It sounded pompous but ever so nice.

'My name is Marie-Claire but they call me "Stip".'

'Stip?'

'That means Chip.'

'I can see why,' I laughed.

We went up a steep street and when we reached the top Stip said, 'I'll go first. It's the house down there on the right. I'll go in and if I leave the door half open, get in quick. If the door closes go back without turning your head and return to the bistro. Those people are trustworthy and will get you here later.'

I watched her hurry through the front gate, cross the garden and go in. As I crossed the garden the door was open and I was literally snatched inside.

Five smiling faces and the smell of roast beef welcomed me. Paul, glowing with happiness, held a glass in his hand. His small, thin-faced, jet-eyed sister Germaine caught me in her arms and smacked me on both cheeks.

A wisp of a girl next to her smiled curiously. 'My name is Francine,' she said in a voice which sang. I looked at her. She was finely built and had baby blonde hair crowning her head; her triangular shaped face had a small straight nose and gracefully arched brows. Her intelligent clear blue eyes looked at me directly but with just a touch of melancholy; her mouth was innocent and inviting; she wore a schoolgirl skirt and blouse.

Stip flung her arms around my neck, 'We've already met, haven't we?' The *pater familias* solemnly said good morning and held out a moist, limp, beringed hand; he held a tinkling glass and chewed on a smelly cigar butt. He wore a dark suit, flashy tie, huge pearl tiepin, silk shirt and pocket handkerchief; he looked exactly like a caricature of the bourgeois in a music hall skit.

I had just entered a forgotten world: a well-heated home with comfortable furniture, copious meals served on beautiful porcelain plates set on starched linen tablecloths, solid silver tableware and crystal goblets filled with vintage wines. I was impressed by the feeling of family happiness which emanated from everyone at the return of one of their own.

They reminisced and caught up with each other until the subject of what to do with Paul and me came up. Then, to everyone's surprise, we discovered that Francine, the candid schoolgirl, had been a member of the Resistance for a long time, had already escorted several British pilots who had been shot down out of Luxembourg, taken couriers, who were on their way to London to Brussels. To her father's discomfort, she calmly began to discuss ways and means of getting identification papers for Paul and me and mobilising a network to get us to France. She sounded so confident and self-assured that she made it seem very easy. Paul and I had only to recover our strength by resting and eating and wait.

The family decided that Paul and I would have to separate for a few days to minimise the risk of discovery. I was to stay with them during the day but would spend the nights with some friends up the road. Paul would also sleep out but 'out' was shrouded in mystery, kept like a military secret, until Francine, who knew everything, told me matter-of-factly, 'Nothing in the world could keep that old tomcat from visiting the gutters to chase all those pussies he's been dreaming about for years.'

I lived as a fully fledged member of the family for a whole week. I spent long hours in a small room upstairs reading, listening to music and chatting with the two young girls. Stip was still in the Lyceum but Francine was preparing for her Baccalaureat so I offered to help her review her courses.

Francine kept me up on current events: the latest songs of Charles Trenet, the latest jokes about Hitler, the latest American novels circulating secretly and the latest dance steps. The latter, of course, had to be practically demonstrated and I, who

had thought that all my sentimental and sensual feelings had
dried up forever, found myself increasingly stirred by the pliant
young girl's body, which I held with increasing tenderness in my
arms. I felt guilty; only a few weeks ago I had wanted to die
when Hanni had been killed. What tricks war played with time
and feelings! Terror, hate and hurt, deep friendship and love, all
vanished so quickly! To stay alive and lucid one had to bury
feelings – to be dug up later, much later, when perhaps they had
lost their sting. In these carefree moments I found something I
could almost call happiness.

One evening Francine was going out to a small birthday party
in her honour. She appeared in a luminous midnight blue dress
which showed off her lovely figure. She was discreetly made up
and perfumed. A diamond clip held her hair in place. She
looked radiant.

'Happy birthday', I said as I embraced her and kissed her
chastely on the cheek. At least that was my intention but, as I
held her close, I was carried away by my reawakening desire
and it turned into a real kiss.

In spite of everything I became impatient to move on and
Francine worked hard to speed up the complicated process of
getting two outlaws into France. One day Paul appeared out of
nowhere, nervous, in a hurry and laughing too much. He asked
a few polite questions but didn't bother to listen to the answers.

'I'm going to visit my parents in Brouch for a few days. Do
you want to go with me, Alec?' He glanced knowingly at
Francine, who blushed scarlet and squirmed in her chair
accompanied by gales of laughter on Paul's part. 'You can suit
yourself, of course, but it might be wise to get away for a while.
Things are getting too hot for comfort around here.'

Francine's father, who was fed up with worrying about
getting caught, was delighted to lend us two bicycles for the
trip.

We packed a change of clothes and a snack and took off. We
breathed in freedom deeply as we glided down the Eisch hill.
Neither of us had ridden bicycles for a long time and we
frequently had to stop to catch our breath. Around 5.00 p.m.,
five kilometres from Brouch, we rode down a lovely road at the
bottom of a gorge which ran parallel to a river whose churning
waters had been swollen by the melting snow. I was gaily

pedalling ahead when I saw another cyclist approaching unconcernedly. A fisherman? Something looking like a pole stuck out
above his shoulders. He was dressed in green – more of a
grey-green really.

Suddenly I stiffened and cried, 'Paul, it's a Fritz!' I stopped and
turned to flee to find that Paul had got off his bike and was standing
by the roadside. I said, 'What the hell are you doing? Let's go!'

Paul smiled, 'Don't be foolish! He's got no reason to be
suspicious of us. Anyway, he can shoot us down like rabbits if
we make a run for it.'

Trying to look nonchalant, he bent over as if trying to adjust
bicycle chains. I was furious. 'Don't you realise that we could
have been far away before he could even raise his rifle to shoot.
Now we're trapped!'

We were still arguing as the German came alongside. Grey-
haired and heavy-set he nevertheless pedalled easily only puffing
now and then. He was stuffed into a heavy coat with his rifle
hanging from a bandolier; he also carried a pistol in a holster
attached to his belt. A satchel was fixed to the handlebars of his
bicycle. He stopped, put one foot on the ground and regarded
us suspiciously. Border patrol! We knew we were near the
Belgian frontier.

'What are you doing here?'

Turned to stone, I could only stare. Paul continued to work
on his bicycle but quickly spoke in the local dialect. 'We're only
going up the road. We're farm workers.'

The Fritz said sceptically, 'On a farm?'

'*Jawohl*' I said, but it didn't seem to make any impression on
the guard.

'Are you from around here?'

'No, not exactly.'

'Your papers, please. Both of you.'

Paul began a rigmarole about how we had both, by some
chance, left our papers at the farm but that we were only poor
farmhands . . .

'Why aren't you in the army? You're the right age.'

'Well . . .' Paul babbled on and on.

'That's enough!' The man was perhaps not very intelligent
but he was no fool. 'Deflate your tyres and walk in front of me.
We'll get everything straightened out at the guard post.'

'Where's that?' asked Paul.

'Just four kilometres further on.'

Maybe we could think up something along the way. We obeyed and began to push our bicycles while the old man followed us. Pushing his bike with one hand, he pointed his pistol at us with the other.

We walked silently for a few minutes and then Paul hissed, 'Do we make a break for it?'

'You bet, but not yet. We are in the perfect trap. There's a cliff to the right and a river to the left.' The small riverbank had been fenced off with barbed wire and the wooded land rose vertically up the cliff. The guard could shoot us down like clay pigeons. 'The lay of the land could be more favourable up the road.'

Paul was so tense he didn't answer. Suddenly he dropped his bicycle over my feet and broke towards the right. I was so surprised I was rooted where I stood. The German reacted quickly. He pointed his pistol at me and said, 'Freeze. If you move you are dead!'

I reacted as if in slow motion. I calmly raised my arms and tried to look innocent. The old man, fooled by my submissiveness, ran after Paul who had about a fifteen-metre lead. While running, the guard fired at him several times but missed. Then I remembered I was carrying Hanni's little gun in the inside pocket of my wind-cheater. It was almost a toy but it was better than nothing. I aimed at the guard and shot once . . . twice. The guard, dumbfounded, turned and saw the weapon in my hand. He returned the fire but also missed. I fired a third time which so frightened the guard, who had not realised that my weapon was a miniature, that he turned to pursue Paul again. Paul now had a substantial lead and was about to take cover in the woods above the road.

I fired once more and then the gun jammed! Not wasting time, I threw the bicycle pump into the river, climbed on the German's bike and took off. I heard two more pistol shots, but the German appeared to have forgotten his rifle so maybe he wasn't so dangerous.

'Please, God, let Paul make it! Let Paul make it!' I prayed as I pedalled as fast as I could and tried to think about what I was going to do. At least the guard couldn't follow me. He was unable to use the bicycles so he would have to go on foot to the guard post to alert the others. That gave me an advantage.

There was no point in trying to reach Brouch, since I had no idea where Paul's parents lived, so I decided to return to Luxembourg, the only place I could expect to get help and wait for news of Paul.

I came to a road-crossing about a kilometre further on and veered right. I bore down on the pedals of the heavy bicycle but made little headway up the steep hill. The road was icy and slick but fortunately empty. My feet pushed and pushed on the pedals; my heart felt as if it would burst; my throat was rasping as if sand-papered; I had to slow down! I was finally rolling over the crest which dominated the snowy landscape, passing through the midst of an enormous beech forest.

The first thing to do was to find a place to hide the bike and then go deep into the woods without leaving any tell-tale tracks. I came to a bridge spanning a frozen creek. I flung the bicycle over a parapet and jumped after it, carefully avoiding the rocks which stuck out through the ice. I slashed the tyres with my pocket knife, removed the satchel and hid the bicycle under the arch of the bridge. I looked through the satchel – it was a real treasure bag: a lunch box, a wallet full of money, identity papers, and a blue sweater. I kept the money and the food, drew the sweater over my shoulder and threw the rest after the bicycle. I ran up the creek, avoiding the pockets of soft snow so as to leave as little trace of my passing as possible. When I was well away from the road I climbed the bank to get my bearings.

I knew I was somewhere in the enormous Luxembourg forest, which stretched from the German Eiffel Mountains to the Ardennes in Belgium, but where was Luxembourg? It should be to the south-west. I saw a red glow over the tops of the trees, which must be the setting sun, and started walking.

The going was hard; the snow had thawed and frozen again several times in the spring weather, forming a hard icy crust which occasionally caved in under my weight. Then I would sink into a bloated mushy mass. I skidded and scraped my shins trying to free my feet from the ice. My shoes filled with snow and I had to lace them tightly in order not to lose them. Worst of all, I was making a lot of noise and leaving a trail that would be easy to follow. I tried to maintain a steady pace and to stay constantly alert to danger.

Darkness settled over the forest but one by one my old friends, the stars, took their assigned places in the constellations to guide me. The night was beautiful but very cold. The soldier's sweater kept me warm as long as I continued moving but the minute I stopped the cold, which must have been minus fifteen degrees Centigrade, froze my perspiration. I saw no sign of human habitation, only a few paths through the forest. I could see very clearly as there was a full moon reflecting its light on the snow. Every so often I would pause and listen; what I feared most were the savage dogs of the border patrol but I heard only a few bird cries, the snap of breaking branches and the hammering of my heart.

I ran . . . walked . . . ran . . . fell . . . ran . . . walked on for hours and hours – how many I never knew as I had sold my watch in Berlin to buy a bunch of flowers and thus could only calculate time approximately by the course of the stars. Suddenly I froze – I heard the barking of dogs and the shouts of men slightly ahead and to my right. Then I saw a dozen flashlight beams. They were searching for something and coming towards me. I quickly retraced my steps, praying they would pass to the side of my tracks so the dogs would not pick up my scent. I shook with fear as the clatter of ice breaking under their feet and the yapping of the dogs became louder and louder. Now they were only 100 metres away. I had to stop or get caught by the searchlight beams. I burrowed into a mound of snow. I was certain that the dogs would find me so I opened my pocket knife – more a comfort really than a deadly weapon – and held my breath. Then a miracle happened. For no apparent reason, the men regrouped, talked, changed their line of search and disappeared rapidly in another direction.

I waited until all was quiet and I was sure they were gone. I scrambled out of the hole and continued. What had happened? What were these men doing in the middle of an enormous forest? On manoeuvres rounding up poachers? On a manhunt? I never found out. I was exhausted but knew that if I stopped I would fall asleep and freeze to death.

At last, the sky began to pale and the voices of the forest announced a new day. I came to the edge of a cliff and sat down on a tree stump. I could see a small village shivering in the bottom of a deep gorge. I could see a main street, two parallel lines of street lights, gabled houses with black tile roofs and the needle spire of a church. It seemed to be asleep but then, one by one, a few windows lit up. At the far end of the village I could see a series of long, low buildings. Glaring spotlights came on and I could see railroad tracks clearly outlined against the snow. A station? No! I heard the sound of clanking metal and a small three-wagon tram car rattled out from a building and took its position at the head of the street – probably its usual starting point. Where was it going? I watched people get on. Then another tram car took its place and the procedure was repeated. I kept track of the frequency of departures and saw there was no checkpoint or police. These people were probably commuters on their way to work.

I decided it was worth a try. I cleaned the mud off my clothes as best I could but my shoes were impossible; they were torn and the soles yawned like a crocodile's mouth. My feet were soaked and half frozen but I would have to deal with that particular problem later. I found a path leading down to the village and also a signpost which identified it as La Rochette, which meant little to me. As I got close to the tram I could read its destination – Luxembourg!

I had been on the move for twelve hours and was so tired that I could barely climb into the middle wagon. It was crowded. Good! The other passengers made way for me and I took my place near one of the windows, making sure that it could be opened.

The ramshackle swaying tram rattled up hills and hurtled down slopes, making frequent stops. Most of the factory workers got off at a place called Mersch and were replaced by white-collar workers going to Luxembourg. The tram took an hour and a half to reach the outskirts, where I got off. A large clock on the façade of a building informed me it was 8.20. Emotionally and physically drained, the relief suddenly hit me and I felt very weak. Taking unfrequented sidestreets I finally came to the beautiful avenue where Paul's family lived. I approached the house cautiously, but then I saw an arm beckoning me on through the partially open door. They were waiting for me!

Francine flung herself into my arms, Stip clung to my neck, and their parents looked on anxiously.

'Thank God you are back, Alec! Where's Paul?' The question hung in the air. Feeling death crawl into my soul, I had to tell them I didn't know.

They told me what they knew. When Paul and I hadn't arrived at Paul's parents' house, they had telephoned the neighbouring farm to ask if anyone had seen two lost 'packages' along the road. No one had seen anyone. Francine had then alerted her friends in the Resistance who had combed the road in a car, but all in vain. The only thing they knew for sure was that the Germans had not arrested anyone in that area yesterday.

Now Stip returned to her post by the telephone while the tears ran silently down her face. I felt somehow ashamed and responsible for all their worries and tried to leave. But Papa stopped me.

'Don't be foolish, Alec. We already have enough problems without you causing us more. No one blames you. Calm down. The police must be completely blind not to have picked you up already. Just take a look at yourself in the mirror.'

I was shocked by my appearance. I looked ghastly! My face had a two-day stubble, my eyes were bloodshot and I limped badly because of my frozen feet. I looked exactly like what I was – a hunted man at the end of his tether.

Francine took me in hand. An hour later, cleaned, kissed and clothed in Papa's bathrobe, I sat at the kitchen table having breakfast. Francine had left to try to get some clothes and shoes for me and to get someone to go to the site where we had encountered the border patrolman.

12.00 a.m. – We got our first bulletin by phone. Paul had not been arrested. He was probably wounded and in hiding. 2.30 p.m. – 'Your package has arrived safely but slightly damaged.' 2.40 p.m. – A stranger rang the doorbell and told us that Paul, along with several other Resistance people, was hiding in a farmhouse and had been shot in the head. 5.00 p.m. – The doctor who had treated Paul came and told us the whole story.

Paul was OK. While trying to escape up the steep, slippery slope he had turned his head to see how far behind his pursuer was, just in time to see him take a solid stance, brace his pistol

with both hands to improve his aim and fire two bullets at
Paul. The first had gone by him but he caught the second
through the bridge of his nose between the eyes. He had been
very lucky as he could have received it full in the face if he had
not turned and bent over at that precise moment. The guard
had then fired his last bullet and given up the chase. Bleeding
profusely from the excruciatingly painful wound and with his
nose hanging by a thread, Paul had summoned all his strength
and struggled to the top and kept on running. He had come
down the slope and crossed and recrossed a creek to hide his
bloody trail. He stumbled on but was weakening rapidly and
feeling faint, so he directed his steps towards a farm he could
see in the distance. It was getting dark and everything was
quiet. He sneaked into the barn, climbed into the loft, covered
himself with hay and fell asleep. The next morning, he listened
to the farm noises and, as he heard nothing unusual, ventured
out to speak to the farmers, frightening them almost out of
their wits by his appearance. They cleaned him up and sent for
the doctor who, after suturing his nose and giving him some
sulfa drugs, went to Luxembourg to tell his family that he was
all right.

When the doctor finished his story everyone was very
relieved, including Papa, who had reverted to his usual self.

'That's all fine and dandy, but what about my bicycles? I'll
have to buy new ones and nowadays they're worth their
weight in gold!'

I became more and more restless as I hung around with
nothing to do but listen to the BBC broadcasts. The printers'
documents were burning a hole in my pocket. Somehow I had
to get them to London. I had asked Francine about sending
them by courier but she said the operation was not secure
enough for documents of such importance. I felt I was wasting
time in Luxembourg; I was itching to move on.

Competent Francine, ever resourceful, found a safe house
for me in Differdange, a small industrial town on the French
border across from Longwy. There I was to wait for Paul to
join me, for my new identity papers and for the 'Pi-men', the
Luxembourg Resistance to pass us into France. I spent a last
quiet day with Francine's family, then went to say goodbye to

the people who had sheltered me at night. How could I ever find words to thank all of them?

Francine came to take me to catch the 8.30 p.m. train. Arms entwined, we walked in silence through the dark streets, enswirled by snow flurries. We were despondent. How long would it be, if ever, before we met again? Francine purchased my ticket in the dingy station and led me to the platform. I took her in my arms and kissed her for a long, long time. I broke away without another word and climbed into the old compartment. I leaned out the window and watched her wave goodbye, blonde hair whipped by the wind, until her small fur-wrapped figure grew smaller and smaller and finally disappeared around the bend.

From the heavily curtained windows of my second-storey room I absentmindedly looked at the small square in front of the house. It had been raining all night and the pavements glistened as they caught the first rays of the sun. A few tender green budding leaves lent a touch of colour to the drab setting. Differdange was an industrial town and its existence depended on the nearby steel mills, chemical factories and iron mines. As a result, it was harsh, gloomy and ugly.

I had been a guest of the gentle Beck family for a week. He was a dentist and she a simple housewife and the mother of their well-behaved, pale little boy. Someone had met my train and told me it would be five or six days before they could make arrangements to get me across the border. The Resistance groups frequently used the smugglers, who abounded in the border area, to disguise their own missions. Having received an 'honest business commission' certain members of the border patrol could be persuaded to look the other way when shot-down pilots, escaped prisoners and special couriers passed through with the merchandise. Unfortunately, one of the trusted guards had gone on leave for a week, and the Pi-men had to await his return.

I had received a surprise visit from Francine and we had shared a few all-too-brief moments. She gave me a more or less adequate set of identity papers and a beautiful wine-coloured corduroy jacket. She had also brought a message from Paul, who said he didn't feel up to going on. He had still not fully recovered from the shock of the shooting and feared that the traces of his recent wound would render us suspect. He and a fellow who was a draft-dodger had pitched a tent out in the woods near Brouch where they spent the day, going in at night to indulge in lentil soup, white wine and soft beds. He thought this would be a fine way to wait out the end of the war and the arrival of the liberators, but he wished me good luck. Now I was truly on my own.

One day a Pi-man came to get me and take me to a meeting of some young patriots. They asked me to teach them to set off plastic explosives, how to destroy a bridge, how to cut a railroad track, how to blow up a car and to help them to find a good dropping zone for the material they were expecting to be parachuted in shortly. I gladly showed them all the tricks I had learned in North Africa but hadn't practised for so long.

Finally I received word I would be picked up at noon. Standing at the curtained window looking at the square, my heart beat impatiently for, if everything went well, I would be on French soil again that very evening. This time the Pi-man was a girl, a big wide-shouldered girl, with cropped hair and big brown eyes dressed in a fur-lined wind-cheater.

She gave me a warm smile and held out her hand. 'I'm Suzon.'

We took the tram to the edge of town and then walked on a wet, hard-packed road until we came to a modest house. An old woman in a checked apron, who had obviously been watching for us, promptly opened the door.

'This is my mother,' said Suzon. 'Have the others got here yet?'

'Yes, you are the last.'

Three men were waiting in the next room. Two of them said hello but the third remained silent. His face was partially hidden by a soft hat.

'Where's Henri?' asked Suzon.

'He's outside waiting.'

'Let's go.'

The first two, typical Englishmen looking rather odd in their ill-fitting civilian clothing, picked up their knapsacks; I picked up my paper sack which held all my worldly belongings, and the third silent stranger lugged a heavy suitcase.

'He's Jewish,' whispered Suzon.

A man wearing sturdy military boots, blue workman's clothes and a cap pulled low over his eyebrows was leaning against the wooden garden gate. Although still young his face bore the marks of the dangerous life he was leading. Winking at Suzon he lifted his finger to his cap to greet the others.

'This is my brother, Henri,' said Suzon. 'Is it all right to go?'

Henri nodded.

'Now, everyone, listen carefully. Henri will take the lead, Alec will follow twenty metres back, each of the others will go ten metres apart behind him and I'll bring up the rear. Be sure to keep your distance. If Henri raises his hand, you freeze. If he points down, you drop down immediately without making a noise. Watch your step because it is slippery and muddy and the path slopes steeply. We'll eventually come to a pile of rusty *chevaux-de-frise* on your right. That's the border. Once across we are in France. We shouldn't meet any patrols but, if we do, it's every man for himself. If they catch you you don't know anything. Clear?'

The small column went forward. Henri walked ahead confidently and every once in a while would turn to wave encouragement. At last we passed the *chevaux-de-frise*, remnant of an obsolete military defence line.

'Thank you, God!' I murmured. I was home! For a moment all the faces of the friends I had made – Coggia, Paul, Coudert, Nicolai, Hanni – flashed before my eyes, and then I was flooded by an overwhelming wave of joy, gratitude and pride.

We followed the small trail as it wound its way up hills and down through undergrowth until it came to a slag heap outside an abandoned steel mill.

Suzon spoke: 'Here we part company. You, Alec, seem to be special; we got word that you are to be handled with care, so you will come with me. I'll take you to a nearby farm where some of our people are waiting for you.'

I spent the night with a Luxembourg Resistance family who gave me a border zone pass the following day and put me on the 12.45 Longwy–Paris Express.

I felt jumpy and hemmed in on the racing train but everything went smoothly when they checked my papers and after a while I fell asleep. When I awoke in the late afternoon the train seemed to be slowing down. I looked out and the names of the passing stations looked familiar: Gagny, Bondy, Pantin and then, La Villette! Now the train rolled along a deep ditch lined with buildings. The jolting caused by shuntings became ever more frequent and made the bogies ring. By now I was hanging out the window, breathing in the city smells and feasting my jubilant eyes.

'Gare de L'Est,' came a twanging voice over the public address system. The overloaded passengers scampered like a frightened flock towards the exits. Walking on air with a smile of bliss on my face, I let myself be carried along by the throng. The guardian angel in charge of drunks and idiots must have taken me by the hand because I never stumbled on any checkpoints. In spite of my conspicuous emaciation, my age and my red jacket I was not stopped by the Feldgendarmerie or the various other police who were everywhere in the station.

I simply walked through the entrance and was stunned by the view. The late afternoon sun cast a golden hue on the old stone buildings. The air was heavy as before a storm and a warm glow seemed to pour from the streets and the walls. The square in front of the station, which usually teemed with traffic, was almost empty. There were only a few cars and some strange vehicles pulled by bicycles. A quilt of silence lay over the city.

Tears welled up in my eyes. It had been four years! If I had known then what had been in store for me . . . Once I had read in the Field Manual that field duty counted double time – only double? No more? I felt a thousand years old!

17

April In Paris

Clickety-clack – clickety-clack – clickety-clack. The Paris–Bordeaux Express sped through the night. Comfortably installed in the corner of a compartment I dozed, rocked by the song of the rails. The blue light, the only one permitted by air raid regulations, cast its wan glow on the faces of the sleeping passengers.

I was glad to be leaving Paris as my joy on arrival had turned into bitter disappointment – I had gone directly to some family friends who had welcomed me and listened appalled to my story. However, I had perceived an undertone of scepticism in their reaction and had been slightly irritated. I asked them to call my mother and to tell her that 'someone' wanted to see her. I could hear a hollow, frightened voice at the other end of the line.

'Oh! Do you have news of Alec? Is he . . . is he dead?'

'No, no! He's all right. Come right away but be very careful no one follows you.'

Half an hour later she rang the doorbell and walked straight in. When she saw me she tried to speak but no words came, something seemed to snap inside her and she crumpled to the floor. I held her in my arms until she came to and we clasped each other in a fierce embrace without saying a word. Neither of us had thought we would ever see each other again.

My mother was born in one of the Baltic provinces but she had grown up in St Petersburg under the iron hand and strict surveillance of her mother and a German governess who had taught her good manners and feminine graces. She had spent her youth reading avidly, devouring French books and playing the piano. She was fluent in four languages and educated well beyond the standards of a woman of her generation. The Russian Revolution stranded her in Stockholm where she promptly married a handsome young French lawyer with temporary diplomatic status without realising that he was as boring as he was erudite. After I was born the couple settled in France.

My parents divorced in 1924 and my mother married a brilliant journalist and politician. When he died in 1933 I became the focus of her attention. We became very close and dependent on each other; I adored her and spent my life with her – until the war broke out. When I enlisted it was against her wishes and we had parted four years ago on a bitter note. Later in the war she had decided to join the French Resistance where her German proved useful. At one point she had been arrested by the Gestapo and sent to Fresnes Central Prison where she had met many other woman Resistance fighters, among them Geneviève de Gaulle. She had been questioned and left in prison for many months. She had known cold, misery and hunger. But one morning she had been set free – by mistake.

We spent a memorable evening together, but the next morning our friends politely asked me to leave.

My joy at arriving in Paris was soured. Most of my friends had left; I called on those who had stayed but they refused to help. Some tactfully explained that they didn't have the money, others simply panicked and turned away . . . Again and again I heard the same refrain: 'Times are hard . . . Of course we are with you but . . . you must understand . . .' I did try to understand but could only feel humiliated and rejected. I was indignant – what the hell had I been fighting for? I was bitter – what else could be expected from a nation where the majority of its citizens had refused to fight?

The French people were afraid, the Germans, their sympathisers and collaborators were everywhere, they were cold and hungry, had settled into a bleak existence and spent all their ingenuity finding something for their next meal. The black market flourished. To be fair, I had never lived under German occupation. It seemed to have sapped the people's spirit and cowed them into submission. They lived in an atmosphere of betrayals, deportations, arbitrary arrests, random police raids, the torture and execution of hostages.

Finally I found true friends. The Heu family took me in without question. It was exceptionally brave of them because the mother was an American by birth, a fact which she didn't even bother to hide, but that put the family, *ipso facto*, under suspicion. One of the sons was away and I was given his room, his clothes and his place in the family. I tried to contact the Underground for help to leave France but its members didn't exactly grow like apples on a tree. I met a lot of 'Café Resistants' and useless 'Bistro patriots' who really were nothing but bags of wind and others who, after endless veiled discussion, were willing to get me to England or Switzerland . . . for the right price, of course.

I saw my mother several times at great risk to us both but we were soon at loggerheads about the basic issue. 'Haven't you had your fill of the war? It'll be over soon. Why don't you stay quietly where you are?'

'What is enough, mother? Is the war over? Are there so many of us that I can be spared and just sit here twiddling my thumbs? Do you think we can simply stand with our hands in our pockets while Allied soldiers die to free us? Our country is rotten to the core. It's our last chance to recover our self-respect so we will be able to hold up our heads when this is all over. And . . .'

'What?'

'Don't you think I have a personal account to settle with the Boche? If I don't keep on fighting to the end I will reproach myself all my life.'

She finally gave in and agreed to put me in contact with someone who knew someone. This time there was no idle talk. I got a seat in a Lysander which made courier flights to London on moonless nights. One night, I was taken by a Resistance man to an empty barn near a clandestine airport south-west of Paris. With the printers' documents taped to my back I waited anxiously. In a few hours I would finally be in London! Never had I been as close to my goal. Unluckily, someone pulled rank on me and I was left grounded, but the printers' documents from Sachsenhausen were taken to London and in spite of my frustration I was very relieved to have achieved what I had promised.

I got hold of a bicycle and while riding through the empty sunlit streets finally found the Paris I remembered and had so yearned for, but I renewed my efforts to get away. I made contact with innumerable strangers, drank gallons of lemonade in pavement cafés, walked to the far corners of the city to hold whispered conversations but all to no avail. I had been in Paris ten days already and it was time I left. The city crawled with German spies, informers and Vichy police.

I decided to go to Bordeaux to contact a couple of people whose addresses one of my mother's friends had given me. I got a better set of identification papers, food coupons, ration cards, work certificates, a Home Guard pass – the full panoply of what the normal Frenchman needed in those times. Then I filled in an Interzone Correspondence Form, addressed it to my friends in Sachsenhausen saying that Scott Free, return address Liberty Street, Paris, was *en route* to his long awaited destination. I then left Paris without regrets.

The hotel in front of Bordeaux station was still open, in spite of the late hour. The night clerk, who looked like a needy student working his way through college, asked how long I planned to stay.

'Only for one night.'

'There's a room with bath on the second floor, a room with shower on the third, and a room with nothing on the fourth. It's ugly, but the windows open on to the roof, which might interest you.'

'Thank you for your suggestion. I'll take it.'

Walking up the stairs I smiled when a very old joke about the Crash of '29 came to mind. It seems there was a hotel clerk who asked the customer, 'Is it to spend the night or only to jump out the window?'

The room was squalid with tell-tale brown spots left by squashed bedbugs staining the wallpaper. The sheets were dirty, the wash basin grimy and the gutter outside the window was solid! I lay down fully dressed and rose at dawn. I had a cup of saccharine-sweetened toasted acorn coffee and barley and saw-dust croissants for breakfast. I looked at a city map to calculate the distance and then at my watch. I did not want to arrive too early at the address my mother's friend had given me.

I found myself in an exclusive residential area in front of a stately house. I rang the bell but no one came. I rang again – still no answer – but I noticed that a curtain in one of the upstairs windows had moved as if someone was peering out. I rang again but nothing! I felt ill at ease and conspicuous. Something was definitely wrong! I walked away and when I thought I was no longer visible to whoever was in the house I stepped into a doorway and watched.

At about 8.00 a.m. a lady holding a little girl by the hand came out. She looked around her anxiously and set out for the corner. I followed her, saw her kiss the child goodbye in front of what was obviously a school and turn to go back home. As she approached me, I blocked her path.

'Madame Ménétrier?'

She was startled and terrified. 'Who are you?'

'A friend of Madame Dupont's, your aunt. I came to Bordeaux to speak to your husband.'

'You must be mistaken, sir, I am only Madame Ménétrier's maid.'

I looked at her more closely. She looked distinguished, was wearing a raglan-sleeved light woollen coat, expensive shoes, a simple gold chain and a gold wedding ring and diamond solitaire on her left hand.

'If you are the maid, Madame, I'm Marshal Goering.'

A slight smile curved her mouth. Then her face became tense again. 'Well, just how is Madame Durant, Tante Marie?'

'No, Madame, I spoke of Madame Jeanne Dupont.'

'Oh, how forgetful of me, does she still live in St Cloud?'

I realised she was testing me. 'Madame Dupont still lives in Paris, 2 rue de la Paix, left stairway, first door to the right on the third floor. She still works at the Caron Pharmacy on the same street and she is very well, thank you. She asked me to give you a kiss for her, which I'd be more than happy to do, and to consult your husband on a personal problem of mine.'

The lady unbent. 'So you are not from the police?'

'Good God, no! Whatever gave you that idea?'

'You see, the police come every day under any pretext to inquire about my husband and I haven't the slightest idea as to where he is.'

'What?'

'My husband disappeared fifteen days ago. The police and the Gestapo came looking for him but he never came home. Someone must have warned him. I'm now alone with my little girl and a baby. I am constantly watched and they harass me every chance they get but I really don't know anything. I've had no news whatsoever. I don't know who you are but if you don't want to get involved with the police I would advise you to stay clear of me.'

'Thank you, Madame. Forgive me. I wish you and your husband the best of luck.' I fled as if she had the plague and walked around for a long time, watching the reflections in shop and car windows, making sure I was not being followed. I then took the bus to the second address.

After a ride of two and a half hours, sitting cheek to jowl with chickens and ducks, I arrived in Marmande on the banks of the Garonne River. Marmande was famous for the role it had played in the religious wars, its 'Chicken Strings à la Marmande' and its eleventh-century Romanesque church. After a twenty-minute walk I came to the gate of a charming villa shaded by big oak trees. I rang the bell and three barking dogs and a sleek, tanned woman came to the gate.

'They're just trying to be friendly. My husband will be home in a few minutes. Why don't you come in?'

The house was very modern: big glass windows brought the garden indoors; there was a profusion of wrought iron, including a chandelier made from a wagon wheel; astonishing things had been fashioned from vine stocks, wood screw presses, cut wooden barrels and carefully damaged copperware – all very nouveau riche. Soon the owner, a lean swarthy man in his thirties, arrived. He had bushy eyebrows, thin lips and black eyes and tufts of black hair stuck out of his open collar. He looked at me, smiled and said, 'Yes?'

I spoke of Madame Dupont with enough details to convince the man and then told him point blank that I was in danger, had no money and had to get into Spain as quickly as possible.

The man rubbed his chin as he listened attentively. 'Did you come directly from Paris?'

'No, I went to Bordeaux first.' And I told him about what had happened there.

The man, in a casual tone, asked a lot of seemingly unconnected questions which nevertheless turned out to be completely pertinent. Finally he was satisfied and held out his hand. 'Pardon me, but one can't be too careful. We'll see about your problems after dinner. At any rate, it's too late to do anything

now. You can sleep here. With a little bit of luck ... I'm
probably more dangerous to you than you are to me, anyway.'
He burst out laughing and slapped me heartily on the back.

After a delicious dinner my host's younger brother joined us
and the three of us talked.

'Is everything ready for tomorrow?'

'Yes, the truck is loaded, the papers are in order. We can
leave for St Jean at 4.30 a.m.'

'Did you load the girders?'

'Of course.'

'All right. Now listen. This gentleman is going with us. On
the way we'll toss him into the current, so put the sawhorses in
the truck so we can hide him. Take along a couple of bottles of
wine for the checkpoint personnel.'

The brother nodded, said goodnight and left. I was in the
dark and waited for an explanation. The man sank into an easy
chair, twirled a brandy snifter in his hand and admired the
golden colour of the Armagnac which reflected the ceiling light.

'My brother and I have a small family business. At first we
were ironmongers, but little by little we have expanded and
now we deal in building construction materials, wine, wood,
just about anything. Our best customers are the Government
and the Germans, of course. We not only make a lot of money
but there are also a lot of side benefits. We always have fuel for
our trucks, passes to get through the forbidden zone, drivers'
licences, etc, which make our lives easier. This allows us to help
a lot of people too. We donate generously to the parish church
fund, to the fire department, to the gendarmes and to any local
charity, so everyone is nice and accommodating to us. You can
call us opportunists, war profiteers, if you like, but ask the
Resistance what they think of us. Tomorrow night, when you
are in Spain, you will be thankful that we hid you under the
steel girders. We are taking you to the Public Works in St Jean
Pied de Port.'

We got up in the middle of the night, had a hasty breakfast
and walked a short distance to a lonely warehouse where we
found the brother leaning against the truck. We said good
morning and the three of us climbed into the truck cab. The
brother drove and no one said a word for a while.

Then the man said, 'Now listen, St Jean Pied de Port is next to the Spanish border. Pamplona is about eighty-four kilometres further up the road which leads south-west. Right now we have nothing to worry about but in an hour we shall stop and put you in the back as we may run into some spot checkpoints when we go into the Forbidden Zone. It might get sticky but don't worry; we know what we are doing. Once we're through, I'll give you more instructions. If we get caught, we don't know you. We've never seen you before. You must be a stowaway who got into our truck without our noticing. Sorry, my friend, but those are the rules of the game.'

We stopped in a small forest off the main road, got out, stretched our legs and had a bite to eat. Then the brothers put two metal sawhorses in the back of the truck and laid steel girders over them leaving a den just big enough for me to lie down in, out of sight. On one side we put another set of girders in such a way that I could worm my way out if need be.

'Well,' said the man rubbing his hands, 'here we say goodbye. Get in and make sure you can get out in a hurry. Relax. We've done this before. We'll cross the German checkpoint in about twenty minutes. Keep quiet and still. Everything will be all right. The Boche don't bother us if we give them a couple of presents. Then we'll go on for another half-hour and when it's time for you to get off we'll knock against the back of the cab three times. You're to return the signal so we'll know you have heard and are ready. Push the girders aside but don't show yourself. We'll stop a few minutes later, then you'll get out quickly and jump over the right side of the truck. You'll see a river below. Don't hesitate; hurry down; just be careful you don't sprain your ankle. You'll be stiff from lying so rigidly in the cramped space and the rocks are slippery. Watch your step when you cross the river as the current is very powerful. The water will come up to your waist. Once across you're in Spain. Watch out for the Guardia Civil. They patrol a twenty-kilometre stretch on the other side of the border and work hand in hand with the Germans. They get a substantial reward for every fugitive they return to France.'

'Are there no patrols on our side of the border?'

'Sure, but never early in the morning. The stupid asses patrol all night so they're too tired to do it in the morning. Trust me, I've no desire to be caught either. I've trusted you and I don't know anything about you, not even your name. It's much better like that. You did the right thing when you came to us. No, you owe us nothing. Just come back to visit us after the war and tell us your story. Now, as they say where you are going, *Vaya con Dios.*'

Very touched, I embraced the two men and climbed into my hiding place. The truck started up, then stopped. The man climbed out and shoved a paper sack into my hands. 'I almost forgot, my wife fixed something for you to eat and said to wish you luck.'

I lay as in a metal coffin and each time the truck hit a hole my ears rang with the clang of the metal girders crashing against each other. I thought about the conversation of the evening before in which the man had defended his position. It was true, they were war profiteers but this was certainly compensated by the risks they took helping fugitives to escape. I was learning not to make harsh judgements such as I had with the STO workers in Berlin.

The truck was stopped only once by a French patrol but after an exchange of pleasantries we rolled on. At the checkpoint entry into the Forbidden Zone one German soldier checked the papers while another climbed into the truck to look at the cargo. I stopped breathing and broke out in a cold sweat, my mind went completely blank. I could not think of what I would do if I were discovered. Then two bottles of wine were dangled out of the truck window and everything was declared *in Ordnung*. The barrier was lifted and I heard guffaws and good wishes follow us. I relaxed. How quickly I had forgotten what fear was like.

Then the truck slowed down and I heard three distinct knocks on the back of the cab. I quickly returned them, pushed some girders aside and held myself ready. I was tied in knots of anxiety. The truck stopped. I stood up holding my small valise and the paper bag in one hand, grasped the railing of the truck with the other and vaulted over, falling flat on my face. For a moment I thought I had broken my ankle as an excruciating pain flashed up my leg. Then I moved my foot; it hurt but I could walk. I stood up and took one, then two steps; I was going to make it. I waved in the direction of the moving truck and began to climb down the fifty-metre high river bank.

Huge slippery rocks plunged down towards the foaming water; it was frightening. I picked up a strong stick to use as a cane. When I stepped into the icy waters of the river the current almost carried me away but step by step I waded across and scaled the opposite bank. I stopped under some trees to catch my breath and look over the terrain. I was drenched. I took off my shoes and shook out the water. Everything seemed quiet so I ran from the river as if the devil himself were after me.

All of a sudden I heard the sound of running water; I was at another river almost as wide as the Gave. There was nothing to do but to wade through the water again. On the other side I ran square into an old man who was leaning against a tree, regarding me with amusement. I tried the Spanish Traveller's phrases memorised from a little book on the train trip to Bordeaux.

'*Buenos días, señor.*'

'*Salut,*' the man answered calmly.

'*Ici, España?*' I asked, pointing to the ground.

'*Non, ici la France.*'

'What?'

'France,' repeated the old man and, seeing the stunned look on my face, he continued: 'Usually the gentlemen who cross the Gave are going the other way.'

Then it hit me like a flash of lightning. The river here made a long bend and I had been in such a hurry that I had not noticed, got turned around and had re-crossed the river – back into France!

The old man tried to comfort me. 'It's not a complete disaster. The German patrol won't be back for a while. You have enough time to get across again. Go on.'

I walked in the early morning sunshine through deep woods and listened to the warbling birds. I walked cross country in the baking heat of noon over sun-scorched scraggly hills and dales and listened to the cicadas' obsessively shrill sound. Once I caught sight of two soldiers whose odd-shaped shiny black helmets revealed them to be members of the dreaded Guardia Civil. I dived into some bushes and waited until they had passed. Another time I almost stumbled into a siesta-sleeping border guard, but otherwise I did not see anyone, any dwellings or villages until I spotted some shepherds' huts nestled into the hills while I was walking in the cool moonlit night.

At dawn, still walking, I began to consider what I was going to do when I got to Pamplona. I had been warned that the Spanish authorities put illegal immigrants in the Miranda de Ebro Camp and I had heard rumours in Paris that the French Consulate in Pamplona had been taken over by the Free French. The nearest British Consulate was in San Sebastián, about ninety kilometres from Pamplona. I could try to get help in either place.

The paths turned into roads, the roads into busy highways as I got closer to Pamplona. Even though I had washed up in a brook and tried to tidy up my clothes, people still turned to stare at me.

At 2.00 p.m., on the corner of a busy street, tired and dazed, I stared at the building across from me. A big brass plate on the wall informed me that here was the *Consulat de France*, a message reinforced by the presence of the tricolour flag which flew from the flagpole on the second-storey balcony. I made up my mind and went in. With its deep red carpets, marble staircase with wrought-iron banisters, brass wall sconces shedding a soft light, the place positively reeked elegance.

I went up the stairs and rang the bell outside an imposing oak door which clicked open. A distinguished man in a dark suit greeted me.

'The Consulate is closed. We open at 4.00 p.m. Would you kindly come back then?' Then, taking a second look at me he added, 'Or perhaps you need immediate attention?'

Bedazzled by the grandiose setting I didn't know quite how to begin and finally managed to say, 'Well, you see, I heard the Consulate had been closed . . .'

'Yes, until 4.00 p.m.'

'No, you don't understand. I mean – uh – permanently and taken over by the – uh – a delegation from General de Gaulle.'

The dignitary remained unperturbed. 'Where did you hear such nonsense? You're the third person in the last two days to come here with the same tale. Sometimes I wonder . . . Just a minute, please. I'll try to interrupt the Consul who is having lunch now.'

I knew I had made a big gaffe but I was so tired and let down that I remained rooted to the spot. I looked up and saw the portrait of a benevolently smiling old man with baby blue eyes and a carefully groomed moustache bearing a military cap adorned with gold oak leaves – Marshal Pétain! I gasped, stormed out the door, took the stairs by fours and flew like an arrow out into the street. There I tried to slow down and only looked back when I came to the intersection. Exactly as I had expected, a dark van drew up in front of the building within a few minutes and four Guardias Civiles ran inside. What a narrow escape!

Two hours later I sat on the train to San Sebastián pretending to do the crossword puzzle in one of the local papers. I hoped this ruse would give me a respectable middle-class air. The small train rolled through wild mountainous country covered with magnificent forests, emerald green fields and small, scattered, austere-looking villages and farms. I got off and walked the last stretch into San Sebastián to limber up my tired stiff legs.

It was early in the summer season but, even so, the heat rose in waves from the asphalted streets and cement pavements. People ambled by in light summer clothes and feeling ridiculous in my heavy jacket, I got rid of it.

San Sebastián was a large seaside resort very much in the turn-of-the-century English style. It resembled Le Touquet or Deauville. Its wide avenues were lined with elegant shops and big hotels. Bathers were taking advantage of the lovely day, lying on the fine sand horseshoe-shaped beach encircled by steep hills which sloped down to the deep blue sea. The last rays of the setting sun bathed the hill which dominated the town.

I sat down on the sea wall. I felt mellowed by the warmth and peace. When night came I went down to the port to eat, then went to locate the British Consulate. Afterwards I found a secluded spot among the rocks on the beach and fell asleep like a baby.

The next morning I washed in salt water and spent my last pesetas on bread and fruit. At 10.00 a.m. sharp I was in the waiting-room of the British Consulate. English magazines were spread out on a round table and I happily leafed through some. I felt as if I was already in England.

The receptionist was busy manicuring her nails. She looked at me questioningly. After so many years of frustrated hopes I swallowed hard before trying to enunciate properly my well-rehearsed speech.

'Excuse me, please, I would like to see –'

The young woman regarded her broken nail and said, 'Are you English?'

'No, but –'

'Are you registered at the Consulate or as a member of a British delegation in Spain?'

'No, but –'

'Then I'm very sorry, but there's nothing we can –'

This time I interrupted her. I pounded her desk with such force that ashtrays, the inkwell and the nail polish flew. The look on my face must have been threatening because the girl shrank in her chair and other people patiently awaiting their turn stared at me. I calmed down. I didn't want to tell my story in public because there might be informers present. I took a printed form from the desk and printed in large capital letters on the back: CONFIDENTIAL MILITARY MATTER – URGENT. I handed it to the young woman and pointed at the door behind the counter. When she still hesitated, I raised my voice, 'Quick. Quick.' I won. She took the papers through the door.

The door opened and a visibly disturbed man emerged, followed by the receptionist who seemed to be taking cover behind his back. He came up to me.

'Are you the one who wrote this?'

'Yes, I did.'

'Is it true?'

'Yes, sir.'

'Well, come along, then.' The receptionist lifted the flip-top panel in the counter to let me in. He took me to a dusty, smoky, untidy office. The Consulate official, a slightly shabby-looking stringy blond in his late forties, showed me to a tired leather chair and sat down behind a table overflowing with official red tape.

'All right. I'm listening.' His voice was pleasantly cordial.

I told my story briefly: studies, war in France, Africa, Gibraltar, Algeria, imprisonment, Tunis, Malta, Egypt, Tunis again, and then the long road which had led me to Sachsenhausen, Luxembourg, Paris and Pamplona. The Englishman listened attentively without comment. When I finished he neither spoke nor moved. Then he lit a pipe, puffed on it and continued lost in thought for a long time. Finally, his eyes focused on me. They were penetrating but friendly.

Taking the pipe from between clenched teeth he said, 'Is this all really so?'

'Yes, sir. Everything I told you is true.'

'You must admit your story is extraordinary – shocking! I cannot do anything for you until it is checked out item by item. I suggest that we put you up in a safe house in San Sebastián while we wait for clearance. It's run by some Free French. They aren't very serious but they are nice. They're here under cover as Red Cross workers and they take care of Frenchmen who escape across the border. They are also in contact with the French Resistance. Now and then we help each other out. I'll give you a letter of authorisation so they'll keep you at our expense. They'll get you a set of Spanish identification papers. It'll probably take a week to get your clearance. If all goes well we'll send you to our Military Attaché in Madrid. Let me speak frankly, if you've been telling me tall tales now is the time to say so. There won't be any consequences. However, if we find out later you've been lying, or have ulterior motives, we'll take very harsh measures. Remember we are at war. Do I make myself quite clear?'

'Very clear, sir.'

'Now to another matter. We expect you to be discreet for the time being. No one must know who you are or where you come from. This is mostly in your interest. Spain, after all, is still an ally of the Axis.'

They drove me to the 'French House', a villa perched high on a hill overlooking the sea, almost hidden by the flowers and bushes filling its garden. The master of the house was called Paget. He had been some sort of non-commissioned officer who had been incorporated into the Diplomatic Service by ruse. He was in charge of the safe house which he ran well if somewhat casually. He took care of French Resistance people *en route* to England, Madrid or North Africa, as well as agents going into France. He lived with his Spanish wife and mother-in-law. The sheets were clean, the food was good and there was plenty of it.

I was intrigued by the people who came and went carrying thick envelopes, by the humming of a generator and the intermittent clicking of a transmitter – not all was as innocent as it appeared in the sunny villa . . .

I relaxed and sunned myself on the beach while waiting for

my clearance to come through. The British Consul had given me money to buy clothes and he telephoned every day. An Irun lawyer was legalising my status in Spain. On the fifth day I was told to stand by, and at 6.00 p.m. a big black British Embassy car came to fetch me. An armed guard sat next to the driver but he never even looked at me. We drove over bumpy roads all night. We went through Victoria, Burgos and other sleepy towns not known to me. When we ran up against checkpoints the police, looking at the diplomatic licence plates, just waved us through. We arrived in Madrid at dawn.

They took me to a hotel in the centre of town where I was ushered straight to my room without even having to register. I found an envelope propped up by the telephone containing a brief message: 'Mr Sleator. 11.00 a.m. You will be picked up at 10.30 a.m.' I fingered the note mechanically as I sat on the side of the bed. I was exultant, I had made it – three months and ten days after escaping from Sachsenhausen! The date was 15 May 1944.

18

The Crossroads Of Spain

The British Embassy, as I had expected, was housed in an enormous imposing building whose long halls buzzed like a beehive, contrasting curiously with the dignified decor. I was taken to a cool shaded office where I was greeted by a wide-shouldered resolute man.

'How do you do? Please be seated. My name is Walter Sleator. I'm the Commercial Attaché but I also take care of other affairs. We can talk about that later. Cigarette?'

I declined and while Sleator got up to search for his pipe I took a long look at him. He had chestnut brown hair, a high forehead, a determined jaw softened by a childish dimple and friendly eyes.

I examined the room. I could see the garden through the half-drawn shades of the two windows. The room was furnished in dark mahogany, leather upholstered chairs, glass-fronted bookcases, oriental rugs and antique engravings on the wall.

Taking a seat, Sleator said, 'Well, let's have your story; then we can decide what must be done.' His French was perfect, with a Parisian accent, on which I complimented him. 'Oh, I lived in Paris for years. I was manager of the Rolls-Royce and Bentley Agency which was at Levallois-Perret.'

The small talk continued for a few moments, then Sleator turned serious. 'Well, time for business.'

I talked and talked while the Englishman listened with his head inclined and eyes half shut; he nodded now and then but never interrupted. When the story was finished Sleator thought for a moment and then looked up.

'And you still want to fight?'

'Naturally, sir, for the same reasons as when the war started, but now I have an added reason – I want to get even for all the kicks I have received during the last four years and now that one can almost taste victory, I want to be there.'

'I understand how you feel. Here's what we can do. I have another less formal and more functional office in town. I will send you over there with instructions to give you a set of identification papers, money and anything else you might need. Then go back to your hotel, lock yourself in and write me a detailed report of your story. I want facts, names and dates. I am especially interested in the concentration camp. I'd also like a plan of the layout of Sachsenhausen, if possible. I want to see you with the report three days from now. My secretary will give you an appointment. In the meantime, give some thought as to what you want to do in the immediate future. So long.'

For the following days I stayed almost constantly in my hot cramped room, which opened on to the courtyard. Then I went to visit Sleator in his other office, an apartment in a beautiful building in the heart of the city, and handed over the report. Sleator glanced through it.

'Very good, thank you. If you remember any other little detail please write it down. Do you have a copy?'

'No, sir, I thought —'

'You thought correctly. I still don't have all the answers from London but what I have so far confirms your story. Now, no more talking about Sachsenhausen.'

'Sir?'

'We've had a meeting about it already as well as a consultation with London. We'll have to consult them again but your report should clarify our attitude. It has been decided that, for the time being at least, you are not to mention this matter outside this room under any circumstances — not only about your own experiences but also anything you may have learned about similar camps in Germany or Poland.'

I wasn't very happy with this suggestion and told him so. Wasn't all the suffering I had experienced and witnessed in Sachsenhausen going to serve any useful purpose? I was overwhelmed with anger and despair.

'Listen, I told you that we haven't made a final decision so come down off your high horse. Stop and think for a moment of what effect the truth might have on the ordinary person; they'd go out of their minds with worry. Think about the reactions of all the Jews scattered throughout the world – especially those in the United States; if this information became public knowledge we'd have a tidal wave of general panic. Think about the morale of our soldiers – do you think knowing would make them fight better? And do you really think making this thing public would affect public opinion in Germany? Do you think the Nazis are going to stop their atrocities because the world is aware? Don't be naive. Give us a little time. I assure you that the matter is being taken up with our allies. Our government has been aware of the existence of such places for some time, though I must admit we've never had such an eyewitness account of what actually goes on there. Believe me, I am sorry to disappoint you but you have to learn that one must avoid head-on confrontations with state policy, especially in wartime.'

Raging inside, I squeezed back tears; I felt crippled. 'Your orders, sir?'

'Rest. Go out on the town but be sure to check at the hotel at noon and 8.00 p.m. so we can get a message to you quickly if need be. Also, be sure to spend the night there. I'll talk to you in a few days when I have received final instructions. Then we'll make arrangements for your future. Sorry, old boy! I do respect your stand. Goodbye.'

He held out his hand. Standing at attention, I brought my heels together, ignoring the proffered hand and walked stiffly out. Once on the street I felt terribly ashamed of my behaviour but then the helpless ghosts of my friends in Sachsenhausen – Coudert, Nicolai, Gallouen, Olaf – flashed through my mind and I felt sick, felt like a vile traitor.

I wandered through streets filled with carefree crowds for a long time until I felt calm enough to take Sleator's advice. I would relax, see the sights and think seriously about what I wanted to do.

I ate at good restaurants, listened to Flamenco music and went on a shopping spree, to compensate for the deprivation I had felt for so long.

A few days later Sleator summoned me. 'I still have no instructions concerning our – er – last conversation but I thought we should see what you want to do so we can start making arrangements.'

'Thank you, sir, but first let me apologise for my behaviour at our last meeting. I'm deeply ashamed and –'

'Forget it,' laughed Sleator. 'I fully realise that if you didn't have such an irascible temper you wouldn't have taken the bit between your teeth and fought as you did. Taking everything into account, you'll do. By the way, I almost forgot to tell you that your famous printers' documents arrived safely and you'll be happy to hear that we have already inflicted heavy losses on German tank units due to them. Just that makes your escape worthwhile. It seems that the fellow who made the delivery has been nominated for a high decoration. Funny, don't you think?'

Sleator called an aide who took me to another room. 'Well, let's see. First I have to know whether you want to work in the British Secret Service, join any active British fighting unit which you might choose – you've certainly earned the right – or join a Free French unit in England or North Africa or any other place they may want to use you. Whatever you decide, we would like you to get a clearance from the BCRA, the French Secret Service. You know their sub-agency in San Sebastián but their main agency is based here in Madrid.'

'Yes, sir, but I've been thinking about a plan which I would like to discuss with you. It concerns Sachsenhausen.'

'You're not supposed to speak about that – not even with me.'

'I know, but I've been thinking that if you parachuted me plus a dozen other commandos into the camp by night with sufficient arms, ammunition and explosives, and clothes to distribute among the inmates, we could take the camp in no time and set the prisoners loose. Can you imagine the consequences? Fifty thousand prisoners on the rampage right in the heart of Germany!'

'My God, have you thought about the losses? Have you thought about what could happen to your friends?'

'I know they'd welcome a chance to die fighting for their freedom. They're condemned to death, anyway. Let me show you what I have in mind. Give me the plan of the camp which I drew in my report.'

'Oh, we have an aerial photograph taken a few days ago on 19 April. Don't ever say we didn't take you seriously.'

'My apologies, Mr Sleator. Let me explain my plan of attack.'

I talked excitedly and the aide took rapid notes of what would be needed: the number and kind of men; the amount of arms and explosives.

'Well, that's enough for today. Don't get your hopes up – the top brass won't like it and the political repercussions would be tremendous because of the loss of lives, but the scheme is just daft enough to have a chance of succeeding.'

The Calle San Bernardino was a quiet narrow street lined with middle-class houses and located in the University quarter of the city near the Plaza de España. About a third of the way up the street one could see a group of people waving their arms in the air, going back and forth carrying packages and suitcases and exchanging information. These were the French of Madrid. The building in front of which they stood housed the Red Cross Social Services. Here the young men trying to enrol in the Free French Services, French fugitives and those released from the infamous Spanish concentration camp, Miranda del Ebro, were received and sent on to new destinations. In spite of the efforts of the Red Cross ladies to maintain some semblance of order, the mood was happily chaotic.

From here secret agents, members of the BCRA, operated undercover. I was introduced to several men wearing civilian clothes who, I was told, were important officers. Colonel Bastid, an ex-director of the Bank of Indochina who himself seemed to have acquired the wizened air of an old Chinaman, smiled mischievously at me.

'Sleator spoke to me and also sent me a copy of your report. Quite a story. We'll have to have a long talk about it as soon as we get the green light from our respective authorities. Tell me, have you decided what you're going to do next?'

'Not yet, but I do have something in mind.' I told him briefly what I had discussed with Sleator's aide. The Colonel thought for a moment and then commented, 'Even if the plan should succeed, no government is going to take the moral responsibility or the political risks. Anyway, you'd be crazy to go back into Germany. The Germans would be only too happy to get their hands on you. In fact, you should be extra careful, even here. Spain and Germany are very friendly even though the current German reverses have cooled the relationship somewhat. Don't count on any help from the Spanish authorities if something should happen to you. You can choose between going to England or North Africa, but think a bit. It's almost the end of May and it will take some time for you to be integrated into a unit which means you'll be at a standstill for a while. I'm fully convinced the Allies will make a landing in Europe, perhaps in France, before the summer is over. If they do, the French Resistance will have a leading role in preparing the landings. We're in dire need of guns, ammunition and radio equipment. The Allies parachute us all kinds of equipment, but we need well-organised teams to pick it up and distribute it. That's the area we have been concentrating on. We need men like you who can become operational overnight. I'm hoping I can persuade you to join us. We'll have a front row seat for the invasion; we'll be the first ones into France. Besides you can be in a front line division without having to go through England. Think about it, will you? In any case, I'd like you to meet some of our officers.'

I met Major Vuillet, a razor-thin man with a wolfish grin and Colonel Richard, a corpulent, clownish and calculatingly courageous man who seconded Bastid's opinions. I left deeply pensive. What had been meant to be a strictly social call had opened a range of possibilities. I was eager to get back into action and was slightly fed up with all the diplomatic pussy-footing that had been going on. I was seduced – impressed by these men with whom I felt completely at home for they were my own kind.

I spent a few sunny carefree days sightseeing in Madrid. One day as I stepped out of the hotel I bumped into a scurrying blondish man. I was about to apologise when I recognised the stranger.

'Ivan!'

'Heron!'

Heron had been my Boy Scout name. Ivan was one of my old scouting pals. He had always been handsome, always an idealist and always a winner. He was the son of Ukrainian immigrants. He had been involved in his father's anti-communist pro-Ukrainian activities but he himself had always been French to the core and had somehow managed to come to terms with both conflicting philosophies. We were overjoyed at having found each other again. Hundreds of questions tumbled out as we sipped our drinks in a small pavement café near the El Prado Gardens.

Ivan spoke of how the Gestapo had begun to take a personal interest in him after he was spotted taking part in patriotic student demonstrations. They kept a close watch on Russian and Ukrainian immigrants. He had gone to Switzerland and joined the American Secret Service. Now he was the proud possessor of a Swiss passport and was presently in Spain on a mission for the OSS.

I told of my adventures. I glossed over the concentration camp episode but I was so happy to be with a boyhood friend that I quieted a small voice which told me not to talk too freely; in any case, wasn't Ivan working with the Americans? Ivan was impressed by what I told him.

'Do you mean you really escaped from a concentration camp? Which one was it?'

'Oranienburg-Sachsenhausen, near Berlin.'

'Oh, yes, we've heard rumours. You must have seen horrors there.'

We arranged to meet again that evening when we reminisced about old times and the war, happy to be together. As we parted Ivan said offhandedly, 'Heron, you seem to be completely in the air. The English really don't know what to do and the French don't have the means to do what they want to do. Would you consider working with us? Believe me, the Americans do know what to do, have the means to do it and don't waste time talking about it. They are the ones who are going to win this war. Would you like me to speak to my Chief about you?'

Taken off guard I said, 'No. Wait a while. I'm already confused enough as it is.'

'Never mind. I'll talk to him if I get a chance. It wouldn't bind you to anything in any case. Let's have dinner together tomorrow and I'll take you out on the town. I'll give you a ring.'

It was late even for Madrid as I walked back to my hotel thinking how happy I was to have found an old friend but feeling slightly uneasy. I tried to analyse what was bothering me but finally gave it up as a bad job and let it be.

Ivan called the next morning saying he was going to be busy all day but confirmed the dinner date. 'We'll have dinner at the Pergola on the Heights of the Coruña. It's cool up there and we

can dine al fresco. The food is as superb as the setting. Will that
suit you?'

'You bet.'

'I'll send a taxi which sometimes does jobs for us to fetch you at
the hotel and you can come by and pick me up. Another man will
be in the taxi but I'll give a note for you to the driver.'

I was waiting in front of the hotel when an ordinary looking
taxi pulled up. A sportily dressed square-jawed man stepped out,
and came up and handed me an envelope containing a brief note
signed by Ivan. I got in the back with the stranger who introduced
himself.

'I'm William Murphy, a colleague of Ivan's.' His Spanish was
strangely accented.

'Are you American?' I asked.

'Yes, I work at the embassy.'

'Excuse me. My Spanish is terrible. I would prefer to speak in
English.'

'Of course,' said the stranger undaunted.

We exchanged a few banalities but I became more and more
anxious. Murphy stumbled over a word now and then; he spoke
textbook English. He definitely did not have an American accent.
Trying to mask my concern, I looked out the window but felt the
stranger staring at me. Suddenly a car cut in front of the taxi. As
the driver stepped on the brakes he swore between his teeth:
'*Verflucht!*'

My blood froze. German! That was Murphy's accent. I was
trapped! I had to get out somehow. If I was mistaken I could
always apologise later. The taxi moved fast through the dense
traffic along the wide avenue but I could see a traffic jam about a
block further on. The taxi slowed down. Now was the moment!

I lunged for the door handle, pulled it down and pushed with
all my strength. The wind caught the door and flung it wide open.
Desperately holding the door handle, I hung horizontally half out
of the taxi. Seeing Murphy go for his gun, I lashed out with both
feet with such luck that one foot caught him on the jaw and the
other caused the gun to fly into the front seat. The taxi braked
and I let myself drop to the street, rolling into a ball.

I hit the pavement hard but managed to scramble up just
before an oncoming car smashed into the open taxi door. I
limped away in the ensuing traffic chaos, at which the Spanish

are so adept, towards a narrow sidestreet and hid behind the open door of a courtyard. Holding my breath I peered through the slot of the hinges and found I was not being followed. I waited for five minutes and checked myself over – scrapes and bruises, pants and jacket torn, but nothing serious. Like a lame dog I slunk through the streets to Sleator's office and luckily found him in.

Sleator burst out laughing when he saw me. 'Who did you meet up with? A Bengal tiger? Here!' He went to a corner cabinet, pulled out a bottle of Scotch and two glasses and offered me a drink. My full confession was followed by a long silence.

Then Sleator said, 'There is nothing to be done. Your cover has been blown. Now listen. You are not to return to the hotel; I'll have someone pick up your things and take them to you at a new place. We'll see to it that all trace of you vanishes from the Spanish police files just in case they are in the mood to pass information on to their German friends. We'll find your Boy Scout friend and take care of him, although he is probably long gone by now. It is imperative that you leave Madrid so decide if you want to join a fighting unit or your friends on San Bernardino Street.'

'San Bernardino, please,' I responded.

'It's probably the right decision for you. Don't budge from your hide-out until you hear from us. I could give you hell for having been so careless and undisciplined but what does it matter now? You're damn lucky to be alive. As far as I'm concerned I'm still your friend. Now get out of here! Good luck.'

I was deeply touched. I turned to go but was stopped by Sleator. 'Would you like a bodyguard for the rest of the time you are in Madrid?'

'No, thank you, sir, but I would appreciate your getting a gun for me.'

'I'm very sorry, that's out of the question. But wait . . .' He opened a drawer and drew out a 9mm revolver. 'This one is personal property and doesn't belong to the service. I hope you won't have to use it.'

'Thank you very much, sir. I'll get it back to you at the Levallois-Perret after the war.'

'Good! I'd like to know what happens to you and, who knows? perhaps I can sell you a Rolls.'

I changed hotels, my trousers and my identity. An anonymous tramp was buried under my name in a small cemetery outside Madrid.

The BCRA got in touch with me, gave me a commission as Captain and sent me in an official car to San Sebastián, where the Paget family received me with open arms.

Two days later I was on my way back into France. An important shipment of arms and ammunition had to be delivered to the Resistance. An experienced man accompanied me to train me in this kind of operation and introduce me to key men on both sides of the border. We were driven to the small Basque village of Burguete, which lay at the foot of the famous Roncevaux Pass. A knotty weatherbeaten old man met us and we spent the rest of the day in his house, speaking in sickroom voices, sipping harsh wine and nibbling at hard cheese and peppery sausage as we waited for evening.

Then the old man slung the rucksack over his back, strapped his goatskin wine bag diagonally across his chest, adjusted his beret and signalled for us to follow him. It was dinnertime so there were few people on the streetss but I still asked the guide if it were not dangerous for us to be leaving so openly.

'We are on the border. Everyone here is involved in some way with smuggling. It's their main source of income and has come to be the regional sport, so that all customs agents have to be recruited from other provinces, which only adds spice to the game. Some other men from the village will join us later. Everyone knows what we are doing but would let their tongues be pulled out before they would give us away.'

The old man who had been listening laughed approvingly. We set out briskly up the narrow rocky path and as darkness fell the sky turned star-studded and festive. Half an hour later we reached a small ledge and the old man hooted like an owl. The signal was echoed back. I could faintly see a few wooden huts and then shadowy figures loomed before me. I counted about forty men who greeted the old man with broad white smiles clearly visible in their dark faces. They talked in Basque and their expressions became grave.

Then the old man turned to me and said, 'Everything is ready. There are thirty-eight of us. We'll be leaving in ten minutes. We have already distributed the loads – thirty-five kilos per man. It's a lot but I think we can do it. There are two scouts at the top who'll brief us before we cross the border.'

I was impressed – thirty-eight men to carry one and a half tons!

'I know, but the grenades, guns and radio equipment are needed urgently over there. We can thank God that we are not carrying explosives this time because we'll be passing through particularly rough country. The men have been well paid for the job and you, as a mountain climber, shouldn't have any difficulty keeping up. Try to be very quiet – the border guards get a good bonus for each arrest. If we run into trouble everyone will scatter. Whatever you do, don't get caught. Use your gun only as a last resort. Darkness is our best ally. Our job is to see that these supplies reach their destination. That's all.'

We set off in Indian file and I watched them pass. Their backpacks were stuffed to bursting; some even had boxes balanced on top which they kept in position by holding with both hands; some had sacks over their shoulders; others had harnessed a kind of rack with cases carefully lashed to it on their backs. They left behind a male odour of sweat and wine. My guide and I walked at the end of the column, with the old man bringing up the rear. We climbed swiftly.

At first I had trouble keeping up until I settled into the familiar mountain-climbing pace. After an hour, the path disappeared and we walked over bare rock and grassy patches. The temperature dropped as heavy flocks of clouds settled down on the heights.

'*Merde!* It's going to rain!' swore the old man.

The rocks became slippery and we were swaddled in a dense cottony fog. At each step we risked sending down clattering rocks. I admired the man walking ahead of me. He took long strides and was so sure-footed he seemed to have eyes on his espadrilles.

The column finally halted two and a half hours later. We were sweating and shivering. The men silently lowered their loads and squatted down. All that could be heard were a few eerie night noises and the wind whipping and whirring around the mountain peaks. The scouts appeared from nowhere and whispered their reports to the old man who spoke to me and my guide.

'Everything is fine. The border guard has already passed, the foul weather is in our favour. We're only two hundred metres from the border but we'll have to hurry. Sometimes freebooters hang around here to try to make a few extra pennies by shooting at us. Watch your step because the descent on the French side is rather steep.'

We crossed the border one by one, regrouped on the other side and started downhill. Suddenly there was the rumble of a rock slide and through the fog we saw the diffused halo of a flashlight beam.

The old man swore under his breath, the column turned to stone. A murmur rippled up from below. Young sixteen-year-old Paco had slipped, had been caught, but his load had gone into the ravine. Panicking, he had turned on his flashlight. Five minutes later the load was recovered and the descent continued. I was soaked and scared, scared of being in German-controlled territory again. I concentrated on placing one foot in front of the other and the wave of fear passed.

After a while, the fog lifted and gave way to a fine drizzle. We reached a pasture surrounding a large sheep farm. Someone whistled softly. A shadowy figure stepped out of the house, waved us into a barn and the men set down their loads. The barn doors closed, the lights came on and I could see the glistening faces of the men as they took off their drenched clothes, brought out their knives to cut hunks of bread, cheese and sausage, and squirted wine from their wineskins down their throats. I shared their rations and we all sank exhausted into the pungent hay which muffled every sound except the monotonous patter of the rain, putting us to sleep.

The shepherd awoke us up at dawn. I looked at the piled-up boxes as I walked out of the barn. They came from England, the United States and, mystery of mysteries, France! We said goodbye to the old man.

'What will you do now?'

'Oh, we'll go back tonight.'

'Empty handed?'

The old man smiled wickedly. 'Oh, no! There are some

interesting things on this side that are in great demand over there. Business is business, you know.'

My guide and I walked through fields down the valley. When we reached the road we found a boy waiting for us with two bicycles. We pedalled for about three-quarters of an hour, arrived at the old ramparts of St Jean Pied de Port and went to Marcel's bistro, which at this early hour was empty. The guide introduced me to Marcel. We exchanged information while drinking a glass of wine and then went on to St Palais.

The owner of this bistro was called Jeannot. He was about sixty, a veteran of the 1914 World War and a *Grand Invalide*. He dragged a wooden leg, breathed with great difficulty as he had been gassed and lacked several fingers from his right hand but his eyes burned with an indomitable fire.

He welcomed me and said, 'We've called a meeting of the local Maquis and Resistance leaders to plan our activities for the next weeks. They should be here soon.'

Six men came in separately. The first two Maquis leaders belonged to the FTP faction, which was mostly communist. They addressed each other as 'Colonel.' The third, a drab-looking man who would never set the world on fire, introduced himself as a captain in the army. Then came a man who just called himself George and whose sole goal in life seemed to be to kill Germans. A doctor and a public works engineer from nearby villages joined them. Leaning against the wall, I looked and listened.

They were all so different. Each had joined the Resistance for individual reasons but they all had one thing in common – they had been indelibly marked by the war. There was an indefinable something in their eyes and bearing and there was grief and hard determination in their faces. It was touching to hear them converse; they spoke as brothers but seemed to be unaware of their brotherhood. They spoke of their actions, their frustrations, their worries, the losses they had inflicted on the Germans, their own dead and wounded or, even worse, captured. They worried about the incomprehension of the general public, the blind fear which dominated the peasants to such an extent that they refused to give them aid of any sort and chased them away. They related the betrayals, the jeopardy in which they had placed their families as well as themselves, and talked about the terror, hunger and cold they had endured. What could compel hundreds of such men to hide in forests, to fight to efface France's shameful defeat and to try to vindicate her honour and obtain her freedom?

I was learning about a side of France which had been unknown to me: Frenchmen who refused to bow to the yoke; hunted men who fought from the shadows; France's small battered band of heroes who fought in the dark and the mud exactly as the famed army units were fighting in Italy and North Africa. It puzzled me how men with a common cause so often split up into rival factions. Ambition? Envy? Politics? Human weakness? Perhaps, but fortunately there was a redeeming side to the questions: this made it safer because the whole organisation did not unravel like a sweater when one link was ripped.

The business side of the meeting was dispatched with efficiency; the distribution of the arms' shipment, the list of what would be brought on the next trip, the plans for immediate actions. Then one by one they left, alone again, to face their individual destinies. I remained thoughtful and was completely convinced of the need of supplying men such as these with arms to wage their battles. The time was ripe to hit the enemy. Although battles were still raging, the Germans were retreating. The Russians had recaptured Sebastopol, Rome was under siege and the Americans were regaining their bases in the Pacific. Now the Resistance's role was vital and I was finally to be part of a group which would help to liberate my country.

Jeannot's granddaughter, a very young velvety-eyed quick-footed girl who had been orphaned and was mistress of the house, served us lunch. Her grandfather proudly told us that she was their liaison agent – she delivered mail, orders and sometimes even arms! My guide departed for Toulouse immediately after lunch. Next day a local guide took me back into Spain by a shorter easier route. During the following days I made various crossings, got to know different routes and different Resistance groups and formed an idea of the intricate network which covered both sides of the Pyrenees.

One afternoon when I returned to San Sebastián I saw a black car parked in front of Paget's house. Colonel Bastid was inside waiting for me with catastrophic news. A Gestapo crackdown had badly broken up the organisation in the Bordeaux and south-west region. Many had been arrested , caches of arms had been discovered, radios confiscated and secret codes seized. Several agents were already on their way to try to put the pieces back together but it was imperative to establish radio contact again. I was to take new codes and crystals to the dozen remaining radio stations and bring back a complete report.

I was exhausted, having made four crossings in five days. 'Do I have time to get a clean shirt?'

'You'll leave tomorrow evening. That will give you plenty of time to memorise your briefing . . .'

19

Happy Birthday

I spent the next day memorising code names, telephone numbers, addresses, recognition signals, radio frequencies and ciphers, and travel itineraries. I also learned the main activities of each group with which I would be in contact. My head felt as if it would burst with all the information but Paget told me not to worry; he was sure I would be able to remember it all and in the right sequence when the time came.

Sitting in the car *en route* to the border I kept on reciting items to myself, but the more I tried to remember the more confused I became. This time I was going the 'Royal Way'; what Paget had described had evoked visions of being carried over the border in a sedan chair but, of course, it was not quite as fabulous as that. It certainly was faster and easier than any of my previous crossings but, since so many people had to be bribed to make it possible, it was used only for ultra-important missions. The 'Royal Way' began in the neighbourhood of Irun and Behobie. After crossing the last bridge over the Bidassoa River, I arrived at the charming village of Ascain in the centre of the Basque country in the middle of the night.

The next day I went on to St Jean de Luz where I met a dead end. I spent the whole day stubbornly looking for the man I was supposed to contact but all in vain. I encountered only closed doors, closed mouths and flitting eyes; fear was rampant and no one trusted the well-dressed stranger who asked embarrassing questions about people it was safer not to know.

I had better luck in Bayonne. I found my contact immediately, gave him new orders and a radio crystal and caught the train for the 110-kilometre trip to Pau. Before getting on the train I took a few precautionary measures. I rolled up the radio crystals inside a handkerchief and taped the small flat package to my belly under my shorts. I changed identity as Paget had given me two sets of papers, hid the extra set in my sock and rehearsed my new role. Name: Verdier, Paul; job: Public Works employee; place of birth: Lorient (the town had been bombed and all records burned); address: Ascain. I was sitting quietly pretending to be very interested in my magazine when suddenly the compartment door was flung open and I saw a tall policeman and a uniformed German wearing a swastika armband framed in the doorway.

'Police! Papers!'

I calmly handed my papers to the policeman who checked them and then showed them to the German, who was getting ready to hand them back when something caught his eye.

'You live in Ascain?'

'Yes.'

'When was this card extended?'

'I don't remember exactly. Last autumn, I think.'

'20 October?'

'Could be.'

'Then it's false. Follow us.'

'What do you mean?' I stuttered.

'I said the card was false,' laughed the German. 'Your forger friend should have known that the colour of the seals is changed periodically. Your stamp is black and the colour for the date it carries was purple.'

Sandwiched between the two men, I was taken down the aisle to a compartment which took up the entire width of the carriage. A sticker on the glass door stated that this car was reserved for Germans. There was a door with a window on each side and a bench occupied the entire length of the far wall. A smaller one was placed next to the entrance door. Two harmless looking German soldiers were sprawled on the longer bench, innocently observing the passing landscape; facing them, next to the window, there was another German soldier evidently in trouble as he was holding his head and looking angry. Next to him was a small skinny guy who also looked upset. I assumed that this man was French because he was wearing a Basque beret and a profusion of decoration ribbons stitched to the buttonhole of his lapel. A German holding a rifle was sitting opposite him while a German policeman scrutinised his papers.

The policeman who had followed me shoved me into the

compartment, searched my pockets, placed everything on the
bench, including my wallet, pushed me down next to the little
Frenchman and went off to sniff out other victims. I had been in
a panic but had calmed down and was now filled with a cold,
calculating resolution. I knew I had to get out of this trap
quickly or I would not get out at all and I was weighing the
possibilities when my neighbour leaned against me and murmured, 'We have to escape. Shall we try now?'

'Don't be a fool,' I whispered. 'Wait a few minutes.'

'Shut up!' shouted the guard. 'Speaking is *verboten*!'

I was worried that the small man might do something foolish,
thus alerting the Germans and ruining my chance for escape. I
examined one of the windows, which had been opened half-way
because of the hot weather. It was an old-fashioned railway
window which could be held open at various positions by
hooking a perforated leather belt through a brass peg below the
window frame. When the belt was unhooked the window
would slide down into the door. The train was rolling at about
sixty kilometres per hour but I thought we were slowing down.
If we were nearing a station then I had to get away now, before
the train stopped. It was slowing down! Forty kilometres . . .
thirty kilometres . . .

'Please, sir,' I said in a sugary voice and raised one finger like
a well-behaved German schoolboy.

The policeman busily examining papers did not even raise his
eyes. 'What do you want?'

'Please, sir. I have to tell you something. It's very important,
sir. You see . . .' I was just talking to gain a little time without
alarming the guard while I got to my feet.

'What is it?' said the policeman impatiently as he stepped
towards me, thus placing himself between me and the guard,
who raised his rifle to make way. I kept my eyes meekly
downcast while, with a sidesweep of my hand, I hit the
policeman viciously in the throat. The man gasped, choked and
fell back on the guard who was caught unaware. I then grabbed
the little Frenchman by his lapels, stood him up and threw him
on top of the heap. The other Germans just sat stupefied while I
took one . . . then two steps towards the window, pulled the
leather strap loose with my left hand and pushed with my right
on the window which slid down with a click. I grabbed the

window-sill with both hands and dived headfirst into space. I crashed into the wind and the roar of the speeding train, twisted, turned in mid-air and landed on my feet! How I had done it I couldn't say but I landed on a parallel track and then fell over on my side. As I bounded up and dashed away I heard the screech of the brakes and saw the sparks fly as the wheels grabbed at the rails.

I headed towards a high chainlink fence which ran parallel to the track. To my right a pile of railroad equipment blocked the view; about sixty metres to my left I could see an opening in the fence which seemed to lead into the fields but to reach it I would have to run in the same direction as the still moving train, and risk being intercepted by the Germans. But it was my only chance!

As I ran a shot rang out . . . another . . . then a volley from the train windows. 'Just what I was afraid of,' I thought as I ran, propelled by fear and sheer willpower. Then I heard a hubbub from the train. The passengers had finally realised what was happening and were gleefully cheering me on through the open windows, delighted that their German masters had been outwitted. The wave of the strangers' enthusiasm seemed to lift me and carry me on towards the break in the fence.

Suddenly I felt a violent blow as of a fist slamming into my shoulder. I staggered, nearly fell but managed to straighten up with a great effort and continued my wild sprint towards the exit. For a moment I thought someone was behind me but when I turned my head there was no one – nothing. Again I turned. Still no one. Twenty, ten, five metres to go. The shooting continued but seemed to consist mostly of small-arms fire – the rifle shots were rare. I felt detached from my body. I could see myself running. I saw the spurts of earth as the bullets struck all around me but they didn't concern me – it seemed to be happening to someone else. The danger had become abstract.

Two metres, one metre – I was cheered on as I hurtled through the opening. I dived into some bushes and disappeared from view. I was on a steep path which rose abruptly through the shrubbery and was bordered on either side by high box hedges threaded with barbed wire. I couldn't get off the path!

I was overcome with panic, my legs began to shake and gasping for breath I slowed down. I could not believe no one was following me. After a few moments I pulled myself together and started trotting uphill at an even pace. Two hundred metres further on the terrain flattened out. I just had to get out of this tunnel of a path! To my left I saw a gate opening on a field but I bypassed it, as I was sure that the Germans would investigate it first. I passed a second gate and finally vaulted a third. I crossed the meadow diagonally, jumped the corner fence and repeated the same procedure twice. I could hear no noise of pursuit; I had only heard three short whistles from the train as if the engineer were wishing me God speed.

A stillness lay over the countryside. I could only hear the drumming blood in my ears. I slowed down to a walk and headed south at a brisk pace trying to make up my mind about what to do. Should I try to reach the Pyrenees on my own? No, it was too far and too risky. Besides, I was on an urgent mission. I would try to reach a village – St Palais. There I could get help.

My concentration was broken when I felt something wet and sticky on my left hand. I looked down – blood! My jacket sleeve and the left side of my shirt were soaked. I remembered the blow to my shoulder; I must have been hit. I fingered my shoulder blade, felt a sore spot in the centre but could not see it. I took out my handkerchief, folded it in eight and packed the wound as best I could. I hoped the jacket and shirt would keep it in place. Now it was imperative to reach St Palais.

I had jumped off the train about twenty-four kilometres from Bayonne. St Palais should be south-east so I had to reach a road to orient myself by the road-signs. As far as I could remember, there were no large villages in the area, which should complicate the Germans' search. I walked – ran – walked – ran up and down hills, through fields and on paths always towards the south-east. I became lightheaded and an old tune resounded in my head over and over again.

I had performed my acrobatic stunt at approximately three o'clock in the afternoon. Daylight should last until around 10.00 p.m. and I had to take advantage of every minute of light as the ground was very broken. At about 6.00 p.m. I began to flag. My throat was parched, my trousers were now soaked to the knee so I must still be bleeding heavily and the expensive shoes which I had bought in Madrid were killing my feet. I started to look around for a farmhouse where I might get some help.

Finally I saw smoke fuming from the chimney of an old house which had completely blended into the landscape. There were no telephone wires so I went up to the door and knocked. A wizened old woman who looked like a witch opened it. Strands of grey hair straggled from her kerchief and in spite of the hot weather she was wrapped in a black woollen shawl. Her jet black wicked eyes widened and she bleated like a terrified sheep from a toothless mouth.

'Get away from here, go away!'

'Please don't shout, all I want is to wash up and rest a bit.'

'My God, look at you, you are covered in blood. You are a bandit!'

'No, no, Madame. I was hit by a German bullet while trying to escape.'

'So you are a Maquis! That's even worse. They do nothing but cause problems for honest people. Get away from here!'

I finally had to bargain with her to let me wash and drink from her well and after much crafty haggling she finally gave me some espadrilles, clean clothes and a hunk of bread in return for my Madrid shoes and Patek-Philippe watch. I felt outwitted and ridiculous, but I preferred that to feeling like a ruffian. As I left I warned her: 'You keep your mouth shut about this.'

'We'll see about that.'

'Listen carefully, Madame, if I fall into German hands nothing would please me more than to confess that I almost got away due to the help you gave me.'

Disillusioned, I continued on my way.

Although I found the going much easier in the canvas shoes, I was still bleeding profusely and weakening steadily. Once I sat down and dozed off and when I woke I had lost track of time completely. It was dark. I was chilled and shivering but forced myself to go on, setting my course by Orion, who now lay very low on the horizon.

Just before dawn I lay down on a hill that overlooked the desolate countryside. The shrill noise of the cicadas was all I could hear. Suddenly I sat up; I had heard a long continuous rumbling from the west and could see flashes of light on the horizon. A thunderstorm? No, the sky was clear and starry. Again the steady rumbling – again the flashes of light. The west? There were long beaches in that part of the country; they could not be more than thirty kilometres away. Excited, I scrambled up and listened. 'My God, they have landed!' The heavy thunder of the naval bombardment intensified, the flashes of light came faster and faster. What day was today? Today was Tuesday, 6 June 1944.

'They have landed!'

What should I do? Should I run to do what I could to help? Impossible! I was too weak and exhausted; I would never make it. I had better go on to St Palais, get my shoulder taken care of and join the Resistance. I was mad with joy. Shouting and laughing, I ran downhill, came to a paved road and ran towards St Palais. It was still dark when I knocked on the door of Jeannot's bistro. When his granddaughter opened the door she blanched at my condition.

'Come in quickly! What happened?'

I sank into a chair. 'Lucy, they've landed! They're here!' I was crying and stammering with joy. I had lost all self control. I jumbled and muttered, 'Alert the others. We have to go right away!'

With great sweetness Lucy calmed me down. 'Let's take care of you first, we can hear what the BBC has to say while I clean you up.' The BBC was off the air; the few live French stations blared their usual inanities.

'It's an operational black-out. It's got to be that!' I declared.

'We'll wait and see,' said Lucy soothingly. 'Tell me, you are not the "gas man" by any chance, are you?'

'The what?'

'Last night we heard about an incident on the Pau–Bayonne train. Near the village called Le Gas a guy is supposed to have dived out of the window and escaped amid German fire and the Germans have been combing the region for him all night. Even the local priest was arrested for joining in the cheering and cursing the Germans.'

'Well, so I'm the "gas man". I also have a piece of lead in my shoulder.'

'You've run more than forty kilometres in that condition?'

Jeannot and his wife appeared and it was decided that I should go to a château near Navareux, a place Colonel Richard sometimes used as a safe house for wounded or hunted Resistance fighters. Jeannot promised to notify San Sebastián about the change in the ink colour of the stamps and to arrange for someone from the network to get in touch with me.

'Jeannot, they have landed!'

'Who? Where?'

Jeannot became very excited but Lucy cut him short, 'Let him be, Grandfather, he must have had a dream.'

I rode a bicycle downhill to Navareux, rang the bell of the village pharmacy an hour later and the pharmacist, sleepy eyed and still in his pyjamas, took me to the stockroom and made me sit down. He asked me a few pertinent questions as his agile hands removed Lucy's bandage and saw that I was bleeding again.

'The bullet has to come out but I can't do it here. You've got a high temperature which means the wound is infected so I'm going to give you a dose of sulfas and take you to a place where you can lie down while I call the doctor.'

He took me to a bistro near the Central Square where the owners took me upstairs and put me to bed. A girl called Line, who had small eyes, a pointed nose and quick gestures, took charge of me. As she worked in the bistro she came upstairs every half-hour to check on me. I shook and sweated with fever. The pain in my shoulder only allowed me fitful sleep and my nightmares merged with my hallucinations so I found it hard to grasp what Line was saying when she rushed in shouting, 'They've landed! They've landed!'

'I know. That's what I tried to tell you.' For me, Line had become Lucy.

'You didn't tell me anything, how could you know? We've just heard it on the radio.'

'I heard them when they landed last night.'

'You're raving. How could you hear anything last night? They just landed at seven o'clock this morning – and in Normandy.'

'But I heard them!'

'You must have heard the storm raging over Bayonne.'

I was silent. I had sunk back into sleep.

The pharmacist came to see me in the evening and, as the doctor still hadn't come, decided to try to extract the bullet himself. He sat me under a ceiling light, opened a sterile pack and took out a canulated probe.

'Hold on. This is really going to hurt but we have no anaesthetic to give you and you mustn't make a sound.'

Gritting my teeth, I steeled myself. The pain was excruciating! The probe went deeper and deeper. My stomach turned over and I felt the probe burrowing into my innards. I tried to hold on but was dissolving into nothingness.

'Look, sir! Look! The probe has come out the other side!' exclaimed Line.

'Good God! Why hadn't the good man first made sure that there was no bullet!' I thought as I fainted.

When I came to, my eyes focused on a new face.

'You have a nasty infection,' said the doctor as he leaned over me. 'We removed strands of horsehair from your wound which probably came from the shoulder pads of your jacket. You're going to need special care. We'll . . .'

I heard no more; I was unconscious again. Whenever I came to during the next three days I was unaware of my surroundings . . . aware only of my misery. The peaceful daytime noises of the bistro downstairs were replaced at night by the rowdy racket and beating rhythms of the percussion instruments of a jazz band, which boomed up from the popular dancehall below my room, and jumbled with the painful pulsations in my head. On the fourth day I awoke to find the early morning sun shining on little Line, who was snoozing in a chair next to my bed. The fever was down, my headache was gone and my shoulder hurt less.

I was taken to the Château de Navareux the next day. A beautiful Renaissance building with round ivy-covered corner turrets stood in a park under century-old trees surrounded by green lawns, white gravel paths and overgrown formal flower beds. The mood inside was harmonious and enchanting; chintz curtains, polished antique furniture, old tapestries from which cherubs, princesses and shepherds smiled, bowls full of roses in every room and books, books, books everywhere. The occupants, two kind, dried-up virtuous middle-aged spinsters called Martha and Anne, took care of me and followed the doctor's orders with stern military discipline. Installed in a soft canopy bed, I enjoyed the quiet, the rest and the coddling. An agent from Pau came and I gave him the radio crystals which I had saved from German hands and all the instructions I had stored in my mind, still surprisingly clear. Sometimes in the evening the doctor would stay to play chess and when I was well enough to walk around he suggested that I should try some fly-fishing in the river to exercise my shoulder. Obediently, I went to the river and with my left arm cast the fishing-line as far as I could and wound it in over and over again. But as the weather was stifling hot and the exercise boring I sat down on a rock, took off my shoes and dangled my feet in the whirling, icy river. I watched the milky grey-green waters crash and splash against the rocks and turn into cottony foam; fascinated, I stared as the current divided, formed half-circles to avoid obstacles and rejoined further downstream. The roar of the river was impressive and seemed to originate in the heart of the mountain but after a while I pulled myself out of my reverie and began to reflect. Since the Allies had secured their beachheads in Normandy, France would soon be liberated and I wanted to be in on that. I had to get moving even if I wasn't completely well. For quite a while I had been feeling that I was wasting time.

For months, for years, I had stagnated in prisons and prison camps; I had hung around waiting to fight like a true soldier; I felt I had been waging a rabbit war – always running. I could remember running – running through mountains, through forests, through cities, through deserts as if the dogs were on my tail; I could remember braving the seas; only once had my dream come true – when I fought with the SAS in the Libyan Desert. Apart from this one episode I had always fought alone – not my fault to be sure – but nevertheless alone. I had struggled time and time again to get off this one-way track only to be swept up by an invisible, relentless, centrifugal force which always flung me back to my starting point. My deeds had earned me nothing but hatred, abuse, shame and useless suffering. I had been rotting in shit for too long. I was no longer the foolhardy youngster I had been. I had earned the right to call myself a man. Now I had to shape my own destiny, to stop being flung about. I had to fight. I recrossed the border and spent two days in San Sebastián.

A change came over me. I was fed up with being beaten, battered, hunted and hurt and I was seized by a cold fury, a loathing for the Germans, whose arrogance was swelled by their victims' abject acceptance that the conquerors were invincible. I was tired of being constantly afraid – tired of being constantly tired.

Intelligence reports gave the Resistance hope that the Germans in the south-west of France were getting ready to pack up. They were regrouping into units, their vehicles were being tuned up, their requisitions had increased; they were restless, their officers' tempers flared, the soldiers' jokes pointed to home. The Germans were being pushed north towards Paris. God willing, this would be the first step towards their Fatherland and total defeat.

I disappeared from circulation without giving any explanation, I was going to treat myself to my war. I went wild. I joined several operations of various Resistance groups and with them blew up railroad tracks, bridges, roads, lay in ambush, hurled grenades, killed, screamed with glee. We killed – killed and ran – never stopping to count the cost – either to ourselves or the enemy. It was Ferryville and the SAS raids all over again, but worse. Destiny had come full circle.

One day two young Maquis and I lay in ambush on top of a hillock above a road, a case of hand grenades open at our side. A convoy of eight trucks loaded with German soldiers and a motorcycle escort appeared. We waited until the first truck was just below us to hurl the first round of hand grenades, then rapidly followed up with more rounds. The leading trucks caught fire and exploded, the following trucks crashed into them and the fire spread down the line. The three of us stood on the hill, in plain view, screaming like madmen, flinging more and more hand grenades, causing a horrible massacre. Soon, however, we ourselves came under a shower of bullets. The motorcycles had given cover to the convoy's last two trucks; the soldiers had dispersed into roadside ditches and were shooting at us, protected by the smokescreen from the burning gasoline.

I screamed over the din, 'That's it boys, let's go!' but as we turned to take flight one of the young men was caught by machine-gun fire and fell dead to the ground. We scrambled down the other side of the hill to our parked bicycles without being pursued. We were sooty and singed, pieces of debris clung to our hair, our eyes were bloodshot, our throats and lungs ached from the acrid fumes.

'Who was the man that was killed?' I asked.

'He was my brother,' answered the Maquis in a strangled voice.

Once, when walking into a Maquis camp on top of a mountain, I thought my time had come and that I had walked straight into a trap. Beneath huge trees, tents had been set up and at long tables gendarmes sat in full regalia: revolvers, braided kepis, whistles and all. My companions laughed at the stunned look on my face. A full brigade of gendarmes had joined the Maquis and brought along all the tools of their trade: bicycles, vans, official forms, seals and inkpads and were now officially misdirecting the German traffic, liberating hostages, manufacturing false papers; in short, the law enforcers were happily flaunting their uniforms and illegally serving La Patrie.

I simply dropped out of sight during the last week of July and first two weeks of August. In San Sebastián they presumed I had been killed. I walked in one morning ashen, exhausted and mute. I had crossed and recrossed the border innumerable times. I was sick to my soul of killing, I was confused, depressed and ached with remorse. I felt like a sleepwalker who had been suddenly awakened, just as I had felt in 1940 when I had come to, beside the hot machine-gun and realised I had killed. What most horrified me was the perverse pleasure which the bloodshed, destruction and slaughter had given me, but such acts were admired in wartime. I had enough reasons to want to get even, but my popular fame filled me with repugnance. I spoke to no one, ate, fell fully clothed on my bed and woke up twenty-six hours later. I felt a little better, morally and physically, but still refused to talk about what I had been doing.

My friends left me in peace and made plans to celebrate my birthday which was on 23 August. That very morning I received orders from Madrid to stand by to go into France with Colonel Bastid, Major Vuillet, Colonel Richard and his aide, Captain Larre. When Paget saw me adjusting my backpack he burst out laughing.

'Today you are crossing the border first class with an official pass so get out of that smuggler's outfit and put on your Sunday best.'

I thought Paget was joking but, as he swore he was telling the truth, I changed quickly. A big white Packard convertible with bright red, shining leather seats drove up at noon. Colonel Richard, grinning from ear to ear, was driving and his beaming passengers confirmed what Paget had said.

'We're going in this car?' I asked, amazed and nervous.

'Of course!'

'Won't we get shot at?'

'No, quite the contrary. They will present arms. We are going to be the first representatives of the Free French Government to enter this part of France, which has just been liberated.'

'And the Boche?'

'Gone! Taken prisoner! Dead! Why do you ask? You should know more about that than we do.'

I blushed and make an awkward gesture. 'Oh, you know how people talk.'

We arrived at the border at Irun in the early afternoon. A Guardia Civil officer stepped forward, checked our papers, looked at the car and its occupants, saluted and signalled for the barrier to be lifted. 'Have a good trip.'

I was almost having a fit. Afraid the Spaniards would hear, I whispered, 'How many times have I crossed this border! But never before have I been this scared!'

Colonel Richard, who was sitting next to me, kept a straight face and whispered back, 'This is just one of the facts we have to accept now. It will be just as hard for us to become law abiding citizens as it was to dive into the cloak-and-dagger life.'

Once across the border our welcome was one of overwhelming cordiality and respectful diffidence. I could not help murmuring, 'Hypocrites! They'd have shot us down yesterday without blinking an eye. Now look at them – scraping and bowing!'

'You talk too much, Alec,' said Colonel Richard. 'Now we are the law. The customs man and police are only agents for that authority.'

A few metres into France the car stopped and Colonel Bastid announced, 'This is your birthday present, Alec.' When I tried to thank him, he continued, 'To top it all, Paris has just been liberated by General de Gaulle and General Leclerc.'

20

The Eighth Of May

As the car carrying the official delegation sped through the towns and villages, I watched France wildly celebrating her liberation. From every building on every street flags flew France's colours proclaiming the jubilation of her people. Everyone had turned out to hail the liberators. Having searched high and low for someone to help me out during the time of occupation, I was amazed at the abundance of so many fighters, Resistance Chiefs, Maquis and freelancers who were strutting and staggering about, heading parades and rousing the crowds with patriotic speeches. Anything which bore any resemblance to military gear had been taken out of mothballs: bandoliers and cartridge belts, boots and leggings, new and outmoded weapons, berets, kepis, forage caps and helmets from both wars. There were few decorations visible but so much gold braid and stripes that I wondered what had happened to all the run-of-the-mill soldiers. Everyone, but everyone, wore an arm-band adorned with the Cross of Lorraine which had been authenticated with some kind of official stamp.

It was a true carnival! Citroens, whose sides had been scribbled in chalk with patriotic slogans and Lorraine Crosses, sped recklessly by and bellicose youngsters perched on the mudguards played at war now that it was all over. People laughed and cheered, the women embraced and kissed everyone in sight, wine flowed like water – this was probably to be the greatest Bacchanalia in French history. Here and there, I spotted a familiar face from the Maquis – the real fighters – but these men were unchanged; I could see them smiling indulgently in wonder at the antics of the crowd. When my eyes met theirs they waved and winked as if sharing a private joke.

After innumerable stops and patriotic toasts the official delegation finally arrived at Pau at the end of the day. The next day, I was appointed Commander of half of the East Pyrénées Region, but while my title gave me ample authority I had few explicit instructions as to what was expected of me so I had to rely on my own judgement and make on-the-spot decisions to fulfil my mission. I found myself trying to solve problems about as difficult as trying to drive a square peg into a round hole. Fleeing war criminals, SS men, Gestapo and notorious collaborators were to be intercepted and arrested at border crossings. Normal commercial relations were to be re-established between France and Spain but, what would happen to my friends the smugglers?

The Spanish Republican guerrillas who had taken refuge in the French Pyrenees and who had become a bone of contention between France and Spain were to be disbanded and disarmed. I went to talk with their chief who was entrenched with his men high up in the rocky mountains.

'Look, Alec,' said Colonel Ramírez, 'you and I know each other well so you're not going to impress me with your arguments. You want us to stop our raids against Franco? Do you think that's fair? France betrayed us in '39 when, after she had offered us asylum, she put us in internment camps; nevertheless we fought with the Maquis. How many of us died liberating your country? And now that you have won your war you want to stop us from winning ours?'

I had to take heartrending decisions – dislodge them from their strongholds along the border, force them to negotiate instead of fight and eventually disarm them. The weight of authority lay heavily on my shoulders.

I got together a band of dedicated resourceful men and convinced the Gendarmes, the Secret Police and the Customs Officials to collaborate and had the satisfaction of seeing these disparate factions working together for once.

After the liberation of Paris the Joint Allied Forces and General de Lattre de Tassigny landed in Provence. Together with General Koenig's First French Army, whose ranks had been swelled by the Maquis, they drove the Germans north with heavy losses. Nine-tenths of France, Belgium, Luxembourg and part of Holland were liberated and the Reich's own territory was invaded. By the end of October Aix-la-Chapelle had been occupied and General de Gaulle had set up the first

All-Party Government. The smell of victory was strong in the air.

In mid-December, when I was beginning to be bored with the routine, a bespangled mothball-smelling general arrived to take command of the border region and I was granted leave. I went to spend Christmas in Paris and to await further orders.

In spite of the battle raging in the Ardennes, where von Rundstedt had launched a counter-offensive which threatened the final victory of the Allies, Paris was teeming with uniforms. Public buildings, hotels, garages, brothels and movie houses had been requisitioned for Army Headquarters, Officers' Messes, PXs, dispensaries and warehouses by the Allied Command. The city's sparsely supplied stores and restaurants were crowded. The soldiers on leave joined in the Christmas festivities but the hard look in their eyes and the lines on their faces reflected their knowledge that the war was still not over. I was happy to be home again, to be with my mother, to see my friends although there were many who would never come back. I longed for a normal life, for a peaceful life, but I also knew the war was not over.

I was assigned as Liaison Officer to the American 517th Parachute Command after the New Year. I was weary of war but felt I could not stand by while the American 'boys', 'Tommies' and Russians were still dying in order to end the war. Therefore when I was asked to volunteer for a commando raid into Germany I felt obliged to go. I sincerely hoped this would be the last of this kind of action for me; I felt I was tempting fate but I knew that I could be of help since I had the training for this type of warfare, had been in Germany during wartime and spoke the language fluently. We were to be parachuted down near Merseburg to destroy an essential factory which had been installed deeply and solidly under-ground. Even though Allied bombers had repeatedly tried, they had been unable to put it out of commission. The raid had been carefully planned with aerial photographs and a scale model of the target built on reports from secret agents. We were to be met by a 'reception committee' which would take us in charge and help us to get out of Germany after we had fulfilled our mission.

We left at the end of March 1945. As we flew into Germany

our convoy was caught in an anti-aircraft barrage, our plane was hit, fire broke out on board and filled the cabin with dense smoke. We managed to put out the fire and were just settling down again when a blinking light indicated we were over the drop zone. We barely had time to hook up our static lines and step out into space.

The drop was a disaster! We were caught in the beams of German spotlights, bullets zoomed by, tracer bullets flared all around us and we almost landed on top of a flak battery. The Commander and three other men were killed, two others were wounded and another had a broken ankle. We had to abandon them. We opened their containers, grabbed the demolition sacks, their revolvers, ammunition and survival kits and ran! Luckily we had landed near a small village and were able to find a car providentially parked on a street; we threw in the gear, piled in it and drove away hellbent.

Twenty minutes later we found ourselves in a deep forest and since we were afraid of running into a roadblock we hid the car and began to walk through the hilly, heavily wooded country. After a while we found a secluded spot and dug into the soft mossy earth. We felt frustrated and guilty because we had had to leave our companions behind and now there was no question of carrying out our mission. While driving, I had spotted the name of a town on a road sign, which together with the indications on the milestones led me to believe that we must be somewhere in the Black Forest, more than 350 kilometres from our target! We decided to hole up for the day and try to make a plan. I estimated that if we were in the south-east of Germany the most feasible thing was to head in the direction of Alsace. Maybe we would get a chance to blow up a bridge or something along the way, but our number one priority was to save ourselves.

That night, a light rain was falling as the three of us set out. Our voluminous greenish raincoats were not readily identifiable in the dark and we decided to keep our uniforms on underneath as, in case we were captured, we would not be executed as spies. We walked all night, taking care to go around the few dwellings we encountered. A deep anger simmered in me. I had sworn never to run from the pack again and here I was doing just that.

At dawn we stopped on the edge of the forest where we had a

wide view of the Rhine valley and hid there awaiting the night. We had three obstacles to hurdle before getting to Alsace. First, the Siegfried Line which the Germans had built to face the Maginot Line. I knew little of this famous defence line, only what I had read in the newspapers at the beginning of the war, but as the Germans were now busily engaged fighting in the north of Russia, the Saar, Lorraine and the Palatinate, this remote section of the border should be relatively deserted. We had crossed the Black Forest without seeing a soul or any traces of troop movements.

The second obstacle was the Rhine. If the west bank of the river was in Allied hands the German side would be heavily guarded. As a matter of fact we should pray that both banks were still in German hands so as not to get caught in the crossfire but, in any case, we would have to make the crossing by boat as the few remaining bridges must be closely guarded. I recalled seeing the Rhine at Basel and Strasburg at this season of the year and was certain it would be at least 400 metres wide at this point with a very fast current owing to the heavy rains and melting snows.

The third obstacle was the crossing of both fighting lines but for this it was impossible to plan; we would have to play it by ear when we could look the situation over and judge the terrain.

We started walking, sensed a town ahead, made a wide detour and came upon a big factory humming with activity. Some bright beams of light pierced the heavily curtained windows and camouflaged glass roof and the grinding of the machines was impressive. As we circled the walls we came up against the factory's giant purring transformer.

It was done quickly. We emptied the demolition sacks: eighteen sticks of TNT, detonators, cables, couplings, more than enough for the job at hand. It was child's play to blast not only the transformer but also two adjacent pylons for good measure. We were treated to a fantastic display of fireworks: shattering explosions from the charges and short-circuit sparks split the night. After a dark silence the factory began to spit out the shocked shouting occupants and we sneaked away feeling that at least we had accomplished something as this factory would be idle for a long time! We never knew what we had blown up – a doll factory, a parachute factory, a music-box factory?

Since it was still raining and dark we guided ourselves by compass, skirting the houses. Everything seemed to be asleep – or abandoned? We crossed a road which ran parallel to the Rhine, saw few cars circulating and came to a vast deserted zone which looked like a training ground. It was criss-crossed by a complicated network of muddy paths which circled bushy mounds of different heights. On taking a closer look we realised these were the sighting turrets for underground bunkers. Everything looked neglected and forsaken but we were wary because here and there we could see dim lights cast by a few light bulbs. A lot of wreckage was strewn around and the ground was riddled with muddy, water-filled shell craters. We were slowly wending our way through when a voice challenged us. We froze and I called back brazenly, 'Shut up, you fool. All's well!' I must have sounded genuine because there was no further inquiry.

We had to bite down on our teeth to keep them from chattering with fear as we continued on. Suddenly we were brought up short by rolls of rusty barbed wire. Openings had been cut through the rolls which could be closed by pulling *chevaux-de-frise* which were placed to one side across them. We had no problem getting through and found ourselves walking amongst the famous 'Dragon's Teeth' – tank traps made of concrete pyramids of different heights and sizes placed helter-skelter which were bordered by deep ditches, but these also presented no obstacle.

I was amazed! The defence lines were less dense, less deep, less massive and less unsurmountable than I would have believed possible. It seemed as if the Germans had built it convinced it would never be necessary to defend their frontiers against invaders. They must have let it go to seed during the fat years of victory and now, when it was needed, it was beyond repair. Through the falling rain we saw ahead a no man's land – shrubby, boggy and pitted with shell holes. It should be easy to cross unless it was mined!

As no one volunteered to go first we drew lots and the task fell to me. I had never been so scared before! I tried to get hold of myself and zigzagged from crater to crater, figuring that if there had been a mine it would have already exploded, unless it had been replaced! There was nothing to do but take a chance! Each time I put a foot forward I was sure it was going to be my last step and I tried not to think of what it would be like to be blown to pieces. I was drenched by a cold sweat, I was mumbling incoherently to myself and I couldn't even think of how to pray.

The two others followed me close enough to try to place their feet exactly where I had and far enough so as not to go with me if I should be blown sky high. I felt as if my entire being was concentrated on the soles of my feet, as if death lurked only centimetres beneath me. I walked as if on eggs and it took me half an hour to cross 200 metres.

We finally arrived at the bank of the Rhine. It seemed as silent and forlorn as what we had encountered before. We were tired and cold, the five hours which had elapsed since leaving our last hiding place had lasted an eternity. Through the dark and rain, the shapes of things we could make out were strange and threatening. We groped around and finally found a small flat-bottomed rowboat which lay upside down with a pair of oars neatly stored beneath it. We turned it over, pushed it off into the river and scrambled aboard. We readied our guns, our hand grenades hung from our belts under our raincoats. The rapid current carried us north and, as we really had no exact idea as to where we were or what we were aiming for, we just let ourselves drift downstream, trying to keep the boat in line with the bank and to ship as little water as possible.

I had relaxed a little after the stress and I thought of Paul who had called the Rhine the Styx. Trying to order my thoughts as to what we would do upon reaching the other bank, I was surprised to hear myself mutter, 'God will provide.' Suddenly the boat crashed loudly against a rock we hadn't seen. It was really more of a shipwreck than a landing and we stepped ashore like drenched ducks. We stood motionless, straining our ears and eyes.

Straight ahead, behind the trees, there was a road and, in spite of the late hour, we could hear the noise of moving vehicles and could see dimmed headlights shining in both directions. We should be getting close to the front lines as we could see brief sporadic flashes of light followed by thunderous blasts, the echoes of a half-hearted battle bedded down for the night. Listening to the volume of the explosions, I deduced we were about five, or at most seven, kilometres from the front. Although exhausted and badly in need of rest, we had to go on to take advantage of the five hours still left before daybreak.

The place would probably be crawling with German troops once the sun came out.

We approached the road and watched cars, trucks and ambulances roll by. Many were camouflaged with netting and tree branches and looked battle-torn. The road itself was pockmarked with shell holes which had been hastily repaired and mud-packed but which nevertheless snared up the two-way traffic. Small bands of infantry walked in single file along the roadside and the headlights of the passing vehicles made their wet helmets glisten and illuminated their war-weary faces. They had protected themselves from the rain with whatever they had been able to find: pieces of tents, tarpaulins, sacks, blankets, so I decided that in our green raincoats we could pass undetected. We started to walk a short distance behind a group of soldiers who were going in our direction. Occasionally we saw the distinctive black leather raincoats and breastplates of the Feld-gendarmerie who were trying to get the bogged-down traffic moving again, but they were too busy even to glance at our trio. We passed several houses whose front yards were filled with disorderly parked vehicles and saw a lot of soldiers going in and out, from which we assumed that these were being used as temporary rain and rest shelters.

We had been walking for a good hour when the traffic began to thin out, became sparser and finally ceased altogether. As we must have been getting very close to the front we left the road and walked in the cover of some bushes. Very warily, very slowly, we moved from one bush to the next, fingers hooked around the triggers of our guns. The visibility had improved a little but not enough to allow us to see a lurking machine-gun nest directly in front of us. The enemy however had seen us coming! We were challenged, threw ourselves flat on the ground but were already under fire. We shot back blindly, aiming at the blue flashes of the bullets coming at us. I raised myself slightly to get at the grenade hanging from my belt and felt an indescribable pain splitting my guts. I felt myself fly through the air but didn't feel anything when I hit the ground.

I was pulled out of nothingness by the sound of a woman's voice – a distressed voice which kept on repeating, 'Oh, my Lord. Number Seven is dying! Number Seven is dying!'

I opened an eye and saw a white ceiling and a spotless white wall above my head. Was I in a hospital? My eyes focused on a white metal headboard and then on a plaque with a number printed on it. I squinted to try to read the number. No. 7. No. 7? No. 7! I was dying! I reacted violently but the sudden movement resulted in an excruciating pain which wrenched a moan from me.

'He's coming to! Please don't move! I'll call the doctor.'

I could now see the owner of the voice, a young nurse who bent over me, but all I could do was to bat one eye to show I had understood her. Slowly I became more and more aware of myself. I was pervaded by an all-encompassing pain, the source of which I finally located in my abdomen. The nurse returned, followed by an intern who lifted the sheet which had been draped over a cradle. He examined me and plunged a needle into my arm. I felt myself slipping back into the abyss but summoned all my strength to mumble, 'Am I really dying?'

'Of course not! What an idea! You've been badly wounded but you're going to pull through!'

Relieved, I let myself slip away. During the following days I was completely confused; I was engulfed in a black stupor, a turbid nightmarish sleep and a burning fever but whenever I awoke a nurse was always at my side. By and by, I came to realise I had an incision which ran from sternum to pubis and another one from side to side, right across my navel; I wondered what had happened and what kind of patchwork had been done to me. Drain tubes sprouted from my belly and each time they dressed my festering wounds I thought I would die of agony. Very slowly I recovered, regained strength and the marvellous joy of living quickened in me. I had often considered the futility of being the last man killed in a war; I was glad I had escaped that senseless fate!

Soon I was allowed to walk around with the help of a cane and to receive visitors who left flowers and much happiness behind.

On the morning of 8 May I could feel something in the air. An electric current galvanised the hospital, I could hear hurried footsteps in the corridors, muffled laughter and cries. The current gathered momentum and exploded into wild joy which carried all before it.

'Victory! They have surrendered! The war is over!'

Everyone cried, laughed and embraced, even the seriously ill seemed to grasp the news and joined in the happiness. I could not believe it had really happened. My war was over!

I managed to get my uniform, persuaded one of the nurses to bind me tightly so I could hold myself straight and sneaked out of the hospital. This was one celebration I was not going to miss! Stunned by the light of the bright spring sun and the street noises, I saw men, women, soldiers, children, nuns out on the streets shouting, dancing, kissing, waving flags, parading, drinking. A sweet feeling invaded me. Now I knew it had been worthwhile! When I returned to the hospital that night I was exhausted, lipstick-marked, pleasantly tipsy and extraordinarily happy. The war in Europe was over, my war was over!

EPILOGUE

Without Drums Or Trumpets

On 16 September I woke up with a birthday morning feeling – this was the day I was getting out of the army. My mind wandered back to the glorious dawn in 1939 when, standing on the Aguille Verte with my friend Albert, I had wondered what destiny had in store for me. If I closed my eyes I could see the fantastic rocky ice-covered mountain peaks which seemed to beckon me. I had come full circle!

Walking on air, I left the Pont de Neuilly Metro Station under a despairing drizzle. A wet wind whipped my face and the trees of the Boulevard du Commandant Charcot had already lost most of their foliage. The yellow leaves ran in streams over the pavements and in the gutters and were carried up in flurries at the street corners. Very few people were out; the city seemed to have shut herself up. I turned a corner, walked along la rue de la Ferme, stopped in front of number seventeen and read a red, white and blue bordered plaque placed to one side of the door: *Demobilisation Centre. Headquarters of the 711th Division.*

I entered the pretentious modern building with a thumping heart, nervously clutching a brown envelope and went down the hall into an office furnished in typical military style. A few soldiers sat reading newspapers, chatting, smoking or just picking their noses, passing the time while waiting for something to happen. I seemed to be the only one leaving the army today. I went up to a desk and handed my papers to a soldier who read them carefully and began to scribble in the proper blanks of a form with painstaking care. He was a nice rosy-cheeked clean-scrubbed well-mannered boy who, when he had finished his homework, carried the papers next door to his superior officer to have them verified and sealed. Then he escorted me to another office where a slovenly army clerk again scrutinised my dossier and handed me 1,000 Francs! – just enough to buy a pair of trousers and maybe a newspaper. Was this my reward for six years, one month and three days – for 2,225 days of waging war, for all my suffering, for all the lost years of my youth? Stifling my anger, I spoke to the clerk who was assiduously noting down in his books the amount disbursed.

'You can't be serious!'

'Everyone says that to me, sir, but don't blame me. I'm only a clerk. I just follow orders. Please sign the receipt.'

I did and turned to go. The young soldier who had read my dossier and had been watching the scene in embarrassment hurried to the door, stood at attention and saluted me as I went through.

On the pavement I thought that apparently nothing had changed in me since I had gone into the building. I was still the same man wearing the same wet uniform with the marine anchors stitched to the collar, the decoration ribbons pinned underneath the jacket pocket, and the red beret adorned with the parachute emblem. But everything had changed! The change had been brought about by demobilisation paper number 945-ex-1 and the voucher for civilian ration cards which had been added to my dossier. I had been someone – an officer in command to be treated with due respect; now I was no one. I had no training, no diplomas. I was an expert at blowing up bridges, stealing cars and killing silently; I was completely unprepared for civilian life.

Then, against all logic, I began to feel good. I was filled with gratitude and hope as I started toward the Metro Station and a new life. Only once did I look back at the place where I had been transformed into an ordinary man again. I smiled to myself thinking I had left the war as I had entered it, alone and unheralded – without drums or trumpets.

Et si c'était à refaire
Referait-il ce chemin?

Ballade de Celui qui Chante dans les supplices
Aragon